Rock Me Gently

Rock Me Gently

A TRUE STORY OF A CONVENT CHILDHOOD

JUDITH KELLY

BLOOMSBURY

First published in Great Britain in 2005

Copyright © 2005 by Judith Kelly

The moral right of the author has been asserted

Bloomsbury Publishing Plc, 38 Soho Square, London W1D 3HB

A CIP catalogue record for this book is available from the British Library

Hardback ISBN 0 7475 7629 7

Export trade paperback ISBN 0 7475 7352 2

10 9 8 7 6 5 4 3

Typeset by Hewer Text Ltd, Edinburgh
Printed in Great Britain by Clays Ltd, St Ives plc

All papers used by Bloomsbury Publishing are natural,
recyclable products made from wood grown in well-managed
forests. The manufacturing processes conform to the
environmental regulations of the country of origin.

To the memory of Glen Fallows

Acknowledgements

Thanks to all my friends for their kindness and support during the writing of this book: Jean Beard, Paula Gascoyne, Carmelle James, Susan Jaume, Gavin Jones, Avlon Rowley, Kathy Stephen and Mair Truelove.

Thank you very much to everyone at Bloomsbury, especially Alexandra Pringle for her enthusiasm and advice, and my editor Victoria Millar for her observant eye.

I am indebted to Lee Weatherly of Cornerstones, Jill Nagle and my agent, Jane Conway-Gordon, for their faith in *Rock Me Gently* from the beginning.

For their invaluable interest, my thanks to my friends from Nazareth House: Ruth Norton, Maria Hart, Maggie Mitchell and Pauline Playford, and from my Hampden Gurney school-days, Jean Wood.

The support of Old Elvians – Pam Cameron, Gale Gerring, Ann Harvey and Judith York – has been of long duration.

And thanks also to friends from my kibbutz days: Cydney Tune, Evelyn Crouch, Nadine Levin and Mark Reifenberg, who provided information and urged me on in the final stages when the going got tough.

Finally and most of all, my debt to Stanley, Anita Gatehouse and Francesca Unsworth, is profound. This book would not have been possible without you.

Prologue

'Do you remember Frances McCarthy?' She asks the question without expression.

I'm sitting opposite the nun who abused numerous children in her care in a convent situated in the sedate English seaside town of Bexhill-on-Sea.

The light is fading, and I cannot distinguish her features. From the sunset through the window, bright glints catch her hooded eyes, which look straight at me, sharp and mocking.

'Yes, of course I do. She was my best friend.' My voice is tense.

She shifts in her seat, watching me. 'Does it bother you that I ask that question?'

'It doesn't,' I say curtly. 'I no longer feel any guilt about what happened.'

I know what she is trying to do, and I want to grab her by the shoulders and shake her until her teeth rattle. Instead, I sit here very still and remember all that I have tried so hard to forget.

For many years I suffered the nightmares born of the time I spent at that convent. The memories that project across my mind are shared by the silent community of victims who once lived as I did, in a world that was deaf to our circumstances. And it all took place in middle England.

This is a true story about love and caring among children in the face of extreme cruelty. It is my story, about the only two friends in my life who have truly mattered to me. One of them died at the age of twelve. The other recently said: 'I'm still trying to get over my childhood, and now I'm ready to go into an old people's home.'

Chapter 1

Let's go so we can come home, let's go so we can come home. I chanted the catchphrase to myself over and over as the Israeli bus began to rumble its way towards Haifa.

It was August 1972, early morning and not yet light. In the waist of the bus sat a party of bearded Jews, Hasidim, like gnomes in black, with curly side-locks, broad hats and dangling fringes. I nodded at them but none responded; they regarded me with an air of haughty contempt. A large elderly woman shifted over in her seat to make room for me next to the window. I squeezed myself in. I hated the sensation of another human being wedged against my side. I could feel my own perspiration and was beginning to smell that of the others. I reflected that I was lucky to have a seat, and with a certain satisfaction watched the aisle fill up with people who had to stand. Sprinkled among them were several young backpackers with Stars and Stripes stuck on their rucksacks. College students, I thought, the types I would be mixing with on the kibbutz. I envied their cool clothes.

I rested my face against the window. It had all been very sudden, my decision to come here. I knew I should feel excited, happy at the prospect of living and working with other young people for six months. It was idiotic to feel apprehensive. Nerves, of course. Life wasn't meant to be easy.

In the seat ahead of me one of the Hasidim read the

Talmud, running his finger across the page. I watched him with envy. That man had a God and a community. He had a belief system in which pain and loss were explained in terms of an inspirational balance sheet, in which everything worked out in the end, and death was not really death. He believed he was one of God's Chosen, whereas I felt like a digit in a random series of numbers. Maybe I should pray. But God would turn a deaf ear to me.

I felt obvious and alone; the only one on the bus without group affiliation. Perhaps I could start up my own group – the Sisters of Reluctant Tourists?

I squinted as bluish buildings and objects rushed jerkily past the windows, all stiff and brittle. Tel Aviv gradually fell away and the scenery outside the bus unscrolled itself like a speeding tapestry. We raced through hamlets of squat houses with corrugated iron roofs, which nestled among secretive woods of aspen and fir. Long stretches of trees with dusty foliage brushed the bus as it passed. And across a golden stubble field, small bands of farm labourers – male and female together – could be seen tilling and sowing, clearing the land of rubble with the shallow blue line of distant hills behind them. Combine harvesters heaved yellow grain and straw, spewing it on to the land. Old men shuffled past, nodding their skull-capped heads. Young, richly bronzed, hard-muscled men in denim shorts stepped into rusting vans loaded with tomatoes.

The talk and laughter of the other passengers faded away as the bus changed to a lower gear and a news bulletin buzzed loudly through the bus. The raspy consonants of the broadcaster's voice made it difficult to understand what was being said. I examined the faces of the other inhabitants of the bus. The Hasid near me hunched his face over a cupped match, sucked the flame in through his cigarette with all his strength, and funnelled the smoke out through his teeth. Time thickened.

4

As the radio crackled on, the other passengers lit up cigarettes from packs tucked into shirt pockets and handbags. Let's have a fag and forget our troubles. We sat in a pea-soup fug of cigarette smoke until the broadcast ended. Had it not been for the large woman sitting next to me, barring my way, I would have jumped off the bus.

The anxiety hit me full blast, without warning. My body was numb, inert, as I felt the slow, rolling pressure of panic building inside me. I could hardly move, hardly breathe. Things began scratching at the edge of my awareness, pulling, tugging at me. No! Not today, not here. I came to Israel to get away from these feelings. Just ignore them, they'll die down of their own accord, I told myself. I must remain composed. I willed my mind to concentrate on the bus's rocking movement. Let's go so we can come home, let's go so we can come home.

Slowly, slowly, the panic ebbed away, and I could breathe again. I wiped my perspiring forehead with my handkerchief and gulped in great lungfuls of cool air gratefully. See? I scolded myself. It's not so hard, if you just try. I relaxed into the hammock-swaying of the bus. It held me suspended between the life I had left and the life that waited for me somewhere ahead.

Suddenly the rattle of the bus seemed a threat from which I must escape, just as I had from England. I was a caged bird wherever I was. I believed myself to be free of all prejudices – I hated everyone equally. As if in response to my thoughts, the bus shifted down a gear and the brakes squealed to a halt. The driver gave a loud nasal shout of 'Kiryat Ata!'

That was my stop. Suffocating with nerves, I felt the blood glowing in my face. I grabbed my things and scrambled out, relieved. I was the only person to get off.

The street was just a long row of squat, rust-coloured shops, like cubes of pink sugar, with green shutters over every window. The bus coughed away in a cloud of dust, leaving me feeling helpless and frightened, like an out-of-season tourist who had lost her coach party. I had not expected this solitude. I had not expected this strange abysmal town. When I had looked at the map of Israel, Kiryat Ata had been marked in quite large letters; I had been sure it must be a civilised place with modern shops, restaurants and banks.

A voice in my head whispered: 'You asked for it. It's up to you now. You're moving forward. That's progress, isn't it?' But from what? Towards what? Did I really want to be here? Questions without answers, they spun in my head. I should turn myself round and go back to England at once, before I got caught up here. Let's go so we can come home. Vainly I tried to recall another of Ruth's catchphrases to calm myself – take the plunge, go with the flow, sink or swim – but stale clichés were no help. I was no longer a child. I was supposed to have accumulated things by now: possessions, responsibilities, goals, experience and knowledge. I was supposed to be a person of substance. But I didn't feel weightier. I felt lighter, as if I was shedding matter, losing calcium from my bones, cells from my blood; as if I was shrinking.

A young man wearing purple braces was bringing out chairs and tables under the awning of a shabby café-bar across the road from me. Propped up in a chair, an old man slept bolt upright. He seemed unconcerned by the clatter of chairs and tables being dragged outside from the café.

The piercing glare in my sun-shocked eyes thumped my head. My featureless thick skirt, long-sleeved blouse and tight shoes felt heavy and inappropriate. For years I had chosen clothes that made no promises. I was ashamed of English holidaymakers who loafed around seaside resorts in beachwear, skimpy shorts and vests in shrieking colours, with too much sunburnt red flesh on view.

I had brought little more than the clothes I stood up in as I had been informed that the kibbutz would provide my work gear. I had wedged my luggage, just a duffle bag, beside me on the aeroplane seat. It was my first flight; at the back of my mind was the thought that if something went wrong, up there in the sky, I'd have my duffle bag at the ready to take with me into the void, using my voluminous skirt as a parachute, leaving nothing of myself behind.

I now stood in the partial shade of a tree, my bag propped up against my leg, as I sucked in the hot, still air. I saw myself for a moment as part of the scene, in the way I sometimes did, and realised I looked like someone lost. There were a few dilapidated shops around, their crumbling walls scribbled with mysterious graffiti. There were no signposts, but I had an idea in which direction my kibbutz lay.

What now? Should I stay, or go?

'Shalom!'

I blinked. The young man, the waiter from across the road, stood beside me, staring at me with a look that was half amusement, half concern. I wondered for an instant how long he had been there. Had I been talking out loud? He said something in Hebrew which I didn't understand.

'English,' I said pointing to myself. 'I'm going to Kibbutz Ramat Yohanan. How far away is it?'

'A few miles,' he said after a silence.

'Is there a bus?'

'No bus for a long time.'

'Is there a taxi I could hire?'

'Taxi? No.'

'Then how am I to get there?'

'You will have to wait for the evening bus.'

'I can't wait,' I said in exasperation. 'I'm two days late already.'

He stared at me with dreamy curiosity. I had been told that Israelis were friendly people, but this man, while not exactly hostile, was not giving me the reaction I needed. He had looked at me a little strangely when I told him where I was going.

Perhaps that was it. I hardly seemed the type to play the part of a pioneering kibbutznik sweating from toil.

I took a breath and decided. 'I shall walk then.'

He raised his eyebrows. 'OK, but be careful,' he said politely.

I nodded. 'I'm here to learn Hebrew.'

'Ah, come in for a drink some time, yes?'

I saw now how foolish it has been not to have arrived at the kibbutz at the designated time. It had seemed less alarming to come at my own pace. I stared through the haze at the road that led to the kibbutz.

'Yes,' I said. 'Yes, of course,' though I doubted I would. When he reached the awning, he turned and gave me one brief, curious glance before disappearing into the dark doorway of the bar. The street fell silent again.

I picked up my duffle bag. Let's go so we can come home. I started down the street, moving robotically, as I had been doing for years. Was I really ready for this world? I didn't know. My intentions for being here were still masked from myself. Maybe I just wanted to belong somewhere, needed to be part of something – the humorous yet sorrowful sound of the Yiddish tongue that I did not even understand, yet always loved to hear from my grandparents; a history that I had been removed from, a history that might not be mine, yet one which I wanted to learn more about.

Or perhaps I was running away from the memories that had threatened to overwhelm me since I rediscovered my childhood diary.

Six months earlier my mother had asked me to help clear out her loft. Together we sifted through old magazines, shelves of dusty jars, a stash of different-sized boxes and strapped suitcases.

I was crouching on the floor when I found the parcel. A brown paper package tied with a piece of string. A sticky label, yellowing slightly with age, bore my mother's round writing in black ink.

'Judith. N. H. Convent,' it read.

'What have you found?' my mother looked up, her lips parted. She stiffened when she saw what I was looking at, and reached out in an effort to lift the parcel away from me.

'Please Judith, don't open that.'

But I had already untied the string, feeling a strange sort of breathlessness as I did so. It did after all have my name on it; I felt I had the right.

'It's all right, Mum,' I said, patting her gently on the arm.

'No, it's not all right,' she said with a sudden authority. 'I should have thrown all that stuff away long ago. There's no point in raking up the past.' Her face was taut with concern.

'What do you mean?' I was sounding petulant now. 'I'm just interested, that's all.' I carried the parcel away from her, out of the loft.

In the seclusion of my bedroom, I let the contents stream to the floor. The smell of mould blossomed upwards. There were a few letters in my childish scrawl and a lot of yellowing newspaper cuttings. 'NUNS PRAY AT SEA RESCUE' the headlines declared. Underneath the cuttings lay a book with a glossy religious picture stuck on the cover. It was the diary I kept during my days at Nazareth House convent. An old photo album revealed the frozen images of assorted children standing stiffly with either beach huts or the familiar façade of the convent in the background. All the photos included black-veiled nuns.

Sweaty and uncomfortable, I stared blankly at the photographs. Many years of carefully guarded emotion struggled for release as the faces I sought burst through the gate of my unconscious, rioting horribly into my memory. Up to that moment, my childhood had been consigned to some much earlier, greyer world. It was my inner country, rarely visited.

9

I sat on my bed, turning my back on the faces. I used to be unable to remember exactly how they looked, and then I taught myself not even to try. Now, in a chance moment, like an unexpected encounter in a busy street, I'd seen them again. The past was swimming back to me, as though the guard had been removed from the gate.

My mother entered the room. 'That girl,' she said, 'the friend of yours who died. What was her name?' She looked at me, a little slyly, as if testing.

I cleared my throat. 'Oh, heavens, I don't remember. It was so long ago. Another lifetime.'

But I knew from the way her face froze that she was anxious. She could see through my lie, and she wondered why I had bothered.

I didn't know, either, except that I believed it was my duty to appear happy. It was the least I could do for her. I didn't want her to feel bad; she had plenty of worries in her life. But even now, so many years on, was I still hiding from my time at the convent?

After she left, I sank down on to my bed again. I picked up the diary. I didn't quite dare open it, not then. It was as if I had been living under an anaesthetic that was only now beginning to wear thin. Suddenly I was frightened of what might await me if I awoke.

Would reading my childhood diary start it all up again? The guilt, the despair that had tinged my days for years. Then I remembered the recurring dream that still preyed upon my nights. I would awake from it gasping and choking, eleven years old again, standing on the jagged rocks watching my life end.

I stared at the faded picture on the cover and I knew that I had to find a way to understand myself.

'Frances McCarthy,' I whispered as I opened my diary.

And as I heard the ragged sound of my breathing, I knew my safe comfortable shell was beginning to crack. I found the knowledge strangely exciting. It was as though memories were returning to me in broken pieces.

'Frances,' I said again.

She had resurfaced – perhaps for ever? – in my mind.

Chapter 2

'Genuflection, girl. I don't suppose you've heard of the word, have you?'

'No, Sister.'

One or two of the other girls sniggered quietly and I could feel a blush burning my cheeks.

'Speak up, speak up. Genuflection is a bow, a bob, a curtsey to the altar. Well?'

'Yes, Sister,' I said louder.

'Yes, what?' Sister Mary said, poking my shoulder with her cane.

'I haven't heard of the word before.'

More muffled laughter from the others. Two of them whispered. Yes, they knew – had never needed to learn nor ever been ignorant.

'Be quiet, all of you,' Sister Mary spat. 'Is there something funny about the word genuflection?'

'I – I don't know, Sister,' I stammered.

'Well, I want you to practise it now. You must learn to genuflect correctly before you go to church again. Practice makes perfect. Do you understand? That way you will learn.'

The convent stood alone at the top of a hill above Bexhill-on-Sea, some distance from the town, and was approached by a long pebbled drive. Mum and I had first entered the building two weeks earlier, blinking in the high, cool gloom after the August heat outside. That's when I became aware of the worrying silence that enclosed the place, broken only by the swishing skirts of a short plump nun bustling along the corridor to meet us. For all its air of piety and polish, I had the sense of being plunged into something murky – a miserable awareness that this was not the holiday camp I had hoped for.

The nun, who introduced herself as Sister Cuthbert, told us to follow her. She had a gravelly voice that billowed out from under her veil. Her big butter-and-egg face looked tightly packed inside her stiff, white coif and her walk was smooth, hurried, like someone who had numerous tasks to perform.

She led us along a long gaunt corridor with creaky floors which stretched ahead with a row of doors leading off on either side. I slipped on the polished floor, but Mum quickly grabbed my arm to save me. We passed a tall statue of a man wearing white robes, his nostrils curved as though with disgust for the rude humans passing below him. Behind his head a golden halo winked, reflecting each flicker of a little glass lamp that burned on the pedestal. I wrinkled my nose at the smell of floor polish mingled with incense.

'This end of the corridor is the children's area,' said the nun in her throaty voice. 'The other end is where the old people live. The children are on holiday in London at the moment, but will be returning next week.'

We followed the nun through cathedral-like archways and turned right at the end of the main corridor. In the dim light I could see dusty statues looming on high plinths, anguished expressions on their stone faces. I held tightly to Mum's hand.

Endless doors opened and closed. Dark empty passageways led into many rooms, including three classrooms. As the nun opened the door to one, she said to Mum, 'So your husband died four years ago, Mrs Kelly? Such a tragedy that he died so young.'

While they began a whispered conversation together, I

thought back to the time when we had lived in a pub in Faversham, and felt sad.

I remembered Dad carrying me up a flight of dark stairs past wooden beer barrels, into a long, smoke-filled bar-room with sawdust on the floorboards. His jacket was a rough tweed that smelt of smoke and had sweets hidden in the top handkerchief pocket. Sometimes he'd place me on the pub counter amid the cozy buzz of noise – small talk, the clink of glasses, the faint rhythmic tunes from a tin-kettle piano – and he'd give me a bottle of cherryade to drink. I called it prickly water. Encased in the warm smell of beer and drunkenness, I watched him down numerous bottles of his own prickly water, with their brass-bright depths. Then one afternoon he lay on the floor and wouldn't get up.

'He was only twenty-nine,' Mum told the endless shadowy strangers who popped in for tea and biscuits. And I had thought then how wrong it seemed to entertain, to eat, so soon after they had put Dad into the ground.

'He drank himself into an early death,' they said. And everyone heaved a sigh and shook their heads. People came and said soft things to me and chatted about him for a bit, then forgot him and talked of other things. For a long time afterwards I had felt, and still felt, torn up inside and that his dying was my entire fault.

Mum and Sister Cuthbert suddenly stopped talking together and looked down at me. Mum said, 'Don't sniff, Judith, blow. What's your hankie for?'

I rubbed my nose with my hand as the nun continued: 'Most of the girls here are orphans. Others have one parent who may have fallen on hard times. We do our best to raise them as good Catholics.'

The classroom had a high ceiling and yellowy-brown walls so dusty they appeared to be dissolving into powder. The room was bare, with a line of plain desks in the centre. A tall smeary blackboard towered at the front; at the back, many-paned windows overlooked the convent gardens. The lower half was made of frosted glass, so the children couldn't see outside. The classroom had an old musty woody smell; if the whole building had an air of gloom, this room was the heart of that feeling. I dismally noticed that most of the books piled in a glass cabinet seemed to be about saints.

A few of the children's chalk drawings were exhibited on one wall. On the other hung a huge wooden crucifix on a chain. An ivory Christ stretched naked, bleeding, elbows and kneecaps jutting through the skin, flesh protruding from open wounds, crowned with thorns of silver and nailed with nails of gold. Although August sunshine was pouring into the room, I couldn't stop a shiver trembling through me.

'See, there is Our Lord always watching over the children,' said Sister Cuthbert. 'It reminds them that home for a Catholic is wherever Our Lord is. And what do you suppose Our Lord was thinking while he was up there on the cross, Judith?'

I looked at the painted wounds. 'Ouch?' I suggested weakly.

The nun pursed her lips and her eyes narrowed sharply. 'No, no! He was thinking: I've suffered this for you. You obviously don't know your Bible.'

'But she's only eight,' said Mum.

'Almost nine,' I said.

'Well, there's time enough to put it right,' said Sister Cuthbert. 'Do you have a rosary, Judith?'

I lowered my eyes. I didn't know what a rosary was. Mum tightened her clasp on my hand. Talking about anything to do with religion made her uncomfortable and self-conscious too.

'Never mind, I'm sure we can provide you with one,' said Sister Cuthbert with a kindly expression.

After we had some tea in the parlour, Mum told me to wait outside for a moment while she had a talk with Sister Cuthbert. I watched them through the open door, and tried to lip-read what they were saying. Sister Cuthbert's mouth was little and plump and curly at the edges and I couldn't understand anything.

Finally the nun said loudly, 'Don't worry, Mrs Kelly, Judith will have plenty of playmates once the children return.'

Fear choked through me. I ran back into the room.

'Mum,' I said, tugging at her to bend down so I could whisper in her ear. When she did, I pressed my face close to hers. I could smell her perfume as I whispered, 'I won't be staying here for ever, will I?'

Straightening up, she took my hand and stroked it. 'Of course not,' she soothed. 'I've told you, I'll be back in a fortnight when I've found us somewhere to live.'

When the time arrived for Mum to leave, I wouldn't let go of her hand; I couldn't let go. She mustn't leave me here, I thought. I might never see her again.

'Stay with Sister Cuthbert,' ordered Mum. 'And don't forget to say thank you for the tea.'

I looked over my shoulder at the silent veiled woman, and my breath caught in my throat. 'Please,' I appealed, my voice wild, 'don't leave me here.'

Mum stood unsure for a moment, staring at me with wet eyes. 'It's not for ever, Judith; it's just until I find somewhere for us to live. Be a brave girl and help Mummy, all right? Promise me to write in the diary I gave you every day. Then you can show it to me when I see you next.' Her voice sounded too loud, nervously cheerful.

When she bent down to hug me, I wanted so much to cry, to hold her close and never let her go. But I didn't want to upset her. I tried to be strong for her sake. I fought back the tears and tried to swallow the tight feeling in my throat, my mouth dry as I stood on top of the front steps of the convent and watched her go. The nun stood behind me and waved.

'Goodbye, Judith, goodbye!' Mum cried out to me, waving her hand before she turned the corner. And then she was gone.

I wanted to please Mum: I wanted her to be proud of me, to stroke my head and tell me how well I had coped, so I wrote regularly in my diary.

17 August 1951
I came here yesterday. Sister Cuthbert gave us tea from a
big tin teapot with milk and sugar already in it. It made
Mum laugh. When Mum left Sister Cuthbert said Oh dear, I
can see someone is about to cry. I said No I'm not and
pretended to be happy. Madeleine and Bridget used to be at
this school. They are on holiday as well. They are taking me
to the beach tomorrow.

19 August
I had my photo taken on the beach. Madeleine asked if I
wanted to stay with the other children. I said no.

22 August
I had a bath today and had to wear an apron in it. We went
to the beach again. The other children come back from
holiday tomorrow. Madeleine and Bridget keep telling me
to stay with them.

Wednesday 23 August
Sister Cuthbert made me write to Mum that I wanted to
stay here with the other children. I don't want to really. I
sent Mum a photo of me on the rocks by the sea. I told her I
looked like the King of the Castle. I wish I could see her and
tell her the truth.

'Sit down, Judith,' said Sister Cuthbert. 'Now, I want you to
write to your mother. You're a big girl, aren't you? You know
what's best, and you know your mother can't really take care of
you right now. So you're going to be a good girl and tell her you
want to stay here, because that's what's right, isn't it?'

I suddenly felt lonely and frightened. A wrenching longing
came over me for Mum's tiny bedsit and gas fire, for the
comfortable smells of her perfume mingled with cigarette smoke.

The nun fixed me with a frown. 'Well, Judith?'

'Yes, Sister,' I mumbled obediently. I wanted her to like me. 'What shall I write?'

'Just tell her that the children have now returned from holiday and you want to stay here with them.'

Dear Mum . . . The other girls have returned now, and I'd like to stay here with them . . . No, it's a lie! I clutched the pen so hard that my fingers ached as I wrote. Sister Cuthbert stood watching over my shoulder. I could feel her eyes boring a hole in my neck. I felt smothered, hot, choking.

To my relief, just as I'd finished writing the letter, the door burst open and a dark-haired girl wearing a faded navy tunic dashed out of it. Seeing the nun and me, she pulled up short.

'Careful, Frances!' snapped Sister Cuthbert. Her fingers hooked around the girl's wrist like a handcuff, jerking her up straight. The girl flinched. The nun seemed to catch herself then, and drew in a deep breath.

'I thought you were supposed to be attending Benediction?' She released her grip, wiping her hand on her habit.

'Sorry, Sister,' said the girl cheerily. I looked at her. I felt no premonition. She had wide dark almond eyes, and her face crinkled when she grinned, showing very even teeth.

Through the door I could see children of all ages falling into line down the corridor, all wearing the same faded blue uniform and knitted berets. The sight of them chilled me: so many empty faces, so many cow-like eyes fixed straight ahead. The bigger children had the look of crushed adults. One older girl of about sixteen sucked her thumb and twisted a strand of hair round and round her fingers. Many of them looked only half-made. I noticed one girl about the same age as me struggling to put on her beret. She had unevenly cut hair, like an upturned lavatory brush. All of them stood in silence.

In comparison, the dark-haired girl's cheerful energy was like an ultra-bright light. Being a little older than me, she took no notice of me beyond a quick, amused stare. 'Sister Mary asked me to fetch the new girl and take her to Benediction with us.'

How did she know I was a new girl? I thought. *The ink's hardly dry.*

'There we are then, Judith,' said Sister Cuthbert. 'This is Frances McCarthy, she'll take care of you. And don't worry, I'll make sure your letter is posted.' She swept it off the table. An aching lump grew in my throat as she left the room in a rustle of black robes, taking my letter with her.

Frances looked at me expectantly. I tried to think of something to say to her, but no words came. Everything in my head felt muddled and wary. Tricked. I'd been tricked into writing that letter. *Mum, please realise that I didn't mean it and come and take me away!*

'Have you been to Benediction before?' asked Frances.

Benny-who? 'I don't think so,' I muttered.

'Well, if you haven't, you'd better stay close to me. I'll show you what to do.'

She led me away, and I followed, dragging my feet, all hopes shattered. Frances had a bouncing sort of walk, all up in her toes. We pushed our way into a vacant place in the silent line of girls who stared at me with a wary, darting-eyed expression on their faces.

'This is the new girl, Sister Mary,' said Frances to another nun who was peering down the row of girls with a frown.

Sister Mary's face emerged from her coif. She squinted and pointed at me with a long yellow stick that curved over at the top like a walking-stick.

'You're . . . Kelly, is that right?'

'Yes,' I said miserably, 'I'm Judith Kelly.' This seemed to offend her. Her face grew hard, and I could tell by the sudden cloudiness of her eyes that she was making a mental note.

'There's no uniform for you yet. You'll have to wear your own clothes for a few days,' she said tightly.

I had begun to wonder how I was ever going to tell the nuns apart. In their black habits, cool coifs and whitewashed faces, they all looked exactly alike to me. But staring at Sister Mary, I thought: *I certainly shan't forget _her_*. Robust with a face shaped like a clenched fist, and a tiny lipless mouth permanently scrunched as if she were about to spit, she eyed the ranks of girls like a cross but efficient policewoman with a truncheon.

Under her stern gaze, my courage left me. She made my scalp tingle with her strangeness. I felt badgered, confused and yearned for Mum.

She sent Frances to search out a hat for me.

'We don't go into church with our heads uncovered,' she said. She emphasised *our,* as if there were other, inferior, bareheaded churches.

Frances returned with an old hat of dark-blue velvet with elastic under the chin. It was too small for me, but Sister Mary said it would do for now.

Suddenly the nun's stick hit the floor with a loud crack.

'All ready? Heads up, mouths shut, eyes forward,' she said. 'Don't gallop at the front. Nor crawl at the back.'

The file of girls trudged towards the convent chapel, which stood at the opposite end of the corridor from the children's quarters. Situated a floor above the old people's area, it was shared by the whole community.

As we climbed the polished wooden staircase to the church, I whispered to Frances, 'Who's Benny Dixon?'

Her dark eyes sparked with laughter. 'Benediction is the name of a church service we go to every day at four o'clock, not the name of a *man*. Didn't you know?'

We passed a cold black marble bowl built into the wall and the girls dipped a furtive hand in the low tide of water and crossed themselves before entering the church. This was the first time I'd ever been inside a church. There was a high ceiling, with lights shaped like dancing ladies hanging down on chains. The altar stood on a dais covered with a white lace cloth and surmounted by a golden crucifix. The room was ablaze with candles and loaded with summer flowers. At the back of the church several pairs of children's eyes peered over a balcony, the sun glowing through three small red stained-glass windows behind them like burning rubies.

Statues hung on either side of the altar. One was a man draped in flowing white robes with his heart showing, his head tilted sideways like a puppy. The other showed a man with cascades of curls falling across his face, sitting down, arms bent as if cradling a small animal, with two children leaning on his knees; underneath, in an ornate Bible-script, it said 'Suffer Little Children'.

As each girl entered the church she paused, curtsied swiftly and made the sign of the cross. I tried to copy them, bobbing up and down and signing myself in a similar manner, but my feet got tangled together somehow, and I fell on my bottom. I scurried after Frances and sat down, cheeks blazing. In the silence I found that my heart was beating violently.

Someone began to speak and I jumped guiltily. I listened, but could not follow what was being said. The speaker appeared to be a priest in front of the altar. A murmur of voices suddenly surrounded me: a dialogue had begun between the priest and the congregation.

Then the piano music started and everyone stood up. I watched what Frances did – stood when she stood, knelt when she knelt. During the hymns she offered me her thumb-blackened prayer book, indicating with her finger which song we were singing, but all I could do was shrug. I didn't know any of the tunes. The songs and prayers were all gobbledegook to me, because they were written in a foreign language.

I sat down and then realised that the others were kneeling. I felt myself becoming red with alarm as I hastily dropped to my knees on the wooden bench, hiding my cheeks in my hands. It was all so strange, and I hoped desperately that no one had noticed my ignorance. But in spite of her jutting coif, which hid her profile, I would soon learn that Sister Mary saw everything.

The priest stood up and walked out. All over. I slumped in

relief as we began to troop out, passing as we did another statue at the back: a woman in blue with a cracked face that frowned beneath her veil. She stretched out her blue arms stiffly towards an injured man at her feet. Below it, on an unfurling scroll, it read: 'The Greatest Of These Is Charity'.

In the refectory, sixty girls stood from end to end along three narrow tables, waiting for the signal for grace. I absent-mindedly sat down on the wooden bench, and then popped up again, mortified by a nudge from the horrified Frances. 'You have to wait!' she hissed.

A tall girl at the centre muttered: '. . . *per Christum Dominum nostrum.*' A loud 'Amen' rumbled from everyone.

I sniffed the air and screwed up my nose. The room had the sickly smell of sour milk.

The children drew out the benches with a noise like the roar of a train and sat down. I remembered how the train had roared like that on my journey to Bexhill with Mum.

A few voices rang out in the refectory but were instantly hushed. At last came the signal to talk, and babble broke out.

I sat in gloomy bewilderment, looking around the long room with its white-tiled walls. Dozens of flies buzzed everywhere. Tea, which the children called 'collation', consisted of two pieces of grey bread that appeared to be curling at the edges, some rancid dripping, and black brackish tea, poured from enormous steaming metal urns into tin mugs. It smelt and tasted like rotten flower-water.

'Give your bread a good bang on the table first to get rid of any ants,' said Frances.

I looked up and down the long table and noticed everyone tapping their bread. I suddenly didn't feel hungry.

Frances began scraping away with her knife at a lump of bread, scooping bits out of it.

'If you eat the mouldy bits, you'll get the gripes, so just scrape it off.' Without looking up she said, 'If you don't eat yours, I will.

23

But you've got to learn to eat things you don't like. And you can't begin too quickly.'

She motioned to the short, stubby girl with thick coarse hair who sat opposite us, grimly tapping her bread. The girl's left hand looked tight and sore. A dark purple bruise clouded the back of it. She was about fourteen or fifteen years old.

'That's Ruth Norton,' whispered Frances. 'One Friday she refused to eat some fish, saying it looked like it had never been alive and she'd just as soon eat carbolic soap. So every day for a week Sister Mary put the same fish back in front of her saying, "Fish is good for brains, which you're badly in need of, and if that plate isn't empty by the end of today, you'll have it back tomorrow." Each day Ruth tried to eat it, but she kept dropping it out of her mouth on to the plate, saying it was too salty. Finally she made herself swallow it and then she spewed it up. Sister Mary forced her to eat her fishy sick.'

I gaped at Frances, who sat matter-of-factly eating her bread and dripping, apparently not overly disturbed by the story. She was casually warning me of a danger, that was all.

'Anyway, if you don't eat, you get a black mark against your name,' she said.

I tried to nibble at a bit of bread. It tasted like old cardboard.

'What does a black mark against my name mean?'

Frances shrugged. 'You'll find out on Sunday.'

Obviously bored with this conversation, she turned her attention to the other girls, diving into their chatter with a laugh. The whole table was ignoring me, their voices and eyes skating over me as though my chair were empty. I laboriously chewed away at the hard piece of grease-spread bread feeling sullen and trapped as I listened to their puzzling chatter.

I had read about boarding schools in Enid Blyton books. Now here I was, actually sitting at a table with the residents of what I had imagined to be a dazzling world. Tears pricked at my eyes. I put my bread down. I couldn't eat any more of it, no matter what they did to me.

'Use a smaller brush on it, that'll work,' Frances was saying. 'Ruth, did you finish polishing the floor of the corridor to the nuns' quarters?'

Ruth's chocolate-button eyes were worried and defiant, but she winked.

'Sure. Just tied the rags to my shoes and skated extra hard. Couple of figure eights and it was done.'

Everyone burst out laughing. I stared down at my plate. They all talked as if they had known each other for ever. I didn't know how to act. If I tried to be funny, they'd call me a show off; if I didn't, I'd be boring. I longed for the day to be over and to be in bed. I realised dimly that their conversation centred on housework. Frances was saying something about a lavatory floor.

'Sister Mary says she wants to be able to eat her dinner off it by the time I've finished,' she laughed, 'so the only way to get the muck off is to scrape it with a knife.'

She turned to a hollow-cheeked girl sitting next to me. Her eyes looked like she'd been raised on fish food: bloodless and watery. There was no colour in her face except at the tip of her nose, which was moistly pink. She had the saddest face I had ever seen, and I had passed a few in the convent that day. Her thick, fair hair looked like it had been cut with pinking shears despite the clips used to tame it.

'Janet,' said Frances, 'can I borrow your penknife tomorrow?'

Janet had rolled up her shirtsleeve and was scratching a pinkscaled sore on the elbow of her papery arm. It looked raw and slimy.

'Course you can,' she said, with a smile that lit up her colourless eyes. 'As long as you don't get caught and have it confiscated.'

'Ta ever so,' said Frances.

I would have given anything to be able to slip in a remark to show I understood what they were discussing. But though I was good at guessing, I couldn't begin to fathom it. So I listened, wide-eyed. Whenever I caught Frances's eye, she looked away. Then she noticed my breathless attention, and took pity on me.

'You'll be told tomorrow what job you'll be doing.'

Without thinking, I blurted out, 'Do you mean the sort of jobs that housemaids do? Don't the nuns employ cleaners?'

Silence. Everyone looked at me as if I had landed from another planet. Frances raised her arched eyebrows, in warning. I bit my lip, searching her eyes for a clue. Then I felt someone kick my leg under the table.

'Are you kidding?' hissed Ruth in a sandpaper voice that should've belonged to an old man. 'Anyone with a ha'p'orth of sense knows that we're the dogsbodies that do all the dirty work here. I bet you've never scrubbed a floor in your life, missy prissy.'

My eyes stung. 'I *have*.' But my voice didn't sound very convincing.

'I believe you, thousands wouldn't.' She leaned across the table and made sniffing noises in my direction. 'Cor! Get a whiff of her!'

Ruth had a flat, dimpled face and almost comically round dark eyes. A scattering of freckles dusted her nose. 'Tell us, do you know what Jeyes' Fluid is?'

I answered, 'No.'

Ruth turned to the other girls and said, 'Oh, I say, she must come from a dead mucky home.'

All the girls stopped eating and looked at me, laughing. I blushed under their eyes. I tried to laugh with them. But I could not because my lips were all shivery. Should I have said yes to the question?

Frances sighed wearily. 'Don't get at her, Ruth. It's not her fault if she doesn't know about the work routine yet.'

'The sooner she gets used to it the better, then.' Ruth took a swig of the bitter black tea from her tin mug and, puckering her bronzed tea-bathed lips, said, 'Yuk! This stuff is strong enough for a mouse to trot on.'

'The milk must be cheesy again,' said Janet.

I tried to think of something to say that wouldn't upset Ruth.

26

Everything in my head was jumbled and arguing. I wondered if it was worth telling them that the children never had to do chores in my London school.

I took another slow bite of bread and dripping. It stuck in my throat. Ruth sat cleaning her teeth with a crust, which she finally gummed into mush and swallowed. Leftover crusts, turned brown by the tea into which they had been dunked, lay scattered on the table. Ruth picked them up and crammed them into her tunic pocket.

A bell rang for grace. Ruth, while stiffly crossing herself, stuck her tongue out at me, then mouthed the words 'What you staring at?' I looked away, feeling as though she had punched me, or pinned a sign to my dress: *This person is to be despised! She doesn't know what Jeyes's Fluid is!*

Section by section, the girls filed out of the refectory, the junior girls last. I asked Frances in a low voice why Ruth didn't like me.

Frances sighed again, looking irritated at my incompetence. 'Don't worry, take it with a pinch of salt. She can't stand anyone here, especially the nuns.'

'Why can't she stand the nuns?'

'She has to work in the kitchen most days instead of being in school.'

I was horrified. 'Why?'

'Because she's left-handed.'

'You're joking!'

Frances's dark eyebrows arched in surprise. She looked around to see if anyone was coming. 'No, I'm not. Sister Mary used to whack her every day in class. She said she was doing the devil's work. Ruth tried using her right hand, but she was no good at it. She's not thick, you know, but she's much older than the rest of us in our class. She's put in with us because the nuns make her work in the kitchen and laundry so much that she gets behind with her lessons. Sister Mary hates her. Sometimes it's really funny, because she'll be writing something on the blackboard with her back to us, and she'll say, "Norton, I know you're up to something over there. Don't let me catch you." She forgets that Ruth's not in the classroom. She's slogging away in the kitchen.'

I bent my head forward to hear better as Frances continued. 'Ruth has a bad chest, you know. She had TB a few years ago. Yet nearly every day she has to go down on her knees like an old washerwoman and scrub every inch of the kitchen floor with carbolic soap. There's a nun at her heels most days, telling her that work is a virtue that will make her a useful member of society. Well, something like that. But if Ruth stops for a second, they hit her on the legs with a cane. But she never cries. Once she had to get out on the window ledge and clean the windows. Another time she had to wash the walls and kill the bugs and flies by squashing them. She's as happy as a skylark most days, but sometimes it gets her down, like today. That's all.'

It was all too much. Awe made me feel weak. How could the nuns do that? 'That must be really rough on her. And so unfair.'

No wonder Ruth acted so cold and angry towards everyone. And no wonder so many of the girls seemed in dread of her. I decided that in future when I saw her frown, I'd climb a tree first and find out what the matter was afterwards.

Frances watched me with an amused, tolerant expression. 'To keep yourself out of trouble, Judith, I'd act the silent sort for the next few days. Copy everything we do. And don't speak to a nun unless it's to answer a question.'

We marched along the dimly lit corridor. The girls broke up into several groups, and Frances gestured for me to follow her. Ten of us trooped down a winding stone staircase to the basement, where passages twisted and turned like a rabbit's burrow. Ruth was in our group, I noticed with a tightening of my stomach; I decided to keep quiet, as Frances had suggested.

We entered a small room with an arched stone ceiling. It was dark and narrow, with green-tiled walls cold to the touch, and smelt of damp and shoe polish. The air in the room chilled me. I shivered and wanted to yawn. The single light bulb had a faint green tinge. It cast the room into shadow, as if it were partially underwater.

Along each wall rows and rows of black boots peeped out of arched pigeonholes. What was this place? I was still looking about me when the girls sprawled together on the dusty, torn sacks spread across the floor and began polishing the boots like professional shoe-shiners. The noise of their chatter filled the room. I side-spied Frances who frowned at me, jerking her head at the pigeonholes.

I slowly pulled out a pair of boots and tried to imitate the others, fumbling as I chose polish and a brush from the wooden box in the corner. *Don't ask why we're doing this. Don't say a word.* I brushed inexpertly at the heavy black boot, frowning in concentration. Soon I had black polish all over my hands and frock.

Amid the swishing noise of the shoe brushes, Frances said to me, 'We come here every evening to polish the nuns' boots, and this is where we tell our secrets.'

I looked up eagerly, relieved to be getting a second chance. 'Secrets? What sort of secrets?'

'Like Frances is Sister Mary's pet,' said Ruth patting Frances on the shoulder and winking at her.

'No, I'm not,' said Frances, her face reddening. 'Go on, Ruth, tell the new girl about that time you caught Sister Helen making big waves in the what's-it.'

'Oh, hell's bells, that story's so stale you could shave the whiskers off it,' said Ruth.

'Go on,' said Frances, 'I want to hear it again.'

Ruth shrugged, brush-brushing rhythmically as she spoke. 'Hell, it wasn't my fault that I caught her reigning on the throne. How was I to know she was in there? I just barged in to find her making a sacrifice to the what's-it god with a wad of Bronco bunched in her hand.'

There was a burst of laughter. 'Oh my God!' I clasped my hands over my mouth.

29

'That's just what she said. The sight of her set my underwear creeping up on me like it had legs.'

'I know what you mean,' said Janet.

'You'd have thought I had the runs or me arse was on fire, I was in such a rush to get away. I really reckoned I was a goner.'

'Why?' I asked before I thought.

A shadow fell over her face. 'Oh, I'm not shovelling all that on to you. You're still green. Best to stay that way for as long as you can. You'll find out soon enough about the nuns. Some of them aren't exactly sane as biscuits.'

'Tell her what happened next,' said Frances.

'Well, I went on running everywhere to avoid her. Eventually I bumped into her in the corridor. She spread out her arms to stop me like someone who wants to stop a bull charging at them. I was putrified. She put her hand on my shoulder and I thought she was about to lose her rag with me, but all she said was, "I'm afraid nature called me on the hop and I had to answer her immediately, but the what's-it's vacant now if you're still in need of it, child." ' Everyone burst out laughing again.

We returned to our polishing. My hands were getting sore from holding the boot and brush so tightly as I scrubbed. Ruth held her nose over a pair of boots complaining that if Jesus had washed twelve pairs of the nuns' feet instead of the disciples', the crucifixion would have seemed like a pushover. Janet put a gleaming pair of boots back into the pigeonholes, and pulled out another pair. 'Come on, Frances, sing something for us.'

'Yes, c'mon, Frances, c'mon!' eager voices seconded this, and Frances needed no further bidding. She put her boot down and began to sing in a voice of pure silver. I felt my eyes widen as the brush slowed and stilled in my hand. She sang with her eyes closed, sitting back on her heels. '*Magnificat . . . anima mea . . .*'

The mysterious song soared and echoed between the narrow walls. Her voice rose and fell and caught in her throat with such pure sadness that I was surprised not to see tears running down her face. As she sang, the other girls stopped polishing, basking in the melancholy song.

'What's that she's singing?' I whispered to Janet. I wanted to know.

'The Magnificat. We sing it in the choir, don't you know it?'

I took a deep breath, blew out my cheeks and puffed. 'No, I don't understand the words.'

Janet looked momentarily puzzled. 'Well, that's because they're in Latin. We don't understand them either.'

Frances stopped singing. Turning to me, she said all in a flood: '*Deposuit potentes de sede, et exaltavit humiles. Esurientes implevit bonis: et divites dimisit inanes . . .*'*

How could she do that? How was that done? How could anyone reel off the words so quickly and confidently? It sounded magical.

'Yes, but what does it mean?'

'Well, the nuns don't tell us that, do they? But I know it off by heart,' said Frances.

'Sing it again,' I said.

'Yes, out with it again,' the other girls demanded.

Frances grimaced and rolled her eyes. Then she opened her mouth and her voice rose loud and proud through the hush of air. It sounded better the second time. It soared; a bird, it held its flight. It tugged at something deep within me. I turned away to put more polish on my brush to hide the tears she brought to my eyes.

Frances finished on a high, wavering note.

'Well sung!' Everyone clapped. Clap-clip-clap. Her song finished, Frances's voice turned matter-of-fact again. 'Someone else, now. Ruth?'

One by one they took their turn to sing a song. They sang 'Greensleeves', 'Ave Maria', 'Danny Boy' and lots of other old

* He fills the hungry with good things: and the rich He sends away empty.

ones. Whenever a song had a chorus the other girls picked it up until a full choir of voices was singing. The songs were sad, the voices thin. I was too shy to join in, and terrified that they'd pounce on me to sing something. I stared down at the boots I was polishing, stiffly humming and nodding my head as though I were having a wonderful time.

'Now it's your turn, Judith,' said Frances.

My stomach kicked in apprehension. I looked at the ten expectant faces surrounding me, all of them waiting for me to sing. Ruth's eyebrows were drawn together in a smirk. I remembered Frances's advice to fall in with everything. Imitate, I told myself. Act. Mimic.

'Go on then,' ordered Ruth.

I struggled to my feet and closed my eyes. What should I sing? I opened my mouth and let out a wailing sound. My voice went up and up, thin and reedy, like a bird's. I tried to imitate Teresa Brewer, but I'd forgotten the words to 'Put Another Nickel In, In That Nickelodeon'. Improvising, my song had no beginning and no end. I felt a bit lost. I began in the middle and made up the words, moving my arms about like a sultry singer.

I opened my eyes to several smiling faces rocking in time to my song. Ruth seemed to be choking badly. Then a shrill shriek of laughter sprang from her throat.

'She can't sing for toffee!' Which took the wind out of my sails.

'Sshh! Go on, Judith,' said Frances. 'It's good.'

I took courage and let my voice ring out. I began to add my own words:

> *I am in the boot-room too,*
> *Polishing a nun's big shoe,*
> *All I want is loving you, and music, music, music.*

Other popular songs flooded into my mind, and I sang fragments of them, too, winding them all together into one crazy song. I knew the girls wouldn't know any of them. I had seen no wireless or a television set in the convent.

'What's she singing now?' laughed Ruth.

'Shut up and listen!' someone answered.

My song ended with the refrain of '*Oompah, oompah, stick it up your jumper*', which earned me wild applause mingled with giggling peals of laughter.

'Thank you,' I said, and sat down again. I felt encircled by the girls' enthusiasm and approval as though by a warm arm.

The juniors slept in the same enormous grey bare-walled dormitory as the senior girls. The seniors each had a tiny thin-curtained cubicle to sleep in; our beds, lined up at the other end of the room, looked exposed, with high black iron bedsteads like something out of a Dickens novel.

My triumph in the boot-room faded utterly as I stood beside an empty bed, staring at the thin mattress in dismay. Suddenly this was all very real, and stark, and horrible. How long would I be here? Mum, please come and get me soon!

Frances came over to me. 'Here, look – we've all got a chair beside our beds, see? That's where your clothes go at night.'

I stared at her. No wardrobe? No drawers? But already I knew better than to ask. I began to take off my dress. I stood in my knickers vaguely scratching my back. I felt sad and very tired.

Frances's hand flew out to grab my arm. 'No, not like that! Look, you put your nightdress on first.' She pointed to an enormous white tent-like thing that was laid across my bed. 'Then you take your clothes off under that. It's a rule: you're never to be uncovered.'

I didn't ask what terrible thing would happen if the nuns caught me uncovered. Miserably, I drew the scratchy nightdress over my head. I told my hands to hurry up, but I was butter-fingered with anxiety as I fumbled with the fiddly buttons at the neck. What a time it took, the great folds of material stifling and suffocating me.

'Don't worry, it gets easier with practice,' said Frances encouragingly.

Draped head to toe in our Victorian nightdresses, we poured into the cavernous washroom, a troop of bare feet pattering on red tiles, and washed our faces and cleaned our teeth in silence. Sister Cuthbert called out instructions: 'Rinse your hands thoroughly, before you wipe them on the towel, then all the germs will go down the plughole. Have some sense, Ruth, it's no use trying to look for them, they're minuscule.'

I cleared my throat and asked Frances, 'Where's the mirror? So I can brush my hair.'

Frances shook her head, and told me what I wasn't surprised to hear by then. 'We aren't allowed to have mirrors. If you're caught with one – ' She shook her head, hinting at terrible things.

As we returned to the dormitory, a bell rang. 'Kneel beside your bed quick,' whispered Frances. I obeyed, dropping my head on my hands. I heard a door open, and then Sister Cuthbert's voice said: '*Precamur, sante domini, hac nocte nos custodias.*'* I felt my shoulders shuddering as several shrill voices answered throughout the dormitory: 'Amen.'

Complete silence followed. Another bell rang, and this time there was a scramble jumping into bed and much noisy pulling-to of the senior girls' curtains. Tucking the end of my nightdress under my feet, I curled myself together under the cold sheets, shaking and trembling. I peered out for an instant over the blanket and saw green curtains round the seniors' beds. The light switch clacked loudly and we were in darkness. I shivered and yawned. My mattress felt lumpy. I thought of my sheets at home, with their smell of fresh air mingling with Mum's perfume. She'd have the kettle on the gas now to make a cup of tea.

Huddled on my pillow, which smelt of dust and age, I watched Sister Cuthbert's huge shadow move across the cracked ceiling. Was it true what Ruth said, that rats ran around the dormitory

* Holy Lord, we pray to thee, throughout the night our guardian be.

at night? She said they could jump on your bed and sever your juggler vein and you'd bleed to death like a stuffed pig. I uncurled my legs and turned over to lie prone in the bed, burying my face in the pillow.

Noiseless except for a vague rattle of beads, Sister Cuthbert approached my bed. I held my breath as the murky figure hovered over me.

'You're not by any chance crying?' said Sister Cuthbert. I could feel her breath on my face. It smelt of peppermints.

'No, Sister.'

'Always answer me with a complete sentence, please.'

I felt her hand on my forehead; her hand felt damp and cold. It slithered down to my neck. Was that the way a big fat rat felt – slithery and damp and cold? Ruth said that every rat had cold slimy fur and red-rimmed eyes.

Sister Cuthbert said, 'Now, tomorrow you will have to be up at five o'clock in time for Mass. Have you practised your genuflection?'

'Yes, Sister, I have practised it a lot.'

'I should think so, too. We don't want you making a fool of yourself again in church. But you are lying in such an odd way. Did your mother never teach you to lie on your back?'

'No, Sister.'

'Answer me with a complete sentence.'

'No, Sister, my mother never taught me to lie on my back.'

'It is more proper that you should.'

I straightened myself out, turned on my back and thrust my feet down into the too thin sheets and scratchy old blankets.

'That's much better,' said Sister Cuthbert, 'and put your hands above the bedclothes.' She took hold of them and crossed them over my chest. 'Now, if our Lord calls you to Him during the night, you'll be ready to meet Him as a good Catholic should. Goodnight, and remember to let the holy name of Jesus be the last word on your lips.'

She sailed silently out of the dormitory. I stayed in my new position for a few minutes, breathing slowly and deeply but awake.

I shall never get to sleep, I thought wretchedly. But even as I thought it my lids grew heavy and my crossed arms began to uncurl. I had just remembered to whisper 'Jesus', when Ruth's gruff voice rang out: 'Night, night, sleep tight, mind the fleas don't bite.'

'Shut it, Norton, you imbecile,' came a voice from one of the curtained cubicles.

Chapter 3

'Are you Judith Kelly?'

I took the hand of the broad-set woman dressed in a shapeless cotton hat and loose-fitting bib overalls smelling faintly of cow dung. Her name was Lorna, she said. She spoke in English, good English.

'Yes. I'm sorry to have arrived so late. How did you know my name?'

'I was told that the only person not to have arrived yet was English, so you aren't hard to identify.' She gave me a smile but I wasn't sure if the remark was complimentary. I felt both reprimanded and looked after. I followed her to the administration office of the kibbutz, smiling and hoping I was making a good impression. She ticked my name off her list and turned to me.

'Fill in this form with your details.'

Name, date of birth, level of education. My pen stopped when it came to religion/race. I bit my lip, gazing down at the form. My initial thought was to ignore the question. But my eyes kept returning to it. *You should put down Jewish*, ran my thoughts. *Why do you resist it? Your place in the world? You keep saying you want a real identity; well, here's your chance to declare yourself.*

I couldn't do it. I left the space blank, and shoved the form back at Lorna. 'Here.'

She stared at me for a moment, and then shoved her hands in her overall pockets. 'Follow me,' she said with a sigh.

I trailed after her to a supply room where I was fitted with two changes of work uniform, bed sheets, work boots, a kibbutz hat, two T-shirts and coupons for the kibbutz shop.

'You can buy all the supplies and toiletries you need there,' she said, 'also wine, beer . . .'

'I don't drink,' I said abruptly.

She looked down. 'Good,' she said with a grin.

As she led me to my room, she explained where I would be working. I was on the Ulpan programme, a six-month introduction to Israel and the kibbutz way of life. 'This week you will be working in the mornings in the orchards or citrus groves, and in the afternoons you will be taught Hebrew along with the others on the programme. Next week you will do the reverse – mornings for class and afternoons for manual work, *und so weiter.*'

We climbed the steps of the accommodation block, which looked like an enormous cricket pavilion. She led me into a small and narrow room with three beds crowded into it. Mine took up most of the wall beside the door. There was a faint smell of cigarette smoke. The curtains were rather roughly pulled back so that the room was a little dark. Several T-shirts and a towel were scrunched up on the floor. A red backpack lolled on one of the two other beds, and clothes hung from nails on the wall.

'Your room-mate is an American girl,' said Lorna. 'The communal shower and toilet is outside, at the end of the corridor.' She nodded in the direction of a lime-coloured door with a porthole window.

'That's about everything, I think. Don't forget that the evening meal is at six in the dining hall.'

'Do I have to pay for it?' I asked anxiously.

'Don't worry, you eat as much as you like for free here.'

I took her extended hand, which felt roughly hewn.

'I hope you enjoy your stay,' she said dryly, and descended the steps. When she reached the last step, she turned, gave me one brief quizzical sidelong glance, and disappeared.

*   *   *

38

I awoke from my old nightmare, familiar as my own skin. I am standing on the rocks, looking down into swirling waters. There is a chain of screams behind me, and I am being pulled in both directions.

Frances's eyes, beseeching me. Don't let go. The waves thumping against the rocks.

The dream lingered, vivid and heavy, pulling me down, making my mouth dry. For a few terror-filled seconds I didn't know if it was happening all over again. Or worse, if time had tipped backwards and it was happening still. The pounding of my dream continued: the heavy tread of boots on the tiled floor. My room-mate, apparently. And even though she had awakened me from the nightmare that had driven me to Israel, instant irritation flared at her thoughtlessness.

Listen, I know you've got good reasons for waltzing in here in your hobnails, but shut up, OK? Can't you see I'm trying to sleep?

I groaned and pulled the pillow tight around my head. Whoever it was didn't take the hint. The cupboard door banged open, and the boots stomped across the room again.

My fingers tightened on the pillow as I seethed. *If you're so determined to wake me up, why don't you just set off a firecracker, for God's sake? That would do the trick.* Nothing outraged me more than a senseless breach of basic consideration for others. I felt ill-used, annoyed and lacerated by the other person's selfishness. Deep down, I didn't believe in their innocence. They're doing it deliberately, my head told me, but I must control my resentment. Don't get angry. It's a luxury you can't allow yourself. It wastes too much energy.

A drawer slammed shut. That did it. I shot up and ran both hands through my wild mop of hair. In a voice ten decibels too low to be audible, I said, 'Don't you see me sleeping here?'

She was a handsome young woman, with a dark plait of hair snaking down her back. She wore a ratty army jacket and stone-scrubbed blue jeans. She jumped slightly at my reaction and then

39

turned to look at me. A T-shirt in her hands, just lifted from a crumpled pile on the floor, was being stretched into shape and folded. Her dark brown eyes squinted at me through round gold-rimmed spectacles with a kind of amused amazement. Then she half smiled at me. She had a good smile, that direct beam of one human being at another.

'Hi! I'm Cydney.'

'Cydney? That's a boy's name, isn't it?'

The teeth went away, her lips filled out, and her manner grew stubbornly hostile. 'OK, so the goddamn boots are noisy, but I've gotta break them in before we start work tomorrow.'

She took a wrinkled pack of cigarettes out of her jacket pocket and lit up. I watched disapprovingly as she inhaled and blew smoke out of her nose.

'Have you ever read what scientists say about the relationship between smoking and cancer?' I asked.

She stared at me. 'Do you ever read what scientists say about atomic pollution?'

I sighed. 'OK,' I said resignedly, 'I guess you know what you're doing to your own body.'

'Can the crap!' she said.

I slumped down on the bed and stared at her in wonder. Here I was in Israel upsetting one of the first people I'd met. Not a good start. Next time something annoys you, I told myself, laugh.

'Where are you from?' I asked.

'San Francisco,' she sang proudly.

'What are you doing here?' I asked, trying to forget the annoyance I felt; I found myself warming to her.

'My parents have just emigrated here. I'm on the kibbutz to learn Hebrew and then I'm gonna go to Jerusalem University.' She reeled off the information in a casual singsong voice as if she'd said it a dozen times before. 'But what I'm really here for is the free love,' she added with a playful laugh.

'I see. How nice.'

'You're English, right?'

'How did you guess?' I said. 'My name is Judith.'

'And what are *you* doing here?'

A strained silence. Cydney stopped folding a T-shirt, looked at me and waited. I racked my brains for the answer. Let's see . . . I recalled some ambitious plans about putting my life in order, but somehow the details had been lost. If there ever were any in the first place. I looked away.

'OK, no problem.' Cydney took a last drag of her cigarette and dropped it on to the floor, grinding it out with her heel. 'Where in England are you from?'

Phew. That was easier. 'London.'

Her eyes widened behind her gold glasses. '*Really?*'

'Yes, really.'

'Yessss! Oh, *yessss!*' she hissed ecstatically. She picked up another T-shirt from the pile. I watched her quick rhythmical movements as she folded. 'It's the capital of the world right now! In the States, every other song on the radio is British: The Beatles, David Bowie, Elton John, and the Rolling Stones. Hey, do you live anywhere near Buckingham Palace?'

'Quite near,' I lied. 'And Ringo Starr lives just around the corner to me.'

'Cool!' she said with genuine admiration. 'Listen, Jude, you'll like it here. This is a real neat kibbutz, you'll see.' She looked up at me smiling, the final T-shirt pinned beneath her chin. She placed it on to the neat pile, patted it and repeated: 'You'll see!'

Chapter 4

29 August
I cried in bed last night. I must have fallen asleep because when I woke up it was morning. I felt so sad inside and felt the sadness would never go away. It's so big and empty here.

30 August
The other girls don't talk to me much. I get up at five o'clock in the morning to go to church every day. It hurts my knees kneeling for so long.

2 September
I learnt to scrub a floor in a passage by the kitchens. I have to do it every day after Mass. I polish the refectory floor after dinner. We slide on the floor with cloths under our feet. And I clean shoes in the boot-room. Some of the girls sing songs in there. Frances has got the best singing voice in the world.

It was impossible not to like Frances. She had something special about her, something that drew people to her. Defining that special something wasn't easy, but when you looked into her eyes, you could always find it. She was open and friendly to everyone, and plucky and attractive and clever without being too clever. Everything I wasn't. The reason I had become a strange object among all the girls was still not at all clear to me – it was partly, perhaps, because the group had been together for years and intruders like me weren't to be trusted, but it was also connected with my distracted manner, which gave me the appearance of being half-witted, or a bit slow. The concept of Latin prayers remained a mystery. Why were they in a dead language which we none of us understood, yet still had to recite parrot-fashion?

As the weeks slowly passed, I stared at the words in the prayer books with increasing desperation. All around me the other girls rolled the words out fluently. It was like learning to read all over again, endless hours of tedious incomprehension. Even in the playground the girls had their own rites and rules, and I was a joke that even the nuns found a bit amusing – dopey Judith. Vacant Judith. Then I became a nuisance, an irritation. I felt awkward, alien, excluded, the outsider.

A hard-eyed girl in my class came up with the remarkable assertion that I was strange in the head, probably mad and the other girls edged away from me whenever I approached. Before long the gossip had spread like wildfire in the playground; it was generally agreed that I was a hopeless dope and more fitted for a loony bin than the convent.

Soon everyone was in on the story. In the playground one day, a girl was explaining to a group what happened to people like the dopey new girl once they'd been sent to an asylum. The girls surged into a knot to listen. 'Look at her!' she said, pointing at me. 'They put them in a straitjacket,' she hissed. 'You know, those jackets that they use for loonies where they tie their arms around their backs –' She demonstrated. 'Well, that's what's going to happen to *her*. And look at her legs. Have you ever seen anyone with legs more like a couple of mop handles?'

I stood apart, listening to the hail of insults, which beat upon my head until it felt bruised. Quite a little band of girls had gathered. 'Dopey!' they chanted. 'Pea-brain!' Some of them threw stones.

I noticed Frances watching them from the playground door. I could hardly miss her: at times she seemed to be in her own personal spotlight. The most striking thing about her was that she always seemed to be relaxed, no matter what she was doing. Now, however, she watched the group of girls resentfully and then walked slowly towards them and pushed through them to the centre.

'Leave her alone,' she ordered in her low, clear voice.

The knot of girls fell silent and pulled back to form a circle around Frances and the ringleader.

Frances leant forward. 'Some people learn things at different speeds, that's all. It's doesn't mean she's mad or weird.'

When she saw that the girl wasn't going to argue with her, Frances jabbed a finger at her and said, 'So stop copying the nuns by calling her names and spreading nasty rumours about my friend.'

My friend. The words haloed in a gleaming glow around me. Every girl heard it. Frances turned and looked at the ring of girls that had gathered. The circle spread wider, as if her glare was pushing them back.

She walked away from them and put her arm around my shoulders.

'Don't you mind them, Judith,' said Frances, who had obviously decided that I was by no means mad and even if I was, it didn't matter. 'You've got to fight for yourself here. You've got to have scars like the rest of us and once you get them, you'll be left alone.'

'I don't want any scars,' I said. 'You'll take care of me, won't you? Won't you?'

Frances nodded and for a week or more we were the centre of attention in the convent. For a while I was afraid of reprisals, but there were none and nobody picked on me again.

After that I just glued myself to Frances. I was like a stray dog,

45

starved and kicked. She seemed to understand that stray-dog feeling and let me hang around with her.

8 September
A nun pulled a girl's hair and she fell on the floor and screamed. She kept on hitting her. The nun's sleeves came off and flew up in the air. I was scared and my tummy was all turning over.

21 September
It's Friday today and instead of fish we had some horrible fried porridge for dinner.

25 September
Precisely nothing happened today.

During my first month at the convent, I began to prepare for my First Communion. The preparations took up much of my time and nearly all of my thoughts. The First Communicants, it was alleged, were a privileged band, set apart from the other girls. I was pleased to be in the company of Frances, and not so pleased to be with Ruth. Although she was six years older than me, she still had not made her First Communion.

'We've decided to give you a chance,' Sister Cuthbert told her, 'although I suspect that you'll never succeed in mastering enough of the catechism to meet the criteria.' Poor Ruth only had two talents: giving Chinese burns and drawing shaggy dogs. I thought it must be because she looked like a mongrel herself, with bright, anxious brown eyes peering through an unkempt fringe that toppled forward over her face.

As First Communicants, we spent extra time in the chapel and had daily interviews with the Mother Superior. We sat huddled at her feet in the sunlit hush of her little office as she told us about the different ceremonies of the Mass and the various vestments worn by the priest. She asked us whether such and such a sin was mortal or venial or only an imperfection. Sometimes she told us stories about saints and martyrs, of good children who had died on the day of their First Communion. We watched as her frail fingers with their thick horned nails twizzled her wooden rosary beads. They were as big as marbles, and clicked as she spoke.

'Don't think that just because you're children, you can't fall down dead at any moment,' she told the ten attentive faces in her thick, woolly voice. Behind her jam-jar spectacles, her eyes looked like big fish in a goldfish bowl as they flickered in the light and darted over our faces.

'God's anger light upon me if I'm not telling the truth – you'll just feel a pin prick and then you'll be gone. I'm sorry to cause you disappointment. But there it is.'

In spite of my outward calm, this revelation spooked me, and I felt my heart fluttering. What if I died before making my First Communion? Would I join the holy souls in purgatory? I started abruptly as I felt a hot hand grasping mine imploringly, and gave it a reassuring squeeze. It was Frances who was sitting next to me. I was relieved to know that someone was just as anxious as I was.

We sat there, gripping hands, gawping around the room. Black velvet curtains on carved wooden rings hung at the tall windows. Somewhere a clock ticked. Incongruously, afternoon sunlight streamed in from the garden outside. I stared at a picture on the wall – a sombre-faced Jesus holding a lamb.

When the Mother Superior smiled she uncovered her big discoloured teeth and let her tongue lie upon her lower lip – an effect that sometimes made me feel queasy. She would close her eyes, nodding gently to herself as she told us one of her special stories.

'Once upon a time, there was a girl called Jennifer,' came her voice from beneath her black veil, 'who, like you, carried out all the preparations for her First Communion with great eagerness. When at last the grand day arrived for Jennifer's First Communion, she made her way to the chapel together with her class-mates also dressed in their white frocks and veils. On the way, Jennifer noticed that someone had carelessly dropped a toffee behind a statue of Our Lord. Jennifer was delighted and quickly picked it up and popped it in her mouth.

'She chewed on it and then swallowed it. It was only after-wards that she realised what she had done. She had broken her fast and could not now receive her Communion. Jennifer struggled with her conscience, but, alas, the terrible little devil of human pride won.'

The Mother Superior stopped suddenly, opening her eyes and glaring at us. '*Who* is making that infernal humming noise?'

At this, Ruth stared vacantly at the ceiling, we all looked at Ruth, and the room grew very silent. Janet, who took all the troubles of the world upon herself, coughed nervously. Her fingers wove together incessantly.

'Well, come along! Who is it?' said the Mother Superior.

There was an uncomfortable shuffling. Janet coughed again and sniffed. All eyes were on Ruth. She had developed a habit of taking off her shoes and rocking slightly, back and forth, her arms clenched around her knees, humming in a monotone. Whenever she felt the nun's myopic stare on her, she remained still and silent. But the minute the nun's eyes closed, she'd begin her rocking movement again, crooning softly to herself and occasionally blowing bored, glassy bubbles through her mouth.

The Mother Superior's gaze rested on Ruth. Her eyes nar-rowed behind her glasses.

'Do you need to go to the what's-it, Norton?'

'No, Reverend Mother,' she said.

'Well, what's wrong with you then?'

'Nothing, Reverend Mother.'

'Stop wriggling about like a parched pea in a colander! I've been told all about you, Norton, so don't think you'll get away with anything. And put your shoes on. If you're going to undress, I shall have to cover up the picture of Our Lord.'

48

Ruth put on her shoes and as Mother Superior stared at her through her black-rimmed magnifying spectacles, I noticed that one of the lenses was cracked clean across and had been glued together with yellow glue, beaded along the mend.

'If brains were water, child, yours wouldn't be enough to baptise a flea. Your behaviour is appalling. I'm reminded of Moses on Sinai discovering the excesses of the Children of Israel. Once again the literal truth of the Bible has been demonstrated!'

Ruth, at that moment, popped a large bubble of spit with puckered lips. She seemed quite oblivious of the bottled rage that bubbled so near her.

'Tell me, do you even know what the Holy Trinity is, you buffle-headed child?'

I saw a quick flash in Ruth's eyes. 'Yes, Reverend Mother,' she said smiling importantly. 'It's the old church at the bottom of Hastings Road, isn't it?' I wasn't too sure if she was joking.

'Oh, take care, child,' hissed the nun. 'One flick of Fortune's wheel and you'll be brought low. Wipe that smirk off your face or I'll wring your ear for you a yard long. I know only too well what the punishment is for your kind of sin. It's written over and over again in the Bible. If I have to speak to you again, you'll not receive your luminous rosary on the day of your Communion. I shall give it to the missions instead. There's enough wickedness in the universe without you adding to it. The Holy Trinity is three, three, three Gods in one. Now to return to my story without any further interruptions, if you would be so kind. The next girl who makes a noise like a wasp when I have asked for silence will get a sharp slap for naughtiness.'

She swept a stern look over us all and closed her long thin lips an instant, but eager to get on with her story, raised an out-spanned hand to her spectacles, and, with trembling thumb and ring-finger touching lightly the black rims, steadied them to a new focus. We stared timidly back at her.

'Where was I before I was rudely interrupted?'

'Jennifer had eaten the sweet and broken her fast, Reverend Mother.'

'Ah, yes.' Fixing her glasses more firmly on her nose, she closed her eyes again.

'Jennifer thought of the chapel, adorned in honour of the First Communicants, of all the nuns, children and town folk who had come to watch the prestigious event – but she did not have the nerve to take off her veil and say humbly: 'I have broken my fast and therefore cannot make my Communion today.' So she joined the other First Communicants in church, and when they went up to the altar to receive the host, she went too, knowing full well that she was making a *wicked mockery* of the Holy Sacrament.'

The Mother Superior paused for a moment, taking us in with accusatory eyes. I gulped and squeezed Frances's hand.

'All her days, Jennifer bitterly repented her wicked pride and weakness, but the tears of a lifetime could not undo the terrible fact that she had made her First Communion in mortal sin. Had Jennifer died before she left the church that morning, she would have passed straight from God's holy table into the fires of hell! For remember, we are as grass which today flourisheth and tomorrow is cast into the oven. Will you two girls stop touching one another?'

Frances and I quickly unclasped each other's hands.

The Mother Superior scanned us triumphantly, her finger wagging in admonishment. 'So remember, children, that the day of your First Communion will be the happiest of your lives, and God could grant you *no greater grace* than to die at the moment when Our Lord is first placed on your tongue.'

There was a silence. The atmosphere seemed full of the sour smell from the nun's black habit.

I felt greatly relieved when her clock clacked and she asked, 'What time is it? Three? Goodness! All stand. Now, why don't all of you make your way to see Father Holland, *quietly*? And I hope I don't hear a noise like a wasp, Norton. As you may know, Father Holland is a priest who is popular for the remission of sins, but clearing up after you lot will be a full-time job. He simply cannot be in the confessional twenty-four hours a day. So remember to help him in his task and examine your conscience daily by asking yourselves the following questions: Do I take the name of the Lord our God, in vain? Do I love my neighbour as myself? Do I covet my neighbour's goods? We shall try to understand these questions fully during the next few weeks so that you may derive from the understanding of them a lasting benefit to your souls. Now off you go and don't dawdle.'

I stared at the floor, pinned to the spot by her words. I did; I coveted my neighbour's goods. I thought of the way I felt if one of us got any pocket money on Sunday. We should have received sixpence each, but a black mark against our name in the nuns' little black books meant a deduction of one penny. By Sunday, most of us had received at least six black marks. I decided that, between one thing and another, I must have broken every one of the Ten Commandments.

I scrambled to my feet with the rest of them, making my way out of the tick-tock musty room as quickly as I could without drawing attention to myself. I had a strange, giddy feeling that after making my First Communion I would never see Mum again. Never grow up, but be trapped here for ever . . .

Frances and I dropped behind the other girls as we headed down the long, draughty corridor towards the priest's quarters. Both of us were quiet, lost in our thoughts. All at once I decided: I had to summon up the courage to tell Father Holland that I could not possibly make my First Communion because my Mother was Jewish. I didn't want to die. I didn't want to go to hell.

I looked at Frances to see if she was still as afraid as I was, but she gave nothing away. She bounced along as usual, her hands deep in her tunic pockets. When she saw me looking at her, she grinned as though she had never been afraid at all. 'Well, what do you make of all this?'

'All what?'

'The Catholic Church. Your First Communion.' Frances had a very grown-up voice, soft and calm.

I frowned. I didn't understand her question. Frances helped me. 'Like, do you believe in the catechism, for example?'

'Well –' I hesitated. 'I . . . don't really understand it yet.'

'You mean you want to believe it? Being a convert, you have to make more of an effort than I do, I guess. And so maybe you even come to believe it better than us lot.'

'But don't you . . . ?'

Frances lifted her thin shoulders. 'Believe it? I don't know. It's too much a part of me. I've been here since I was two. I'll never get away now. I don't think I want to, either.'

'Really?' I stared at her, appalled, as we walked down the corridor. Shafts of dusty sunshine slanted through the windows, so that shadows and sunlight alternated across her face.

'No, why should I want to leave? I was sent here years ago because my mother was too ill to look after me, and *that* hasn't changed. She lives in a mental hospital. An asylum called Netherne. It's in Surrey. I can only remember seeing her once, a long time ago. She was wearing a red dress.' Frances trailed a finger along the wall as she spoke, her face creased in thought.

I took a deep breath, and checked to see that the other girls were still far ahead of us. 'Frances . . . do you think the nuns are too strict?'

Her eyes widened. 'Too strict? They only lose their tempers with us because they care.'

'They've got a funny way of showing it,' I said. 'All they do is shout, shout, shout, yet we're told to speak in lowered voices.'

'That's to keep us out of trouble. I'll tell you a secret, if you promise not to let on to anyone else. I mean, sometimes when Sister Mary loses her temper and hits me, she tries to make it up to me afterwards and says things like, "Did I hurt you much?" and "I'd like to be your mother and kiss away all your tears." She kisses my forehead and sometimes she kisses my hands. Once she kissed me for a long time on my mouth. I don't like it much, but I don't dare stop her.'

I tried to think of the right thing to say. Was it right for a nun to kiss you? Was it like when I put my face up to Mum to say goodnight and then she put her face down? That was to kiss. Mum put her lips on my cheek; her lips were soft and sticky and they wet my cheek; they made a tiny little noise: plock. Is that the way Sister Mary kissed Frances? Why did she do that? She wasn't her mum.

For some minutes I walked deep in thought, and the only sound our footsteps on the creaky wooden floor. The air in the corridor chilled me. It was wettish.

Then I burst out: 'No, I'm sure it's not right. I've never seen such horrible treatment of children in the other schools I've been to! If a nun hit me with a cane the way you told me they hit Ruth, I – I'd snatch it out of her hand and chuck it out the window!'

Frances smiled knowingly. 'No, you wouldn't. What good would that do? The nuns would just get another cane; they've got dozens of them. It's much better to put up with the punishments they dish out – that way you keep everyone else out of trouble.'

I remembered the sound of Sister Mary's cane when she was giving the order for the girls to move to church: whistle, crack. That was the sound you heard but if you were hit then you would feel a pain. I wondered what the pain was like. It made me shivery to think of it, and cold.

Bewildered, I shook my head. Frances seemed to understand it all so much better than I did. 'What about your father?'

'I don't know. I . . . well, I haven't got one.'

'I haven't got one either, not now,' I said to make her feel better. 'My mum brought me here by train. I was really pleased, I thought it was a surprise holiday.'

I heard the resentment in my voice and a sudden flood of anger arose in me as I fought back the tears. I looked away from Frances to hide them. I wasn't sure how Mum had planned everything to be. All I knew was that those plans had seemed to go terribly wrong. After I'd been at the convent a couple of weeks, I'd begun to realise that something big and irreversible had taken place. Life had stopped in its tracks, without explanation.

I'd now been at the convent for a full month, and still hadn't heard from Mum. Nothing that had happened during that month at the convent had helped ease my anxiety. The food was tasteless, the rat-ridden dormitories horrid and the atmosphere everywhere charged. There was always a sense of impending danger and I couldn't bear to live my life in such a way for much longer.

Frances stopped walking and touched my arm. 'Judith? What's wrong?'

I shook my head, but the emotions overwhelmed me. I turned quickly away, pressing against the wall and burying my head in my hands as I burst into tears.

'Why doesn't my mum *write* to me?' I sobbed into my hands. 'I've written to her twice already, and she hasn't sent a word . . .'

Frances put her arm around my shoulders. 'She probably has, Judith! Listen, Sister Mary always holds on to our letters for ages. I'll make sure you'll get them soon, all right?'

I looked up, my tears still wet on my cheeks. 'Will you? How?'

Frances shook her head. 'Wait and see, but I do promise it. Look on the bright side.'

I took a deep breath, wiping my eyes. 'Oh, well . . . that's all right then.'

I said it offhandedly, trying to be brave. Crying didn't go over too well here; I had already found that out. I had cried on many occasions during my first days at the convent. Lonely. I felt it all the time, down to my toes. The other girls, who looked on crying as a weakness, ignored me. Ruth called me a grizzle-guts, telling me I'd end up with water on my brain.

Now Frances rewarded my show of bravery with a smile. I managed a smile in return.

'That's better,' she said. 'It'll be all right, you'll see. Now come on – let's hurry, or we'll be late for Father Holland.'

'What's he like?' I asked as we arrived at a carved wooden door.

'Oh, he's a completely different kettle of fish to the nuns,' she said. 'You'll see.'

Father Holland, inky in his cool parlour, cooed rather than spoke. He allowed us to wander around his spacious rooms, gasping at the crowded clutter of gold-framed pictures, glittering statues and candles. His rooms had a bedroom smell of ancient fabrics and dust. When we got bored with gawping around, we slid over his polished wooden floor between one magic carpet and the next. He smiled at us and waited patiently, crooning a hymn to himself.

'Shall we start?' he said finally. 'You, my child – what's your name?'

One by one, we told him our names. He sat back in his armchair, his hands behind his head, his colourless eyes looking at us over his half-moon glasses. Beside him on his desk stood a teapot, a plate filled with biscuits and a fruitcake. We sat on the floor at his feet and fixed our hungry, mournful gaze on the cake.

He pulled out a large white handkerchief and blew his nose energetically. 'Now then,' he said, 'I am going to tell you about the charity and unselfishness of Jesus, about the Lamb of God and about mercy and forgiveness.' He plunged into a lecture, his gentle voice quivering with emotion.

I sat very still as he went on, my forehead drawing together in concern. I knew very well that the nuns showed neither forgiveness nor mercy to Ruth for being left-handed. None of it made any sense to me.

'Now, the catechism,' he urged us, busying himself with the teapot. He poured the milk in a thin high stream and dropped three lumps of sugar into his teacup. Picking up his cup, he jiggled it in his hand before taking an enormous mouthful and swishing it around his teeth.

We chanted the lines of the catechism in bored, singsong voices, our attention focused wholly on the cake as he brought out of his pocket a big penknife. He couldn't resist displaying its beauties to us – the corkscrew, the tweezers, and the blade that shot open and locked when he pressed the catch with his red bulging fingers. Then he cut himself a slice of cake and ate it, spewing out crumbs as he chewed.

He must have been aware of us watching him like waifs peering at a glutton through a restaurant window, because he smiled.

'Can I press you to a slice of cake?' he said. He gave us each a piece.

As the others munched, I thought my chance had arrived to have a private word with him. Quickly wolfing down my cake, I stood up and sidled around the side of his desk.

'Father, can I ask you something?' I whispered breathlessly.

'Well, now.' He turned his round, sleepy face to me. 'And what do they call you, again?'

'Judith Kelly, Father.'

'And what's troubling you, Judith?'

'Forgive me Father –' I glanced at the others, and then hissed quickly in his ear, 'I don't think I should be making my Communion because I might fall down dead.'

His head jerked back as he stared at me.

'My goodness,' he said at last, 'that's an odd thing to say. Who put that in your head?'

'Also Father . . .' I looked down, my voice dropped even lower as I mumbled. 'I can't take Communion because my mother's Jewish.'

He frowned and patted my arm. 'Very good, my child, very

good,' he murmured. Clap went his hands and he told the others to leave and to take the remainder of the cake with them. 'I'll eat it otherwise,' he said, patting his big stomach. 'Go on, now. I'll remember you all in my prayers.'

There was a general hubbub as the girls walked out the room carrying the cake. Frances looked over her shoulder at me as she left. I had already confessed my fears about Communion to her, and I nodded in answer to her unspoken question.

When everyone had left, Father Holland leaned back in his chair and picked at a tooth with the tweezers from his penknife, his breath whistling slightly between the gaps in his teeth.

'Now then, young lady. As a Jewish child, your mother has loved you enough to place you in a Catholic convent. I know it must be a huge leap of faith for you – right over the edge of reality. You'd do better if you accept the Communion. That's what you need. No matter how hard an uphill climb you may find it. God has not chosen an easy path for you, Judith. Being a convert, you have to make more of an effort than the others.'

'That's what Frances said,' I blurted out.

His pale eyes clouded. 'Frances?'

'McCarthy.'

'Ah, yes. Well, she's quite right. And making your First Communion will be your first step along the path to goodness, won't it? You'd have the sacrament inside you. That would be something, eh? Your mother will be most pleased.'

I nodded doubtfully, still seeing the dancing flames of hellfire. 'Perhaps I needn't take the host on my tongue. I'll make sure it goes underneath.'

'Oh dear, dear me,' he groaned. He rubbed his hand through his silver hair. 'Judith, when you make your first confession, you must confess to these sinful fancies and all the sins of your past life. Meantime, I don't want to hear any more of this nonsense. It's for your own good, that's all.'

The room was very quiet as he spoke of the nuns' goodness towards the children. It was impossible to repay their years of selfless devotion, but I could show my appreciation of them by making my First Communion without any fuss. I didn't want to argue with him because he was the kindest grown-up I had met in a long time.

He packed some biscuits into a serviette for me and we walked together out of the chapel building. As he left, he touched my head. 'Bless you my child, I shall pray for you. And don't worry, because it's all part of God's mystery. As the dove alighted on the ark after the flood, bringing hope to those within, so too he settles our fears and calms our troubled thoughts.' I was genuinely sorry to part from him.

After the shadow of his room, the sunlight outside dazzled me. With the heap of biscuits clutched in my hand, I thought maybe I wouldn't die after all if I made my Communion. But even so, I decided to write to Mum and ask her.

As I headed towards the convent front door, I placed my prayer book on top of my head. I had to walk to the front door without it falling off. It was a small, shiny book, not the best kind for carrying on your head. I imagined that there was a bomb in the book and if it fell off my head I would explode. Steady was best, not too fast, not too slow. I knew that, but as I approached the front door my steps quickened, trying to get to safety. Panic. The book slid off my head; I caught it.

Uh-oh! Death.

Frances was perched on the front steps, waiting for me. I grinned happily when I saw her. My feeling for her was one of pure admiration. It wouldn't have mattered if she had never spoken or even looked at me, provided I could bind myself to her by private allegiance. But she seemed to be seeking out my company more and more and I was grateful.

She made a sourpuss face as she stood up, brushing at her tunic and glowering at me. 'What were you talking about for so long, anyway? I've never had a private talk with Father Holland once and I've lived here years.'

'I told him everything,' I said confidently.

'Everything? Even about not wanting to make your First Communion and all?'

'Yes, even about not wanting to make my First Communion and all.'

'Did you tell him about not taking the host on your tongue?'

'That too.'

'And what did he say?'

'Not much. He just gave me all these biscuits,' I said holding up my bulging serviette.

She studied the serviette with a baffled frown. Clearly it was beyond her. As we climbed the steps into the convent she shook her head.

'I don't know, some people have all the luck. There's no advantage in trying to be a good Catholic. I might just as well be a sinner like you.'

Chapter 5

As soon as I mentioned Buckingham Palace and The Beatles, Cydney's manner towards me changed. She became friendly, looking at me with a mixture of shyness and faint curiosity. I felt guilty for misleading her. I knew myself to be secretive and dishonest.

'*Yesh*! *Yoffi toffi*!' she said with a smile. We started at a brisk pace down a path.

'What does that mean?' I asked.

'*Yesh* means cool. *Yoffi toffi* is nice toffee.'

'I see,' I said, feeling bemused. 'Where are we going?'

'To eat. It's six o'clock.'

'But isn't the dining hall over there?' I said pointing in the opposite direction.

She made a face. 'Yeah, but we're going to the volunteers' camp where they make real chow. The others from our Hebrew course are there. All of us have only been here for a day or two, but we already get along real fine.'

So I allowed myself to be herded down the pathway, though part of me wondered at the fact that I could still be bossed around by women like Cydney.

The kibbutz looked like a big park, with ragged green lawns, trees and water sprinklers. The resident kibbutzniks lived in rows of cream bungalows with red roofs. Beyond a meshed wire fence lay a bright rectangular swimming pool, where several children and adults splashed up water like chips of glass in the sun. At the far end of the kibbutz, we came to a square of wooden houses. Cydney pointed to a group of five or six people hanging around chatting, oblivious to us.

'They're what we call "volunteers". They work six or eight hours each day, but get more leisure time than the Ulpanists do.' The volunteers were a fascinating assortment of hangover hippies, burnt-out runaways and tourists who came and went looking for the unwired world, moseying around in flowery long-haired groups dressed in paisley and denim.

A delicious smell wafted over to us as a girl in a long sixties Judy Collins dress, with her blonde hair braided and wrapped around her head like a golden crown, stirred a pot of communal stew. Further on, I could make out the shapes of people seated and standing, and heard the sound of chattering voices, punctuated by explosions of laughter and underpinned by the strumming of an acoustic guitar.

A bunch of people wearing brightly coloured T-shirts and shorts were having a barbecue. They all looked upsettingly young, no more than teenagers, though I knew that most must be in their early twenties. I felt my mouth jerk into a premature smile, as if practising, and made it stop. It might look funny to appear with a big smile already stuck on.

I need not have worried because, just as we came upon the group, someone threw a cupful of something at the barbecue. Orange flames erupted with a *whump*. Everyone jumped back, yelling and hardly noticed as Cydney and I joined them.

Cydney grinned and rested her hand on my shoulder.

'This is Jude, my room-mate. She's so British, she sounds like the Queen of England.' Everybody laughed, and those sitting hopped to their feet. All extended hands to me.

'Jude. Great to meet you. I'm Rick,' smiled a sunburnt man with long blond hair. He was slim and long-necked, with big prominent lips. I smiled back, murmuring something inane.

'Hi! My name is Mark,' said a strikingly handsome Jim Morrison look-alike.

'Paul,' said a third, with a grip like a vice. He was about seventeen years old, with crazed brown eyes. A scarf was tied round his head and his reddish brown hair hung over it in strands. 'Hey Jude! Let me guess which part of England you're from,' he said. 'London. Right? Forget London, man. This is where it's at.'

I wondered what the Queen would say in such circumstances.

'Wonderful,' I kept saying. 'How lovely.'

Cydney pointed to a young man with a whiskery face and bright blue eyes, playing a guitar.

'That's Michael,' she said. 'He doesn't speak much, he just plays music.' Michael raised the arm of his guitar in acknowledgement. 'And this is Mario,' continued Cydney. 'He's from Uruguay and doesn't speak English.' Mario was heavy-set, his blond-flecked hair and beard accentuating cornflower blue eyes. He nodded at me without offering his hand.

Two women drifted over to the group, their suntanned skin shining like caramel. They looked at me curiously.

'Hi,' said one. Her dark fringe fell into her deep brown eyes. 'I'm Nadine, and this is Evelyn, she's from England too.'

'Oh jolly good! Whereabouts in England?' I asked in my best English accent.

'Southend,' replied Evelyn. She had black waist-length hair and couldn't have been more than eighteen.

'Ah yes, Southend,' I replied. 'That bleak seaside town so beloved of fixed caravan sites and Punch and Judy at the end of the pier.'

They all burst out laughing.

'Far out!' yelled Cydney.

But Evelyn just looked at me with cold disgust and whispered something to her companion. Turning to me, she said, 'Do you normally speak like that or is this for our benefit?'

An undertone of hostility threaded through her voice. My

stomach tightened. I forced a laugh from the back of my throat and turned my attention to the smoking barbecue. Forget it, forget it. But I felt outnumbered, as if they were all a different species.

Everyone sat down cross-legged on the grass, staring at me as though I were an alien fallen from the sky. I suppose I was, in a sense. They began to ask me questions in their rolling American drawl. Why had I come to Israel? Was I some kinda dropout debutante? Were my parents very rich? Did they own a goddam country estate? Their attention was turned on me full force. I felt ambushed. Too much interest brought out every ounce of reserve I had, made me unable to think, to formulate answers, even to hear the questions. I stuttered replies, shook my head, finally just looked blankly back at them all. Everywhere I turned there were faces that expressed the sheer golden, self-satisfied joy of good health: their hair shone, their colouring was rich and their teeth were strong. I was alone, separated from everyone by an aching void of loneliness, but I deserved it. I did not dare to look them in the eye. I did not want to contaminate, did not wish to find further evidence of my lack of worth. Everyone here is an adult, I thought, whereas I am merely in disguise. Probably they thought I was a weird frump, sort of like their high school teachers. It had been crazy to think I could fit in here. I was beginning to sweat. I felt as if I was at the dentist, mouth gawkily open while some stranger with a light and mirror gazed down my throat at something I couldn't see.

'Why don't you say something?' Evelyn demanded, 'You do, after all, speak the Queen's English, don't you?'

I looked down at my feet in their thick brown shoes and traced a pattern in the dusty red soil. Probably she's out to get me now, I thought, and probably she'll succeed. She thinks I insulted her, yet I never intentionally insulted anyone. I sometimes thought that I didn't have to say a word to offend people, that my existence itself offended them.

64

'Hey! Don't pressure her, man!' Rick said. And I breathed again as their attention shifted. Plates were passed around and food from the grill slapped on. Warm bagels and large ladlefuls of various kinds of salad were heaped on to my plate.

Michael began to quietly strum The Beatles' song 'Yesterday' on his guitar.

'That's gross, man, it's giving me bad vibes,' said Mark. 'Don't you know any Doors music?' Michael thought for a moment and then plunged into a rousing rendition of 'Light My Fire'.

To my relief, they all began to talk to each other as though I didn't exist. They were explaining their plans for the future, holding them up to each other like crystal treasures. They took it for granted they would always be useful and busy. They were versatile and thought they might do all sorts of things in the future. Archaeological digs, university, European travels, skills to be learnt, intellectual heights to be scaled. I felt envious of their belief in the future, and wondered at their confidence, the sort that planted trees for a hundred years ahead.

'We'll all be working our asses off every friggin' day during the next six months,' said Mark. 'Morning, noon and night.'

Rick shrugged. 'No problem, man. I'll work and study, I'll never quit.'

'Yeah, you'll be perfect.' Cydney gave a mocking nod, her eyes gleaming behind her round gold spectacles. 'Hey, you guys, I was rapping with Lorna and she told me that we're never to venture into the Carmel Hills without an armed soldier.'

I cleared my throat. 'Why?'

'Because there's an Arab terrorist group based in a village that overlooks the kibbutz.'

Mark yawned. 'Well, I don't hear any sounds of gunfire or explosions. Only the crickets and the flies.'

I felt my skin prickle and the familiar rolling pressure of panic building inside me. I didn't operate on the same frequency as these people. Dimly, I noticed Cydney staring at me with concern. I hunched my shoulders, half turning away. I wanted nothing from anyone but indifference. It was easier to handle; I was used to it. Indifference, or something more definite, like the strong waves of unfriendliness I could feel coming towards me from some of the group. They obviously didn't like me. Why? We hardly knew each other.

'Hey Jude, more food?' said Cydney, 'You look like you need building up.'

'No, thanks, I've had quantum sufficio,' I said, hoping to raise another laugh. 'Any more and I shall bust.'

But no one even looked at me, and the two girls, Evelyn and Nadine, exchanged a grimace. Even if it had been funny, they still wouldn't have laughed. What was the expression that Ruth used? It was like putting a poultice on a wooden leg. Well, that was too bad. So what? They could all go to hell. I didn't care.

The evening wore on and the lowering sun lit up tiny insects in the evening air as they described arcs and things unknown. Michael played his guitar, and some of the others started to sing along, their voices mixing with the crickets. Occasionally someone would fumble the words, and then they'd laugh and tease each other. I sat hugging my knees. The distance between us was insurmountable. I did not inhabit the same sphere.

Finally Cydney turned to me. 'I guess we should go if we have to be up by five tomorrow morning. We gotta be in the orchards by six to pick apples.'

'Super dooper, Gary Cooper!' I said and they all burst out laughing. But to my ears, the sound was false.

Chapter 6

29 October
Every day someone gets hit. Sister Mary hit us all last night with the cane. We stood in a circle and held out our hands. My thumb is still swollen.

3 November
Sister Mary banged my back against the wall. She hit my face. My nose was bleeding. I was really scared because it hurt. She put me in St Joseph's cupboard. Why did she pick on me? It's not fair. I was sent to bed and some girls made a cradle for me.

Winter was darkly on its way and the convent was large and draughty, with treacherous cracks that the cold air crept through. Standing huddled against the wall in the playground one day, with patches of ice still on the gritty concrete, I thought I would never be warm again. My hands were bluish with cold and I dug them deep inside my tunic pockets. I remembered with longing the unbelievably luxurious clothes I used to wear: knitted mittens, thick woollen socks, my red pixie hat.

The playground was just a bare yard, surrounded on one side by squat thorn bushes and on another by a row of tall poplar trees. The afternoon sun did little to contain the cold wind whipping around. My feet felt so numb I thought they would fall off. I stamped them on the ground. The steam came out of my mouth like cigarette smoke. I put my fingers to my mouth like I was holding a cigarette, and breathed out.

Groups of girls circled around the bushes, eating leaves and calling it bread and cheese. Bored of my fake cigarette, I began chewing the ends of my hair, a habit I had acquired recently during punishments of silence. These were moments when time seemed to slow down to a stop. Just one word from a nun, and we had to stand still with our hands on our heads for ten minutes or an hour or two hours or however long she said, until the silence became thick and crushing. I had felt it like a tangible thing, swelling like a balloon under so much emptiness.

At those times, my life stretched away in front of me, every boring bead-like minute of every boring bead-like day lining itself up to be got through. Now I always had one lock of hair that was pointed and wet.

Almost three months had passed without any word from Mum. Whenever I thought of her it was like a vacuum pushing in my chest. Was Sister Mary really hanging on to her letters, like Frances said? She had no right. Or was it just that Mum hadn't written to me? I felt a rage rising in me as I stood against the cold playground wall.

Shoving away from the wall, I threw out my arms for balance and began to spin wildly, round and round. The cold air pulled against my arms, trying to stop them from going so fast, like dragging them through water. I kept going, faster. Eyes closed, little steps in a circle, my heels scrunching on the gravel, really fast – the convent, trees, the hedges all waiting to stop my feet. So what if Mum doesn't write? I don't care, I don't care – I tottered and fell to the ground, on my back, gasping. I could almost feel the spin of the world beneath me.

I opened my eyes. Dizzy. I had to lie there till it was over, trying to grab and hold on to the swooping red-brick building and grey clouds through force of will. Close your eyes and you're powerless, at the spinning world's mercy. Stuck in the convent. Stuck on the ground.

I felt sick. With an effort, I kept down our dinner of mediocre potatoes, shreds of rusty gristle and ponky cabbage, all mixed together and served in a mess from a huge aluminium pot.

Staggering a little, I stood up. No one was taking any notice of me. I felt warmer, at least. I leaned moodily against the wall again, watching as some of the girls slid on a frozen puddle. Frances beckoned to me to join them; I shook my head. She shrugged and carried on playing. She was used to my moods by now.

Suddenly Sister Mary came swishing into the playground with giant strides. I blew warm air into my hands, making a loud hissing sound as she thundered past me, her long rosary beads clattering as if in protest. *Your fault,* I thought sourly. *It's all your fault that I haven't heard from Mum yet . . .*

The nun froze, fixing me with a stony stare. She beckoned to me, holding out her forefinger and curling it up like a worm. Terror clutched me by the throat. Had she read my mind?

'You, what's-your-name, come here quickly when I tell you!'

'Me?' I pointed to myself.

'Yes, you!'

I went forward very slowly.

She drew herself up stiffly, glaring down at me. 'I have read the letter you wrote to your mother yesterday.'

'Why?' I protested with a surge of anger and defiance.

'I'll ask the questions and you'll give me the answers. I examine every letter you write here. If I do not approve of it, then I will not send it. Why did you ask her if you should make your First Communion?'

'Because . . . she may not want me to.'

'Why not?'

I bit my lip. I had hoped that Mum would come and take me away from the convent once she heard I was to make my First

69

Communion. But my plan had gone awry. My ears buzzed and Sister Mary's voice began to sound distant.

'Your mother goes to church, doesn't she?' I heard her say.

Some gut feeling told me that I was approaching dangerous ground. I tried to evade the question. 'I think she believes in God, Sister.'

'I should hope so, too. But does she go to church?'

'There isn't one of her sort where she lives.' I faltered for a second. 'She – she believes that there's more God in trees and birds and caring for people than in churches and synagogues.'

Sister Mary's nostrils dilated. Her clenched-up face tightened further, if that were possible. 'In *what*?'

'In trees, and . . . and birds.'

'No. You said than in churches and *what*? What did you say?'

I swallowed. My throat was sandpaper. 'Synagogues. That's what they call my mum's church.'

'Who do?'

'Jews. My mother's Jewish.'

Sister Mary jerked backwards as though I had slapped her. 'Nonsense!' she hissed. 'You've been poisoned by the devil! Don't you know that?'

'But,' I stammered, 'it's all right, Sister. There's nothing wrong in it. My mother says that Our Lord was a Jew.'

She let out a roar of rage and charged at me, her mouth twisted with fury. 'Blasphemer! Devil out of hell!' she screamed, almost spitting in my face.

I whirled around to get away from her, but she grabbed my hair. She snapped my head back, so that I lost my balance, staggered, but she was holding me up by my hair and pulled me to my feet. I cried out as I felt a chunk of it tear away.

Abruptly, she grasped my shoulders and slammed me against the brick wall. Once, twice. I lost count. The pain in my back felt red then purple and all I could do was gasp. It felt as if my throat was being squashed into my chest and I had lost the secret, the

70

rhythm of breathing. Behind it, there was only a hole, filled with pain.

'Stop it! Stop it!' I could hear myself screaming as if it were someone else's voice. Sister Mary's face twitched violently. She hit me in the face.

Crack!

A great stillness enveloped my shock. I clutched at my face. I wouldn't take my hands away, not for anything. My nose, what had happened to my nose? It felt as if it had been pushed right into the interior of my head. Blood ran through my fingers. I tried to pull myself up. I didn't know I was screaming, the others told me later. My chest ached and tears splashed into my mouth.

'I want my mum,' I wailed, my voice hoarse as a pink bubble popped out of my mouth. Bent over, half standing, half sitting, I looked across at the other girls. My eyes met theirs in mute appeal, but what could they do? I was alone. All around me, I could feel their fierce sympathy reaching out to me, but nobody moved or made a sound.

Sister Mary took hold of my chin, yanked it up to make me look at her. She was a blur of black and white. I could hear her breathing heavily. She bent down, stared into my eyes for a moment, and said in a tight, soft voice, 'Do you understand? You're a wicked child. I have torn up that letter you wrote to your mother. You will rewrite it without mentioning your First Communion. Do you understand?'

I shook my head and shrugged, confused and sore.

'And if you ever write such things again . . .' She made some sort of signal over my head.

I nodded slowly. Now I understood. She would murder me.

'I'm sorry, Sister. I'm really sorry.' My teeth were chattering.

She grabbed my arm and dragged me off to a cupboard built into the wall, just inside the entrance to the playground. She unlocked it, pushed me inside. I heard the lock click shut.

The daylight disappeared. The cupboard was cold and damp,

and smelt like mouldy earth. Outside in the playground the senior girls' voices cried out: 'All in! All in!'

Then a nun's voice: 'Get in with you! In, in, in!'

Then the coughs and voices ebbed away until there was silence. Apart from a crack in the door, there was no light. I whimpered, a cupped hand still protecting my nose. My skin itched at the thought of spiders and creepy crawlies swarming up my legs in ticklish streams. To drive them away, I began to stamp my feet in a steady rhythm. My nose pounded to the beat of my feet. It had stopped bleeding, but felt sticky and swollen.

I wiped away the drying blood with my sleeve. Nausea soured my throat, and I tried not to gag. I wanted someone to hold on to. Anyone. But now I really had turned into a bad person, and nobody would want me any more, nobody would like me. What should I do? Maybe even Frances would chase me away. No one wanted a friend like me.

I forgot the bugs and curled up on the floor. When would it be time to come out? Stifling darkness pressed down on me. I hugged myself, shaking. I felt like a different person lying there in the dark; it was as though I had said goodbye to some central part of myself, leaving an unfamiliar shell.

I remained curled on the floor, breathing in the smell of dirt and mould, for what seemed like hours. I listened as hard as I could for footsteps. Everything stayed quiet. I don't know how long I had been there when I finally heard a click in the lock and the handle snapped down.

It was still daylight. I pulled myself stiffly to a sitting position. Attempts to open my eyes brought bright lights and shooting pains. I groaned and then made out a large figure looming above me, black on white. A pair of clean lace-up boots, shiny and hard as a man's.

Sister Mary leaned over me. 'Right, upstairs with you. Wash your face and go straight to bed.' Her voice wobbled as she spoke.

I felt her hand tug my arm. I stumbled out of the cupboard into the daylight and gasped as hot pain shot through my eyes. What had happened to my eyes? The light stabbed like needles, even through my closed eyelids. Guided by Sister Mary's hand, which now shoved me insistently towards the stairs, I put one hand against the wall to support myself as I struggled upstairs towards the washroom. My tongue felt like a lump, and my mouth was glued shut.

A nun met us on the stairs. I stopped and looked up. It took me a moment to focus my eyes. Then I saw that it was Sister Cuthbert staring down at me with an anxious look on her face. Sister Mary put her finger to her lips and took the nun to one side, speaking quietly.

I stood clenching my teeth together, staring at Sister Mary as her whispered voice rose and fell. Finally both nuns looked at me. Sister Cuthbert motioned for me to come closer.

I swallowed, and stayed where I was. Sister Mary would kill me if I said anything to the other nun. Sister Cuthbert beckoned again, more urgently. Slowly I fought down my fear. I went up to her. She smiled sympathetically as she scrutinised my face.

'Oh dear, oh dear, we *have* been in the wars.' The sympathy didn't seem to belong; it could be peeled off her eyes like a plaster from a grazed knee. 'Your face is very swollen,' she said, as Sister Mary glared at me sideways, from behind the jutting edge of her headdress. 'You must have taken quite a tumble, but you'll live. Best go and sleep it off.'

'Yes, Sister,' I whispered. I couldn't look at Sister Mary. I had the sense of being hemmed in by evil. *Things are so wrong here. Things are so wrong, and I'm so scared . . .*

I hobbled rather than walked the remainder of the way to the washroom and the rescuing darkness of my bed. I wrapped myself tightly in my blanket. My stomach began to make crawling sounds. The rustling on the other side of the dormitory sounded suspiciously like a mouse scurrying across the hollow floor. I lay with my knees up, as close to my body as I could get them. As well as biting my fingernails, I'd developed a habit of sucking the tops of my arms, which were now covered in small bruises. I squeezed my eyes tight shut, as if somehow blindness would protect me.

Nana and Pop. Nana and Pop. I chanted their names over and over. I took out each memory, caressing them like favourite photos. I didn't want to lose or forget anything, because I wanted to get out of here, I wanted to get back to my grandparents. I'd been so happy living with them after Dad had died. The only way I'd find my way back would be if I remembered everything about where they lived.

I closed my eyes. I could see every detail of their house in London, as clear as a picture – the balcony with the geraniums, the kitchen with the sun streaming through the windows – and I could walk every room blindfold. I remembered all the familiar sounds of the area of London where they lived: The cries of the newspaper vendors in the languid evening air; the last few birds in the street, the bustling of traffic and the murmuring of the sky before darkness spilt over.

All these sounds marked out a familiar road. Then, bedtime was the time when I used to feel happiest. Cosily tucked in by Nana with a kiss on my forehead, and a night of easy, dreamless sleep to look forward to.

I shivered as I lay in the dormitory. No matter how hard I tried, I couldn't pull these two worlds together. Nothing connected to anything else any more. Nothing was in its right place. That life was no longer mine. There were no feelings left. I couldn't even feel my breathing; I couldn't feel my ever-present hunger or the cold.

I hunted in vain for some thread I could hold on to. I could only get away from this unbearably strange present by going back to the images of my past: a world whose rules were slowly disappearing.

'Nana and Pop,' I whispered into my blankets. 'I'm so sorry.' I gave a quiet sob. My nose still throbbed. I curled myself into a frozen ball, praying to forget the convent.

*   *   *

Nana and Pop. I couldn't think of one without the other. They were always together. I carried their picture in my memory like a black-and-white snapshot when the shadows look harsh under the gloss: Nana, walking her two Dalmatian dogs along the pavement in Connaught Street, London; behind her Pop's out-of-focus Bentley, ice-cream white, with a shiny chrome fender. And then black and white fleshed into colour and I saw Nana dressed in pale green and cashmere. A brooch or a jewel pinned on her cardigan. Pearls around her neck. A flowered scarf. Her ripe nut-brown hair, with only the faintest tinge of grey at her temples.

Every night I got trapped in the same dream, finding a path that led to a precarious bridge, curving high over the Thames to London. Every night I almost made it across the bridge, and every morning Sister Mary woke us before I could cross it and find my way back to Nana's house.

Mum and I had lived with Nana and Pop for four years after Dad died. Nana had been ready and willing to take us in when we had nowhere else to go.

'Judith, your bedroom has a balcony that overlooks the main street,' she declared when we first arrived. I bounced up on my toes, thanking her, and then I looked at Mum and wondered why she wasn't excited about living in such a big house. When she smiled at Nana it was only with her mouth, not her eyes.

Pop called himself a 'schpieler'. He ran his own betting offices in Mayfair and Brighton, and each day he held my hand as we walked to the Hampden Gurney School, near Marble Arch. I loved London, with its jungle of packed red double-decker buses grinding nose to tail, the continual murmur of dragging sounds, the silvery sigh of Pop's car. He was big and safe, with twinkling dark eyes that smiled down at me as I skipped along at his side.

Sometimes he'd let me play in his car, holding on to the steering wheel and pretending I was the driver. He'd take me with him to his betting office in Bond Street, where I'd watch him taking bets from low voices that burred like bees over the telephone. Framed around his office walls were images of long-dead horses standing with their meek heads poised in the air as if listening for the shouts of the vanished crowds. I loved to listen to the rise and fall of Pop's voice as he bawled orders, and was sure I could do it just as well, given the chance. When he gave me a toy red telephone of my own, I picked up the receiver and said: 'I'll have two shillings each way on Salamander running in the 2.30 at Epsom.'

Pop loved this story. He told it to all his friends, and they teased me about taking over the family business someday.

Every evening we'd sit at the dining table with its starched white cloth, and Pop would talk to me like a grown-up. He'd peer at me over his copy of *The Winner* and joke: 'Do you know how many horses owe me money?' or 'Never gamble, it's a mug's game.' And after dinner he'd brush my hair with his hand, muttering something in Yiddish.

Nana was an avid reader, and it was she who whetted my appetite for books by giving me *Alice's Adventures in Wonderland*. Mum had read this book when she was a child, and now she loved to show off and quote the first page to me word for word. When Nana gave it to me she put a drop of honey on the inside cover saying, 'Eat!' because in her view, learning was sweet.

Together we'd retreat up the stairs to the drawing-room. It was large, glowing with colour, and a place in which I always felt secure. On the landing enormous Chinese ginger jars gleamed like fat-bellied gods. There were eight of them, on rosewood plinths, and I gave a name to each one. In the drawing-room we would sit on a little Chippendale sofa, beside which stood a marquetry table and a collection of snuffboxes.

Once I surprised Nana when she had not detected my approaching footsteps on the thickly carpeted floor, and she declared, 'You don't have to go tiptoeing around here. I don't like surprises!'

'Maybe I should wear bells round my ankles,' I laughed.

'That's a good idea. Shall I tell you a story?' she asked.

'Oh, please!' I climbed on to her lap.

Every strand of her hair was in place, dark and shining.

'Do you know what a *zaddik* is?'

I frowned. 'A *zaddik*? No.'

Her warm face tugged into a smile. 'A *zaddik* is a holy man.'

'Like a priest or a rabbi?'

'Yes, that's right. Well, this particular *zaddik* was not only a wise man, but also a great human being with an enormous love for all of God's creatures, even the weakest and smallest. He felt so responsible for them that he didn't want to hurt even the lowest ant. You know, there are some people in the world who take advantage of those they have in their power and enjoy it, but not this *zaddik*. He had bells put on his shoes, so that when he walked, the ants could scurry out of the way and they always felt safe in his kindly presence.'

On the word 'scurry' she ran her fingers up my arm, which made me squeal with delight.

On Friday afternoons, Nana had a housemaid who helped to clean the house from top to bottom before the Sabbath. Fridays were hustle and bustle. The silver had to be polished; the candlesticks especially had to be nice. In the kitchen there was busy to-ing and fro-ing, and slowly the entire house filled with the familiar Sabbath smells of roast chicken, gefilte fish, kishke and the challah baking in the oven.

After the meal it was always 'our' Friday evening. We'd walk through the packed streets of the West End to Piccadilly Circus, full of coloured advertisements all made up of changing lights, amid the swish of cars and taxis and the jangle of human traffic. The glossy terraced houses stacked up and down the streets. The shops in Oxford Street, all powdered and rouged, bursting with fabulous knick-knacks; the cold splendour of Marble Arch and the gleam of Hyde Park all against the backcloth of a racing sky

– To me this was the greatest show on earth, and much more exciting than either the theatre or the cinema.

Where was Mum was during these outings? I supposed she must have come along with us sometimes, but in my memory it's just the three of us, Nana and Pop and me, walking between them and swinging on their hands.

My special time with Mum was when I returned home from school and told her about my day. Then something happened that really shook my foundations with a bang – Mum found herself a boyfriend. From that moment on I began to see less and less of her and things were never quite the same again. She was engrossed in a world of her own. There were days when I didn't seem to exist; she would look right through me or walk around me, wearing a smile that bulged with secrets. I was invisible. Something or someone was definitely making my importance shrivel overnight.

A car revving up in the street or the jangle of the doorbell had me looking out of the window at the top of a tall man's head. With his dark hair and a big smile, he was the spitting image of Gregory Peck. I watched as he opened his woody car door and helped Mum inside. When the sound of its engine had faded away I'd slump back from the window knowing that I'd not see Mum for a couple of days.

Now when Mum made a rare appearance, my ears buzzed whenever the phone rang. Then she would usher me out of earshot. 'Upstairs, Judith!' she'd say, pointing her finger at the ceiling.

When she caught Mum on the phone for the umpteenth time, gentle Nana actually raised her voice: 'A little less time on the phone and a little more with your daughter would make life easier for us all.' Listening from the top of the stairs, I nodded self-righteously to myself. Nana was right: Mum should spend more time with me. Things should be like they used to be.

Mum stopped going out so much, but she and Nana didn't stop arguing. Hearing high voices from the kitchen one day, I went downstairs in the hope that the sound of my tread might stop them. I stood outside the door and listened. Nana's low voice muttered in uncomfortable bursts. I told myself that they were talking about Mum's work, and grafted random words to the music of their voices, as a songwriter might. But just when I thought I had understood, the rhythm and pace of the altercation changed, and I had to start again. It was a tiring game. Finally, footsteps – slow, reluctant, deliberate – approached the stairs and I raced back to my bed.

The front door slammed. Lying awake, I listened to Nana and Pop moving around in the study below. Their voices were louder than I'd ever heard before. I could hear individual words quite distinctly: *This man . . . I told her . . . for Judith's sake . . . you shouldn't have . . .*

I didn't mean to fall asleep, but suddenly I felt exhausted.

I found a hiding-place where I could spy on the grown-ups' conversations. A cubbyhole inside Nana's larder which, when opened, released an earthy, sweet smell. The larder was stacked with biscuit tins, brown bags tied up with rubber bands, squat jars of jewel-like amber marmalade with curls of peel.

Under the bottom shelf where bunches of dried herbs lay, I discovered a little cupboard. I'd take off my shoes and open the little door, turning its round brass knob to release the secret tongue inside. I had already worked out the best way to sit, with my knees drawn up as far as my chin, and crept in head first, reaching out to grab my sandals and pull the door shut after me.

I fiddled the tongue back into its wooden groove to close the door and waited. And waited. Each minute I heard the long hand on the kitchen clock click forwards a notch, and tried to amuse myself by counting the sixty imaginary seconds in between. *Forty-one . . . forty-two . . .*

All at once Nana swished in, flip-flopping in her house slippers, her skirt brushing against the kitchen table as she passed. The sound of water running in the sink, and then a deeper sound, like water filling a container. Making tea by the sounds of things. I squinted my eyes as I hid, piecing together the action. More footsteps, and Mum came in. I knew it was her by the way she cleared her throat.

'I've had enough of this. What have you got against Michael, anyway?' Mum's voice was a furious whisper. My teeth chattered. I let them.

I heard something slam on the counter. Nana laughed coldly.

'Michael? I've nothing at all against him. What I object to is that your – *infatuation* means that you never see your daughter any more.'

'How dare you accuse me! She's perfectly well taken care of!'

'Yes, by me! Because you're never here! I've already *raised* you; I'm hardly keen to do it again!'

'I'm here all day! Just because I go out the odd night – '

'This isn't what you promised me when you moved in, was it?' Nana's voice turned scathing: ' "Oh, Mum, it's just for a little while, just till I'm back on my feet, and you'll never even know Judith is there, I promise!" *Ha*!'

Their voices broke through whispers and became shouts. I didn't want to hear any more. I crouched there, flushed and frozen, holding my breath. I had to stay stone still. If I stayed very still, they would stop.

'Shut up,' I whispered. 'Shut up, shut up.'

A final angry voice, and then they left the kitchen, one after the other. It had worked. I hugged my knees, pressing my cheek against them. I don't know how long I sat there. Long enough to be cold. No voices, just shuffling and creaks. I could move now; the worst bit was over.

When Nana cuddled me now, it was as if she were hanging on to me. The silences were the worst, waiting for the arguing to start again. I began to spend hours making faces in the mirror to ease the tension building within me. It gave me the chance to try out different ones: faces that I could replace, so that I could believe I was a different person. After trying three or four different faces, or ten perhaps, or twelve, I would decide I liked only one of them – the one that made me look good – and would try to make it come back. But once the face had disappeared, there was no way to retrieve it.

Other children had nice smiles. Not me. Perhaps I would always be toothless. Nana had exchanged my milk teeth for three sixpences, saying they would grow again, but now I doubted anything she said. I wanted them to grow again so that Mum would notice me.

When Nana caught me staring in the mirror, she warned me that if I looked at my reflection for too long I would see the face of the devil and that would bring bad luck. No one guessed that my reflection in the mirror already doubled into the rough red face of the devil galloping towards me. It grew monstrous, the hairy jowls palpitating, every deep wrinkle swelling around its immense Cheshire cat grin.

I painted a picture of what I had seen in the mirror: red-rimmed, glassy eyes, an oversized blood tear dropping from one of them. A face that stared directly at me, encased in fury. It was as angry as I was sad.

Crimson paint was haphazardly spattering Nana's kitchen table as I listened to Mum and Nana arguing again.

'I'm fed up with your spying on me, day in and day out!'

I heard a plate being cracked down on the dining-room table so hard that it smashed. I kept my head down, feeling with every word they spoke the knot of hatred building between them. There was no time to lose: breathless with anticipation, I painted at breakneck speed.

Then I heard Mum calling to me: 'Judith, put your coat on and put anything else you want to take with you into your satchel, then come down here.'

I ran to her with burning cheeks. 'What's happening, Mum?'

She stood proud and furious, glaring at Nana. 'We're leaving here for good.'

My first thought was a happy one – Mum was taking me with her. Then Nana grabbed hold of my arm. 'Go back upstairs and finish your painting, Judith.'

Mum kept silent, watching me and waiting. I was like a juggler keeping two objects airborne at opposite ends of the stage, moving quickly from one to the other to avert disaster. I tried to balance myself neatly in the middle of them, but the lopsided tug-of-war that followed was won not by Nana's need for me, but by Mum's hesitancy, which I interpreted as her wish to abandon me. I couldn't breathe for fear of losing her. I had already lost my dad and now my mum had my double love. I wouldn't let her go without a fight.

I resolved the tussle by yelling, 'Mum, Mum, she won't let me go with you!' as Nana wrestled with my arm. In my heightened vision of terror, the two contestants seemed like ugly giants. I didn't want to break down in front of them. I clenched my jaw until it felt sore.

'Wait outside, Judith.' Mum gritted the words out tightly. As I turned to leave, Nana stood aside to let me pass. I was numb. They were both angry with me. With one last glance at Nana, who looked at me as if she was about to cry, I left.

Mum found a posh hotel for us to stay in for a few days, and then moved us to a dingy one with a tiny bed and a window with a view of a brick wall. Each morning, before setting off for work, she left a plate of sandwiches on the bed for my lunch, along with a magazine to read. I flipped slowly through the pages, looking at the elegant models in their stylish hats and dresses. If Nana and Pop wanted to find us, they wouldn't know where we were. Yet though I spent anxious hours waiting for Mum's return, I locked the door to make sure they couldn't take me away from her.

'Will I be going back to Hampden Gurney School soon?' I asked her after the fifth day on my own.

'Not yet,' said Mum. My relief was mixed with secret disappointment. Relief that Nana wouldn't come and take me away yet worry that I might forget how to read. Or write my name. Or tell the time. Or everything.

'But when, then?'

'I don't know at the moment.' Mum was losing patience. Her eyes looked slightly red, with shadows under them. She turned away, stubbing out a cigarette.

'Never,' I muttered under my breath.

She didn't answer. A few minutes later, I knew that she was in one of her distracted moods again and lost to me. When I asked her if everything was all right, she just muttered 'Yes, yes,' and moved away to stare out the window, with its dismal view of crumbling bricks.

Some days we trudged the endless concrete of London looking for a permanent place to live. Walking beside Mum with my satchel bouncing on my back, I watched London change its colour. As the solid mass of its wilderness closed around us, I saw clumsy drunks lurching sideways through dim doorways and beggars hawking for pity; rubbish-ridden streets where most of the people looked worn out and so closed in on themselves that I wondered if they were sickening for something.

London seemed like an old man with manky breath. Along the pavements blobbed with spit, the wrangling voices of foul-mouthed spivs emerged from fag-fumed pubs and dark alleyways. Packed tube-trains where crowds swayed against one another, heads solemnly averted. Smells of petrol, coal smoke and plaster dust filled the air. Mum and I looked at numerous tiny rooms for rent with paint peeling from their walls in brittle flakes, single black bedsteads with striped mattresses rolled over, greedy coin-eating meters. And notices in the window declaring 'Room to Let – no Irish, children or animals'.

When she saw the fourth such notice, Mum stared at it blankly. 'No children?' she said, incredulous, her voice rising to a shout. 'Why not?' She made a megaphone with her hands to her mouth and shouted toward the top stories of the block: 'Why no children?'

I took fright and pulled at her dress. Don't shout. Don't shout, I prayed. Mum, flushed with anger; me with my eyes on the ground, pretending I wasn't with her. Her voice rang through the street. The pavements were crowded with people, throngs of them, advancing and retreating, hurrying on, turning aside; in the road lorries ground their gears, moved forward, stood idle, their exhaust fumes rising in the air. A few of the people passing by saw Mum calling out. They ran over and said, 'Come on, we'll help you shout.' And they joined Mum in the middle of the street. Someone said: 'One, two, three!' and everyone shouted together: '*Why no children?*'

Every now and then somebody new came along and joined in. Before long, I had lost my embarrassment and was soon shouting louder than anyone. '*Why no children? Why no children?*'

Bulldozers and steam hammers were digging the road. Noise throbbed everywhere. Someone said, 'There's a policeman coming!' Mum and I stood for a moment, jostled on every side by the jumbled voices of the dispersing crowd. The broad space around us seemed to narrow. The dazzling sunlight darkened. Mum seemed suddenly to chill.

'It's a real lark, isn't it, Mum?' I said, trying to cheer her up. But I shouldn't have said it because Mum started to cry. I couldn't think of anything to say except, 'Oh Mum, please stop crying,' which made her cry even harder, so that her shoulders shook.

The policeman just looked at us and went on his way.

One day Mum returned to the hotel, her face alight with a smile. 'I've found a room, in Gloucester Place near Baker Street.'

'Am I allowed to live there?' I asked.

'Not really.' She was throwing clothes in the suitcase, not looking at me. 'I've told the landlady that you're going to a boarding school soon, so just play along if she asks.'

I sank on to the narrow bed, digesting this information. 'Can we one day live in a house of our own with a garden?'

'All right,' said Mum, folding my cardigan. 'We'll get a proper garden. It won't be too big – just the right size for the two of us to sit out in.'

'Do you mean all right yes or all right maybe?'

'I mean,' she said, closing the suitcase, 'all right hopefully. Now remember, you're to tell the landlady that you're going to a boarding school soon.' And immediately she went and seated herself by the window and turned to face the street. She no longer seemed to be thinking of me or, for that matter, of anything, and she even looked over at me from time to time with an odd expression, as if I was now in the way. When I sat down next to her, she appeared to be seized with some sort of anxiety, and occasionally she would glance furtively out the window, her eyes feverish.

I wanted to believe she was only stalling for time by telling me to lie to her landlady. I wanted to trust her. But my dreams that night were of a bulldozer rumbling loudly towards me churning up the road in which I stood.

Nana and Pop. Nana and Pop. I'm sorry. I want to go back to you. Please forgive me. I lay in the chilly, unforgiving dormitory, watching my breath and the ice forming on the windows. I drew the blanket over my head and remembered Hanukkah with Nana. I wanted peace, but my imagination slumped at the word. I closed my eyes and tried in a half-hearted way to picture 'peace' – behind my lids I saw a grey darkness going on and on without end, a place I'd not known for a long time, a place that now seemed far stranger than any wonder of the world. I opened my eyes again and immediately fear moved in my veins, for there entering the dormitory were several shadowy figures. I shrank into my bed. Something appalling had happened which I could not at that moment remember. A sense of a changed world, like my first day in the convent. I closed my eyes again. I had a violent headache and my back was hurting. Then I suddenly remembered the afternoon in the playground and more vaguely my time in St Joseph's cupboard.

'How do you feel?' someone asked.

'Terrible!' I felt weak and sorry for myself. The darkness crouched behind the girls, thick and heavy. Carefully cupping the sides of my mattress and stretching the blankets tightly around the sides to make a crib, they rocked me slowly from side to side. *Hush, hush, hush,* they soothed. Frances, Janet and the other girls from my class. I rested my head on my pillow as sleep overwhelmed me again, great clouds and folds of sleep like a warm fog.

'Shh, Judith. Shh,' murmured Frances. She stroked my head.

The cloud of confusion dissolved as I realised that I had been accepted, as if into a united family, because of what had happened. I had become part of the pattern. I felt a strange relief.

Chapter 7

'So, are you ready to work?' said Cydney.

Everyone was ready except me. I was seated on the edge of my bed feeling groggy as I laced up my boots at five o'clock in the morning. My God, the last time I got up this early was at the convent for morning Mass. I stretched, yawning. My body was made of stone.

'I didn't expect it to be so cold in Israel,' I groused.

'Let's go.' Cydney ran a comb through her hair and turned to smile at me. 'It'll soon be too hot, believe me.'

We met up with a group of assorted volunteers and kibbutzniks. In their crisp shirts and shorts, with their sun-bleached hair showing under the brim of their cotton hats, they were like a herd of happy cattle. In the distance a red tractor catching the first rays of the dawning sun droned towards us. Its driver, a kibbutznik, bathed in coral light, came down the dusty path between the cornfields. He put the tractor in neutral, waved to us, then gestured with his arm towards a trailer on the back. We all piled in. The tractor then sputtered and pulled out like a tugboat on choppy seas. Down to the orchards we rumbled, passing citrus groves and avocado trees, holding on for dear life against the crazy vibrations. The kibbutzniks with their powerful voices and their strength greatly impressed me, but they had nothing to say to us.

'They're very aloof,' I said to Cydney swallowing a yawn.

'Yeah, they think we're soft, spoilt members of the bourgeoisie who'll run away from Israel after a few weeks.'

'They may be right there,' I said. 'I mean, look at those two girls from New York, they look like those twenty-first century Barbie dolls with their shiny blonde hair and blue eye-shadow.'

'Sure, grim,' sneered Cydney, squinting through her spectacles. 'Their T-shirts are so tight, they're cutting off the blood flow to their brains. I give them two weeks.'

We both laughed, the early morning breeze tousling our hair as the tractor plummeted on.

'We'll only win the kibbutzniks' approval by proving ourselves to be good workers, and those two won't get much done in those shoes.' Cydney pointed to their high-heeled sandals. The two girls sat across from us, talking animatedly to each other, blissfully unaware that their fate had already been decided for them.

'How many hours are we scheduled to pick apples for?' I asked.

'Four,' said Cydney, 'It'll be back-breaking work.'

She was right.

We were each given a bucket-like shoulder bag for the apples. When they were full we were told to place them gently in the trailer at the back of the tractor. 'And we want to see this trailer filled by the time we finish here,' said the foreman.

A haze hung over the orchard, which stretched endlessly before us, heavy with fruit.

Back and forth we toiled, picking and dumping. The sun rose, turning the sky into the clearest, palest blue. Soon I could feel the blistering heat, a ferocious furnace burning my skin. It was only seven o'clock but already it was so hot and humid it was like breathing soup. After the first hour, the two Barbie dolls, no longer neat and clean, leaned against the truck, sulking and comparing blisters and broken fingernails. I had blisters too, but I kept picking steadily, aware of the kibbutzniks' eyes on us.

Four hours later even lighting up a cigarette was a monumental effort for Cydney. As I combed the leaves and twigs from my hair and wiped my hand, wet with perspiration, upon my T-shirt, I realised how much I had enjoyed getting dirt on my face and under my fingernails. Hard work, but it felt simple, natural. I was burned by the sun and my eyes, hair, and lips bore the ravages of dust and wind. My blood was jumping yet, even though I may have looked like a free soul, inside I still felt dirty, contaminated, harbouring a guilty secret that I didn't feel any-one else would understand. I smiled uncertainly at Cydney as we made our way unsteadily to the dining hall, where we ate an Israeli breakfast of fried eggs, sliced cheese, cucumbers, olives, tomatoes and gefilte fish.

'Not ready to give up, then?' She grinned.

'Nope. Not yet.' I leaned back in my chair and put the heel of my hands into my eyes and rubbed them. I was dying for a hot shower and some sleep.

But by no means was the day done. It was just beginning, in fact, because after breakfast, it was time to learn Hebrew. The class was a hotchpotch of nationalities: Italians, Indians, Spaniards, Russians, but mainly Americans. Many of them were Jews. Here they were, members of the group I had dreamed of declaring myself part of – they were here in force, but being Jewish was the last thing they wanted to talk about. Whatever they were, their respective ethnicities had been left behind.

As I took my seat in the classroom, my stomach pulling nervously, I willed myself not to panic. Across the aisle from me sat an older woman, a refugee from Russia. I watched as her thin fingers gripped her pencil, her brow furrowed, her mouth pinched. Tough mind, mature soul. Bitter experience had given her a wisdom that I still lacked. She looked very much alone, and it made me ashamed of my own fear.

A list was passed around. Once our names were down we were officially enrolled. Even if I was here under false pretences, this place was to be my lifeline for the next few months: that was something no one could take away. A temporary safe haven.

But the Hebrew letters stood before me like black iron gates, refusing entry. I stared at the blackboard as Teliela, the young Israeli woman whose misfortune it was to teach us, scribbled words and phrases down and did her best to keep the Americans from making asides in English. English was a forbidden language in class.

The thick flat heat hung over the classroom, and I stifled a yawn. If I was honest with myself, I was less interested now in learning Hebrew than memorising the lyrics to the Joni Mitchell songs that I'd heard at the barbecue. The best music to make love to, according to Cydney. I much preferred the comforting golden-rich strains of the Yiddish that I'd heard with Nana and Pop to Hebrew. Their words had soothed me and assured me that I was a good girl, and that all that mattered was that I should be healthy and happy; the thick and slippery formality of Hebrew evoked in me no such response.

On my way out of class a week later, Teliela stopped me.

'Judith, could I have a word with you?'

When the others had left, she smiled and said, 'I don't know if you've heard, but newcomers from the Ulpan are often assigned an adoptive family on the kibbutz.'

'No, I hadn't heard.' It sounded horrible. My stomach tensed at what I knew was coming.

'Well, the idea is that you have a home to go to, you know, instead of just the compound. Tea and chats.' She beamed at me. I could feel my bristles rising with alarm and indignation. I nodded stiffly, crossing my arms over my chest. Tea and chats, my God. I just wanted to be left alone.

Some of my reluctance must have filtered through. Teliela's smile faded as she looked down at a piece of paper. 'You've been allotted an elderly kibbutznik; a woman called Miriam. She specifically requested that you become her kibbutz daughter, if you're willing. I'm sure it would do you the world of good to have a little chat with her.'

'I don't think I would have anything to chat with her about,' I said, trying to prevent my voice from sounding aggressive.

'Well, you know,' said Teliela, 'I thought it might be nice for you, because she's a very astute woman. People often go to her for advice or help about anything that's troubling them.'

She held the slip of paper out to me.

'I have no troubles that I care to discuss,' I said. I was rigid with hostility, shuddering at these phrases. I didn't need anyone to meddle with my mind and heart. 'I don't have to have an adoptive family, do I? I mean, I'm just here to learn Hebrew, I don't –'

'Well, you don't *have* to, but it's certainly recommended,' said Teliela. 'Think it over anyway. Perhaps it's the sort of idea that takes some getting used to.' When I still hesitated, she shook her head and said, 'Miriam is very highly thought of here, you know. She's practically a legend – she was one of the pioneers of the kibbutz, living in tents in the early days. She doesn't often volunteer to adopt a newcomer. But she asked for you especially.'

Why would she ask for me? Despite myself, I was flattered. Slowly, I reached out and took the bit of paper.

At four o'clock I stood on Miriam's veranda overlooking her garden. I didn't want to go in. I felt like Teliela had tricked me somehow. It probably wasn't even true that Miriam had asked for me – why would she? I scowled at the door and then sat down on the creaking sofa-swing, dangling my legs so that my sandals hung loose. Beside me, a low round table was covered with a faded cloth, embroidered in the centre with flowers.

I swung rhythmically back and forth. Of course Miriam hadn't really asked for me; Teliela obviously felt sorry for me and had pressured her into it. She was possibly dreading this visit as much as I was. So I'd just go in and tell her thanks but no thanks, and that would be the end of it – then I could go back to the business of disappearing.

Determinedly, I pulled open the screen door and knocked on the inner door. Nothing. I turned the knob, but it didn't give. I pushed harder, and it opened. The screen door clattered shut behind me as I stepped inside.

I was in a small living-room with a table strewn with books, a floor lamp, a large, comfortable sofa and a shiny little sideboard with a crumpled lace cover on it. There was a small desk, the top open, stuffed with papers and a general dotting of china ornaments and knick-knacks. A pedestal fan rattled softly, moving the thick air around the room. From inside another room, mysterious shuffling sounds were issuing. I peered in, letting my eyes adjust to the dim light.

A scene from my local library confronted me. The walls were creaking with shelves bursting with books. In the midst of it, an elderly woman stood, bent over, her back to the doorway. She was intent upon her labour and had not heard me enter.

'Em, hello?'

She turned around slowly. She was wearing an open-necked summer frock with pale washed-out flowers upon it. Her freckled face was handsome, with deep concentrations of lines around her eyes. Her life had clearly been uphill, painful. A worked and working face. Her reddish hair was parted in the middle, wrapped round her ears and held in a bun at the nape of her neck. Her features expressed energy and goodwill.

'I know,' she said, 'you must be Judith.'

Her eyes, a compelling blue verging to violet, looked directly at me. A powerful blue spotlight.

I shrugged. 'That's right.'

'Bring that chair over here and tell me about yourself while I sort out these books,' she directed me. She had a German accent. 'I run the kibbutz library from here and several books have gone missing recently. I need to sort out which ones.'

'They've been stolen?'

'Looks like it.'

She moved around the room, lifting books, setting them aside.

I should have offered to help, but couldn't be bothered. I leaned against the table and practised what I was about to say to her: *I'm sorry, but there's been some sort of misunderstanding and . . .*

Miriam moved to a small sink, half-hidden in the corner behind a huge pile of books. 'Would you like some tea? How am I going to sort out which ones are missing? Did you say yes or no?'

'What?'

'Or coffee? – I think there's some. Would you please sit down?' she said pointing to a tubby mound of worn velvet with leather arms. 'You're staying more than five minutes, I hope.'

'I need to get back soon. I have some studying to do.'

She peered at me with a disturbing blue gaze as if it could pin me to the wall. 'You don't look like a Jewish girl.'

I didn't reply. People here were always telling me that, and I hated it. It made me feel like an intruder. I yearned to snuggle into the comforting folds of acceptance . . . and at the same time, all I wanted was to be left alone.

Hopeless. I didn't know what I wanted. I looked away.

Miriam didn't seem to notice my discomfort. 'How are you getting on with the people on your course?'

I shrugged grouchily. 'Oh, it's all right. The Americans always grumble about the minimalist living arrangements and austerity of life in general, but I don't mind it.' My voice had become terribly, terribly British again, clipped and formal.

She slid a book into place on a high shelf, stretching on her tiptoes. 'I've noticed that you're on your own a great deal. Haven't you made any friends yet?'

I bristled under the attack of questions, but somehow didn't have the courage to tell her to back off. 'My room-mate, Cydney, is all right. But I'm a bit of a loner, I suppose.'

Miriam smiled. 'You look sensible enough to me. Maybe you're an introvert.'

I found it difficult to settle, wriggling in my chair and looking steadily at the bookcase in front of me, floor-to-ceiling, jammed with books. It was suddenly impossible to tell her that a mistake had been made, not given the way she was bustling about, so efficient and matter-of-fact. I waited, breathing, thinking nothing but breathing, reminding myself that release was inevitable soon.

'Do you enjoy the kibbutz way of life?' she asked.

'Oh, it's great. But a bit . . .' I fell silent.

Her eyes were fixed upon me thoughtfully. They held me still. 'Don't like too many people around?' she suggested.

'Mmm.' She was a mind-reader. I stared at her blankly. That was indeed one aspect of the kibbutz that I couldn't get used to. Everyone was so *sociable,* so bouncing and friendly. If I left the door to my room ajar, everyone going past would look in, yell, 'Hey, Jude!' and come in to talk, gossiping about everything and everyone. An endless fund of stories to be told. In order to get any privacy, I had to shut the door and pretend not to be there. I had begun to wonder if I was there myself.

'You like privacy. Something we have in common,' said Miriam.

I looked about me, taking in the narrow window to the left of the bookcase. Sunlight streamed in, cutting a bright path across the tiled floor while the rickety fan hummed. I was conscious of my awkwardly outstretched legs, my flushed face, the stuffiness of the room, to which the open window seemed to make no difference, and the fact that I felt small in the low chair.

'People always want me to be something I'm not, and I find myself going along with their false ideas of me,' I blurted. I felt my cheeks scorch. What made me say *that*?

Miriam continued to stack books, unfazed. 'Why are you here if you don't feel you belong? You look like a person who day-dreams.'

'I'm not a dreamer. I hate dreams,' I said bitterly.

'Is there anything you care for or want?' She watched me as though I was a new and curious animal.

94

'To be null and void,' I said without hesitation.

'Dead?'

The sound of the word seemed to draw my eyes to the window, which looked out over the distant hills.

'No, no,' I said, 'not that.' I gave a small shiver.

An oppressive silence settled over the room. I crossed my legs, uncrossed them. Another endless grilling process, like when I first arrived on the kibbutz. It tightened me up. How I hated this type of conversation. I felt sick with embarrassment and shame and a desire to get away and assess what all this was doing to me. I cleared my throat.

'I just meant . . . that I find it difficult to connect with people here, to make friendships.'

'Well,' she said, 'maybe you should forget about yourself and take more of an interest in others.'

'Yes, you may be right.' Helpful. She was trying to be friendly, only I was too strange, too alien.

More silence. Staring at the teetering bookcases, I tried to make out the titles of the books she was stacking. They were too far away. I fixed my eyes on the burnt spot on her lampshade instead.

'What kind of music do you like?' she said. 'I have a good many records here.'

Oh, leave me *alone,* why can't you?

I shrugged. 'I don't know. Folk rock. Joni Mitchell. Whatever's around, I suppose.'

'You don't like classical?'

'I'm not too familiar with it.'

'Do you like Mozart? Haydn?'

I opened my mouth and closed it again. I tightened my grip on the arms of the chair. The leather was sticky and wet under my hands. I licked my lips nervously.

'What time is it?'

'Going so soon?' Again I found myself enveloped in her piercing gaze. I could not meet it directly and focused my eyes

95

to the left of her face. I put my head in my hands and rubbed them over my face, over and over again, to feel something beyond that terrible trapped feeling.

'What a fantastic view you have,' I said, sensing that I should make some sort of effort before I went.

'Fantastic?' Miriam enunciated the word with a tone of distaste. 'You can't live on a view,' she said, 'however "fantastic" it may be.'

Even when I made the effort I couldn't say the right thing. I stared at her hopelessly, feeling tongue-tied.

'Look, I don't mean to be rude,' I said flatly. 'I just don't like being bombarded with questions.'

Miriam shook her head. 'Then what are you doing here?'

'What I'm doing here,' I said, 'is that I was told to come. It wasn't my idea.'

She nodded. 'I see. Orders, eh? So suppose you didn't have to come. What would you be here for?'

'I wouldn't.'

I unwound my legs and stood up. A couple of sparrows sat squabbling and pecking restlessly at the window and then flew off. I fumbled for an excuse to leave. 'I'm afraid I have to go to the dining hall now,' I said to her. 'I have to make an early start tomorrow.'

'I'm going there too. Let me walk with you,' she offered.

'It's all right. Really. Thank you anyway. I must be off now.'

She nodded slowly, watching me. 'Well . . . come here whenever you wish. Spend as much time as you like reading, playing my records or helping with the library. The door is always unlocked, even if I'm not here.'

I thanked her and left. What I did share with her but didn't want to acknowledge was a sense of waiting in loneliness, though for what I couldn't say – perhaps to learn who I was?

Relieved to escape, I decided I would never go back.

*   *   *

In a moment I was out of her house, careless now and tossing my hair. I walked along briskly, smiling to myself, but I didn't know why. I began to run and when I reached the path leading to the centre of the kibbutz, I stopped. I felt an uncomfortable sensation, which amid all the wild emotions that were rushing about inside me, I could only recognise as the feeling of being observed. I turned around, but realised people on the kibbutz were strolling by, intent upon their business. No one even glanced my way. Some rode on clumsy old bikes, wearing cloth hats and pedalling slowly. The dusty path I followed wound through the settlement. Beside the plain houses stood potted poinsettias. The air was sweet, and the sun, like mild alcohol, made me yearn for good things. Suddenly this temperate Mediterranean evening, the orchards and the workers steering their bikes fluttered like tissue paper. What was there to keep them from all blowing away?

Chapter 8

26 December
I went to midnight Mass on Christmas Eve. I got up at six
o'clock the next morning. Sister Mary woke us banging on
a chamberpot. She thought it was funny. I didn't. After
Mass I got my sock from the playroom. It was hung on a
string. I got an apple and orange and two old comics. Nana
gave me a pillowcase full of toys when I lived with her and
Pop.

30 December
I had to go and see Sister A. She said I should have to write
my letter to Mum again because I said: I hope you had a
happy Christmas, more than I did.

23 January 1952
Frieda fainted in Mass today. It's not fair that we have to go
to church so early.

6 February
I was scrubbing the floor when a nun made me pick up a
pile of tea leaves covered with ants from a drain. It was
horrible. She said I was lazy. She just stood and watched me
do it. I prayed, Lord, I take this for my sins.

Frances loved my stories of London life with my grandparents. Before she had met me, she had pictured London as some underground city with dark, foggy streets, pickpockets and thieves fleeing across the rooftops with sacks of swag. Now she couldn't get enough of its glories as seen through my eyes.

I told her of the excitement of shops like Selfridges, and about the Christmas pantomimes I had seen at the London Palladium, cocooned within its cosy plush and gilt, watching the faces of actors and actresses I had seen previously only on the cinema screen. I told her about restaurants such as Lyons' Corner House with its sea of tables covered with crisp white tablecloths. I told her of the orchestra playing amid the glittering chandeliers and cool palm trees, of white-capped waitresses silently serving Knickerbocker Glories in tall glasses.

She listened agog, her dark eyes wide. 'Have you ever been to the zoo?'

'Yes, but I didn't like it.' We were standing in the playground, watching Ruth and the others play hopscotch with a piece of broken glass.

Frances stared at me as though I were a gibbering idiot. 'You didn't *like* it? Why not?'

I shrugged. 'The horrible stink.'

But it wasn't just the stink. I remembered the expression in one monkey's eyes as they quietly, wearily, turned in their sockets to follow the visitors' movements. The little sad creature with its paws clinging to the wire meshing filled me with an irrational horror. I'd liked Pets' Corner – the rabbits – the shop; I'd loads of money then, I could buy loads of sweets – but all I could remember was the smell of the zoo and that monkey's eyes.

I tried to explain to Frances what I meant, but I couldn't.

Sister Mary covered the blackboard with chalk strokes, making great sweeping arm motions like the conductor of an orchestra. On either side of her nose the skin hung down, like the jowls of a bulldog. She wrote up a simple sentence with such cold rage that

I felt my heart-rate jump. I looked around and saw the heads of my classmates bent as they scraped feverishly in their notebooks. Ruth, tongue writhing, was stabbing away furiously with her pen, trying to keep up. A raging concerto was in progress: we, the orchestra, playing our half-witted instruments. I sat there like someone who had somehow stumbled into the pit during a recital and been waved into a chair. I should imitate the other girls and pretend to play, I decided. I thought about becoming invisible. Slowly I opened my exercise book and with my mouth puckered, I began to write.

My pen scratched half-heartedly across the paper and came to a stop.

'Your handwriting is deteriorating, Kelly,' said Sister Mary looking over my shoulder. I looked at my page in dismay. She was right: the letters were no longer round and beautiful, but spidery, frantic, and disfigured with blots of blue-black ink where I'd pressed down too hard on the steel nib. 'You must try harder.' I felt the creep of eyes on my back. The breath across my neck. I could hear the creak of her heavily starched wimple. I curled my fingers under. I thought she might be looking at the raggedy edges of skin around my nails. Everything I did was heard and seen by Sister Mary and would be used as a black mark against me.

If only I had a magic carpet that could fly backwards in time. I could go back to Mum, stop her from ever leaving Nana and Pop. Make things the way they used to be.

I'd now been at the convent for over nine months, and had not received a single word from her. I bit my tongue and blinked. It was my birthday, and I mustn't cry. I gulped in disappointment, and quickly started to write again, though the words blurred on the page.

Frances's desk was almost touching mine. She lowered her head, watching Sister Mary carefully. When she was sure the nun was looking the other way, she put her hand in front of her mouth and whispered, 'Judith . . . have you received anything from your mother for your birthday?'

I felt on edge, like fingernails on a blackboard, but managed to shake my head. Tears filled my eyes. I tried to blink them back but they would not stop, and I hurriedly wiped them away as they spilled down my cheeks. Frances sat there helpless, watching. But just before she shot her hand in the air, she gave me a wink and did something with her finger against the side of her nose that might or might not have been scratching it.

Sister Mary frowned slightly. 'What is it?'

'Please, Sister, can I be excused? I need to go to the what's-it.'

'You know you should have gone before,' Sister Mary said, lowering her eyes.

'But Sister . . . please, Sister . . . I didn't know before.' Frances said with a martyred sigh.

Sister Mary looked up and in her eyes I saw affection turn to distaste and distaste to anger. 'Whose fault was that?'

Several furtive heads turned to look at Frances along the row of desks. Frances was the only one who would dare to make such a request of Sister Mary. The rule was that no one ever left the classroom. Only my pen scratched on uninterrupted, my hot cheek resting on my fist, my brow furrowed with false concentration, a model picture of effort. I didn't dare look up. I had learnt that it was best to keep perfectly still and anger no one. I put on my best behaviour, tiptoeing about in a world of eggshells, praying that things wouldn't crack.

Sister Mary's palm slapped her desk. The class jumped. 'All right! If you must, but you know perfectly well that it goes against the class rules. Go! But try and be quick.'

When the door closed, faintly rattling the glass window in its insecure frame, the chalk resumed its attack on the blackboard. Every now and then Sister Mary cast a sideways look over us, like a blinkered horse, in a manner both suspicious and severe, as if she were thinking that all children were insects that would turn and bite her if she didn't get them first and squash them hard.

No one took any real notice when twenty minutes later a nun

called Sister Columba entered the classroom, her habit whisking impatiently against the door. Opinion amongst the children was unanimous that poker-backed Sister Columba was the meanest nun that ever lived, but I had yet to experience anyone as bad as Sister Mary. The class clattered their pens thankfully into the grooves of their desks and stood up. Sister Columba strode briskly across the room, and I would certainly not have stared at her but for the expression on her sallow face, and the way it affected Sister Mary.

Sister Mary put on a soft-soaping smile and then, in a voice of obvious alarm, said, 'What is it?'

Sister Columba leaned close to her and whispered something in her ear. Sister Mary's fawning measly quarter-smile froze and I would not have thought that her fist-like face could have turned any redder, but it did. There was a sharp hiss as Sister Mary drew an outraged breath. She stamped her booted foot, bruising the wooden floor.

'*What?*' We flinched as her voice boomed like an organ into the classroom. It took ages to die.

She looked at us, and we stared fearfully back at her.

'I'm going to leave you for a while without any supervision', she rasped. 'And I don't want bedlam here. You are to continue doing your work in *complete silence*.' She paused here to survey our faces, as though to judge our worthiness to carry out such an extraordinary task, and apparently found us up to it.

The two nuns exchanged dark, conspiratorial looks and with great solemnity walked out of the room. What a din their habits seemed to make, crackling and rasping; how their heels pounded on the wooden floor. The door's glass rattled again as it was closed.

'Good riddance to bad rubbish,' whispered Ruth across the classroom. Then there followed an instant of dead silence, ruffled by mouthed exchanges to each other behind hands, with eyes rolling. The whisperings subsided, only to bubble up a few seconds later, simmering and gradually increasing to boiling point.

'What do you think happened?'

'I haven't the faintest.'

'Did you see her face?'

A breathless discussion ensued. The consensus was that something huge, really huge, had happened. I became anxious because there was still no sign of Frances, but I said nothing.

Ruth slumped down, closed her eyes and rubbed her head animal-style on the wood of the back of her desk.

'There's big trouble brewing,' she said in her husky voice. 'I can feel it in me bones.'

Ruth had recently run away and had been caught wandering through the town. She had been brought back to the convent in a police car, making her a scandal and a heroine for several weeks. That's why she was in the classroom again. Normally she'd be scouring baths and washbasins, polishing and dusting, and even coping with clogged-up drains. But now the nuns had to keep a close eye on her. While the nuns whacked us all, they took particular delight in the cruelty they showed towards Ruth Norton. It was all meant to make Ruth beg them to stop, beg them to leave her alone, but through it all, she never lost her sense of humour. Yet there were times when I saw in her face a sort of low silent rage, as if some other creature might break through, a wilder beast; it was the look I had seen on the faces of some caged animals in the zoo.

'Them nuns are all habit with no fizz in their think tanks,' she said boldly propping her feet up on her desk.

'Where's Janet?' someone whispered.

Janet was so thin, she seemed like a piece of white tissue paper and it was difficult to notice when she was missing from class. Ruth's eyes assumed an intent scowl. I knew it well. She looked like that when a nun barked 'four nines?' at her; her eyebrows knitted, awaiting inspiration.

'I think she's in the dormitory standing with her sheet over her head because she wet her bed last night,' said Ruth.

Janet had a weak bladder and wet her bed quite often. As a punishment, the nuns made her stand for hours wearing the wet sheet over her head. I liked Janet because I had never heard her speak badly of anyone, other than to say a nun had not been nice to her. She also had a pet frog. She kept it in a cardboard box, which she hid behind some trees in the playground. She fed it slugs and squashed flies through the hole in the box and also poured water in through the hole every day to keep the poor creature moist and happy. All the girls admired Janet for looking after her frog so well. Do you ever feel, she asked me once, that every animal in the world needs protection? I knew what she meant and it was a terrible feeling. And even though she herself was always hungry, she refused to let her frog starve.

As we waited for Sister Mary's return to the classroom I folded my arms and put my head in the hollow. All the desks were scarred and spotted with ink and smelt the same: spicy, like the ground under a tree. Sometimes the wood was discoloured, bleached from the sun. There was a groove for your pens and a hole for a tiny porcelain inkwell. Ruth occasionally drank the ink and poked out her blue tongue at us. Sometimes she even ate the paste issued to us as glue. She said she preferred it to our porridge. With my head on my arms I licked the desk, but it just tasted bitter.

An ominous sound then became audible far away in the convent. We all looked at each other, listening. There was a dull rumbling, which became the sound of running feet and raised voices. I felt a kick of fear as if it were the onset of some appalling rebellion. The running feet and voices came nearer. Then the classroom door burst open and Sister Columba came running in. She was dragging someone after her by the hand. It was Frances.

'Here she is, here she is!' cried Sister Columba. She thrust Frances forward.

The class leapt to its feet, the wooden seat-backs clattering as they snapped back. Sister Columba looked now as if she were completely mad, her pasty large-nostrilled face twisted and almost grinning. She produced a bamboo cane from the folds of her habit. My heart hammered at the walls of my ribs.

Sister Mary arrived at the doorway, studying her fingernails as though she had just discovered them, a crooked smile on her face. Behind her stood Janet Dover. She looked so chalky pale and stiff I thought her blood must have turned white. Tear tracks ran down her face. She was sent to stand beside Frances. What had they done?

Sister Columba tapped her cane against the palm of her hand. I had learnt by now that a cane could lacerate the skin. It caused severe black and scarlet bruising that took two weeks to disappear, and all the time during those two weeks, you could feel your heart beating along with the wounds.

Turning to Janet and Frances, Sister Columba said, 'You girls are the lowest of the low. Guttersnipes. What do you have to say for yourselves?'

Frances said in a soft whining voice, 'Me and Janet are sorry, Sister, we promise we'll never do it again.' Her hands twisted in elaborate shapes of pleading. 'We only climbed through Sister Mary's cell window to get our letters. We weren't going to steal anything.' It was like the plaint of an animal.

Sister Columba stared at her for a few seconds and said, 'You have both behaved deceitfully and you know it!' She moved towards Frances and dealt her a savage kick in the side which briefly tumbled her over on to the floor.

Then, turning to Janet, she tapped her lightly on the shoulder with the end of her cane, a broad smile on her face. Janet looked straight ahead, her hands twisting her handkerchief round and round unhappily. I saw a muscle jump in her jaw.

'And what do *you* have to say for yourself, Dover? Are you ever going to be saved from the hot nook of Satan?' she asked, the smile still on her face. 'It doesn't surprise me that your mother never wanted you. You filthy slut, always wetting your bed.'

Janet's jaw twitched again. She scratched her nose.

'Don't pick! Don't fiddle!'

'Yesssister,' Janet mumbled. She began to wheeze, her breath coming in small bursts. I saw Frances shut her eyes.

Sister Columba then advanced on them screaming, 'We do not tolerate such goings-on!' Her words were slathered in spit as she lunged at the two girls. Snorting with effort, she raised the cane high above her shoulder. It made a loud swishing sound, and there was a piercing crack as it struck each of the girls in turn. The blows immediately caused red marks to appear on their legs and arms and their eyes welled with tears. With every blow, the nun's rosary beads clinked together, making a noise like gnashing teeth; her face was red and quivering.

Sister Mary stood beside the door, her eyes opaque and glinting like steel, her tongue licking at her lips.

Both girls staggered. The thin muscles of Janet's legs buckled under her and she then crouched on the floor, hands over her head, but Frances stayed upright, parting her feet for a better grip. The nun's stick streaked back and forth in a rain of blows, again, again, again, again, again. With each swipe Frances's dark hair jumped, but her body and head hardly moved.

Janet, whose face had been pale then red, burst into high-pitched hysterical sobs. She howled half-angry, half-frightened, wailing 'Oh! Oh! Oh!' She then staggered to her feet and fell against the wall with her hand over her mouth, biting her palm in an effort to stop herself from screaming. Sister Mary hurried forward and, grasping Janet by the hair, dragged her into the middle of the classroom. Sister Columba was instantly behind her, taking a thick cloth from her pocket, wrapping it around Janet's mouth and knotting it secure from the back.

Sweating profusely, her hot hue reflected in her white wimple, Sister Columba resumed the flogging of the two girls. But just as the beating had begun to take on a rhythm, Frances slowly straightened to her full height. Head up, chest out, she seemed to tower over Sister Columba even though the nun was taller than she.

Turning, the nun concentrated her cane on Frances alone. Frances stood very still, glaring at her, until with a cry of fury and her jaw hanging wide, Sister Mary ran forward again and pushed Frances to the floor.

'Get down, you little tyke!' she screamed.

Her eyes glazed and lips trembling, Frances immediately struggled to her feet again.

A gasp of dismay ran across the hot classroom. Some of the girls were crying. Ruth, as always, was stiff as a statue, her face twisted into a mask of hate. I kept my head tilted upwards, my eyes on the ceiling. My ragged fingernails gouged into my palms, willing Frances to stay down.

Sister Columba stood still for a stupefied moment, her beady black eyes gleaming. She opened her prim, rather savage little mouth and was about to say something, but before she could, Sister Mary grabbed Frances and pinioned her arms from behind. She then bent her double with her backside uppermost, holding her against her chest. I could see the top of Frances's white legs shining under the glare of the outside light.

'Give her a good hiding!' shrieked Sister Mary.

With a whistle of wind, the blows of the knotty cane lashed against Frances's buttocks with such strength that it almost knocked Sister Mary off her feet. Each blow brought muffled gasps and low moans from Frances's mouth like those of a sick animal. Smarting under the blows of the cane, she began to buck desperately.

Sister Mary's face was gleaming with sweat, her eyes alight with glee. The blows finally stopped after a dozen shots had found their mark.

Puffing and blowing, with white saliva dotting the corners of her mouth, we heard Sister Columba say: 'I think you have both learnt your lesson now.' She nodded to Sister Mary who released Frances and untied the gag around Janet's mouth.

'This class is dismissed!' Sister Mary screamed.

Then both nuns swept out of the classroom tossing their veils and slamming the door behind them.

Frances sagged to her knees and toppled over. A few of us rushed forward to help her and Janet to their feet. With great presence of mind Frances delegated some of the girls to help Janet to the dormitory.

'But keep your voices down and make sure you're not seen,' she told them through dry and puffy lips. Her eyes looked mad, scared and sticking out, her pupils huge as though she'd been in the dark and the light had been turned on.

As the girls left, she buried her face in her hands. I put my arm around her shoulders, and she seemed to lose consciousness for a moment. Her body felt so light it was like hugging a bamboo chair. Very far away, I heard children moving, heard someone whispering, heard a door shut.

When at last she raised her head, I said, 'It's all over. It's all over.' I repeated it again and again, in a soothing, almost hypnotic voice, rocking her back and forth. That was when she let go and wept.

We sat like this for a long time, until Frances's tears were almost spent.

'My head hurts,' said Frances finally. 'And I feel really sick.'

'You'd feel better if you lay down upstairs,' I said. 'There won't be any nuns around for a while. You know they always make themselves scarce after a flogging.'

'Yes, they get upset,' said Frances. 'If we'd hit someone like that we'd get upset too.'

'I don't think I could ever hit anyone,' I said.

'Nor could I.'

When we reached the dormitory, she entered like a heroine, to a soft fluttering of applause from the other girls. She drew a finger over her lips, and told one of the girls to keep a lookout at the door for the approach of any nuns.

In silence, we fetched wet towels and dabbed water on Frances's swelling scarlet wounds. In between them lay mottled purple bruises. I winced feeling the blazing warmth from the swellings. Janet sat on her bed, eyes closed, arms around her shins, rocking and rocking, crooning to herself in a soft nasal tone. Frances lay unmoving, eyes closed, breathing deeply. I blew into her hair.

'You were very brave,' I whispered, squeezing her hand, 'but you should have stayed on the floor when Sister Columba pushed you down.'

'Yeah, then Sister Mary wouldn't have had to squash you against her titties and shown us your bare bum,' said Ruth. 'She's dead kinky. Do you think she's going through her mental pause?'

Frances's eyes flew open. She lifted her head. The other girls hovering around at once began telling her to lie back. Instead, she half sat up.

'Shut up, Ruth,' she said in a low, serious voice, gasping a little as she spoke. 'It's not fair, it's your birthday, Judith. I saw three letters for you from your mum in Sister Mary's cell, and a birthday card. They had all been opened.'

'The sly old dirtbag!' said Ruth.

'You did it for my sake?' I gasped. Pride swelled within me for having such a friend. At the same time a tidal wave of relief almost knocked me off my feet. Mum had written! She had been in touch with me after all, she hadn't forgotten me. I squeezed Frances's hand, unable to thank her.

Like stray cats, we piled ourselves around Frances on her bed. Others had made Janet's bed into a cradle and were gently rocking her. With her eyes dry now, Frances outlined what had happened.

'It was like this, see,' whispered Frances cautiously, looking over her shoulder at the dormitory door. 'I knew Janet was in the dormitory doing wet-bed punishment and I knew she would help me. I sprinkled a bit of sugar I'd taken from the kitchen over the dormitory floor leading up to Sister Mary's cell. Then me and Janet climbed through her porthole window. We managed to look through a few letters. We saw one for Janet from her brother. Then Janet found some long woollen bloomers that smelt of mothballs. We were doubled up laughing at them when suddenly from the dormitory came a loud sound, *crunch*! It sounded like a giant was walking on stones. Then we heard the high-pitched voice of Sister Columba in the distance. "Who did this?" she was shrieking. She went crunching through the dormitory. "Where are you, Dover? Own up immediately! Step forward now or woe betide you!" Then she saw us through the window. She looked like she had steam coming out of her nostrils. First she made us sweep up the sugar and then she marched us to the classroom, and brought out Sister Mary. She just glared at us.'

'Sister Mary called Janet a slut,' I said. 'Do sluts live in slums?'

Crows of stifled laughter.

'Shut up, Sister Cuthbert's coming!' hissed the girl on lookout. We all leapt off the bed as Sister Cuthbert entered the dormitory quietly on her fat little buttery feet. Frances and Janet were too given up to misery to move.

The nun said in a calm voice, 'So this is where you're all hiding out.' She looked first at Janet and then at Frances, and smiled, a full flat mouth on a chunky chin. 'Those are good tears that you have both shed. You all understand very little yet, but one day you will understand the significance of all this.'

None of us replied. Scanning us with her small fat-encircled eyes, Sister Cuthbert went on with a chirpy wag of the head: 'You are feeling that Janet and Frances have been unjustly treated – that no offence could deserve so great a punishment. But you must believe that all this is for their own good.'

We stared at the nun, flummoxed, not daring to interrupt. She came forward and rested her plump pink hand on Janet's forehead.

'God asks very hard things from us. The sacrifice of what we love and the sacrifice of our own wills. The sisters here are only trying to do their best for you, even though at times our treatment may seem a little harsh. *Vere dignum et iustum est* – It is indeed fitting and right. To learn, one must be humble. But life is a great teacher. I won't ask you the reason why you were beaten, but I am sure you must have deserved it.'

I stared at the nun's face. It was pale and controlled, yet glowed with an extraordinary cheerfulness.

'Many things must have happened to you here at the convent, which have seemed unkind, unfair even. But very few things have happened by accident – I am speaking to you as if you were adults. McCarthy, the fact that you are gifted with a wonderful singing voice is going to your head. You're all puffed up with conceit. Tell me, what on earth do you think you will do when you leave the convent?'

Frances said she wanted to be an opera singer.

Sister Cuthbert tutted. 'Your attitude only confirms what I have said. Puffed up with conceit. Yours is strictly a bathtub voice. Learning classical singing is not an option for you. We like our opera stars to have studied music at a very high level. The way you're going it's the sweetie factory or work as a shop assistant for you, my girl.'

Frances shrugged, tears in her eyes. 'Well, you asked what I wanted to do. I want to be like Maria Callas.'

'Opera? Maria Callas? I've heard some things in my time, but that takes the biscuit. You need to be rich to be an opera singer. Don't you know that opera is the most expensive noise known to man? However, you do have one quality, which I think will help you through life: I believe you are fundamentally honest. But there is a quality you need more – we are trying to teach you by easy ways, but today you have had to learn it the hard way – the quality of humility.'

'But Sister Cuthbert, it's not fair, we didn't deserve to be so badly beaten,' Frances choked out suddenly.

The nun appeared to think for a moment. Then shaking her clasped hands before her, went on: 'No, I don't want to hear any complaints from our little opera star. You must have deserved your punishment. Forgiveness is for Almighty God, who sees into every heart, not for me. *Corruptio optimi est pessima.** Hands up anyone who knows what that means.'

We stared at her blankly. She stopped shaking her clasped hands and putting them to her brow, looked eagerly at her listeners out of her small eyes. 'I mean, a Catholic is more capable of evil than anyone, I think, perhaps – because we believe in Him – we are more in touch with the devil than other people. But we must hope,' she said mechanically, 'hope and pray.'

Frances muttered weakly, 'It's not fair.'

'No, and life's not fair, but I am not going to discuss the wicked, foolish things you and Dover have been up to. The nuns have a huge responsibility', said Sister Cuthbert flicking her veil over her shoulder, 'overseeing the welfare of all your souls. In other schools, you would be expelled for your misdeeds, but as many of you are essentially orphans, it is not possible. Therefore you should not complain. You are not really entitled to complain, because you are lucky children: think of all those orphans who have been shipped off to Australia. It's happened here before and it could happen again.'

We all listened to her words intently, for Sister Cuthbert was the only nun we came close to trusting. But she was a grown-up and all grown-ups were dangerous creatures at this school. She could be blunt and forceful and often she would say to us: a hard life strengthens the character. She wasn't Sister Mary and Sister Columba, who were like the darkness when the night-light went out in the dormitory or the frozen blocks of earth I had seen one winter in a graveyard; you just had to endure Sister Mary and Sister Columba when they were there and forget about them

* The corruption of the best is the worst.

quickly when they were away, smother the thought of them, ram it deep down. Sister Cuthbert was attempting to do away with the white cotton frocks that we had to wear in our weekly pea-soup baths, which smelt like dirty teeth, the same water shared between us all. But she made no attempt to do away with the system of spying and violence to which all the children were subjected. She lacked the desire or conviction to question it, let alone bring the abuse to the eyes of a higher authority. She had more to lose than to gain by such confrontation and would be out-nunned, out-manoeuvred and out-foxed if she dared.

Questions surged within me as she spoke. Were we really wicked? So wicked that we had to be beaten like criminals? Did it please God to see us broken and battered? I stared at the floor, unable to ask them. Afraid to know the answers, maybe.

Sister Cuthbert hurriedly left us alone again with instructions for us to return to the classroom, with the exception of Janet and Frances. Ruth gazed after her, her lip curling in slow scorn till her face resembled a devil's mask.

'Three chairs for Sister Cuthbert. It won't be long before she'll need a crowbar to help her through the door-frame.'

I sat for a moment on Frances's bed in silence. Her eyes seemed lifeless, stripped of their usual vibrancy, emptied of their spark.

'Sister Mary had better not come and kiss me to try and make it all better tonight,' she whispered through clenched teeth. 'If she does, I'll bite her lips.'

Her head lolled on her pillow as she sank into a bruised sleep. Before I left her, I pressed my face to a window and looked across the gardens to the quiet road that ran alongside the convent. We were forbidden to play in the gardens, but I liked looking at them. A broad stretch of carefully tended green grass with winter trees beyond. The sky full of swift black-and-blue clouds, the sunlight muted. Then a fine rain began to fall from the high, veiled sky as a few gulls flapped over the ground, screaming distantly. They're a long way from home, I thought, there must be a storm looming at sea.

It was another planet out there. The outside world had become merely a dream, like something you read about in a book.

Chapter 9

Mornings on the kibbutz were fast replacing night as the worst time for me. My brain seethed all night, hurling images at me, parts of which I remembered on waking.

I dreamt that I was standing on the rocks, but I couldn't make it on to the beach because of the see-saw sea surrounding me. An audience of not more than a few dozen people were standing on the sand. My mother was there, but she was talking to a nun whom I did not recognise. I couldn't understand what they were saying, for the words were in a foreign language – or several languages. The nun, still faceless, turned to me, a dark shape shimmering in the heat. She came closer and said, 'I don't understand a word you're saying. Why can't you speak properly?'

I awoke to a terrible sense of failure, my bed crumpled and undone, the very image of restlessness. I lay for hours desperately trying to find a way back into the dream to utter some words that the nun might understand.

Keeping my dreams at bay took energy that I didn't have. I would crawl out of bed in the morning exhausted, feeling like a zombie.

This week the morning started with Hebrew class and I was late again. Teliela stared at me pointedly and called me outside the classroom. Sudden terror engulfed me. My throat thickened as I followed her to the veranda.

'What's the problem? Why are you always so late?' She inclined her head, waiting for an answer. She wore a faded T-shirt and threadbare shorts. Increasingly I had begun to eliminate whichever clothes I had that did not fit in with the others' – to the first class I had made the mistake of wearing a sensible blouse in a neutral shade of beige, but I learned quickly. To prove my allegiance, I switched to a black T-shirt, but I still could not work up the courage to wear jeans. Instead I wore a dark skirt. Cydney, noticing my transformation, asked: 'So who died?' 'You look like you're in mourning.'

In her kibbutz uniform, Teliela did not look like someone to be feared, but I stood mutely, sick with fright, waiting for the axe to fall. At best, I could be put to work scrubbing the dining hall for a week; at worst I could be thrown off the kibbutz. Behind me I could feel everyone looking at me through the doorway.

I shook my head. I still felt drained and battered from my dreams of the night before. The craggy rocks, the ocean whipped into a frenzy at my feet, the terrible feeling of being pulled in two.

'Judith!'

'Sorry,' I muttered.

Teliela tapped her fingers against her arm, contemplating me. 'And what's this I hear from Miriam? She tells me that you're avoiding her.'

A flash of anger. 'I didn't ask to be her kibbutz daughter.'

Teliela shook her head, clicked her tongue in disapproval. 'I don't know,' she said. 'Look, I'm wondering if the kibbutz life isn't too much for you.' She leaned back against the veranda wall. 'You've got to make more of an all-round effort if you want to stay on here.'

She wasn't throwing me out. Not yet. I let out my breath at last, but slowly, slowly. Keep calm, don't beg.

'I'll work,' I said. 'I want to work.'

Her dark eyes scanned me, weighing me up. Finally she

nodded. 'OK, then. Make more effort to be on time and more effort to get on with others here.'

My shoulders wilted with relief. I nodded and turned to go back into the classroom. Her hand on my arm stopped me. 'Judith . . . I can't force you to spend time with Miriam, but I wish you would. She wants to get to know you. She thinks you have a lot in common.'

Her words froze me, an accusing finger pointing to dark secrets. 'Why would she think that?' I struggled to say. 'She hardly knows me.' My voice had a hounded quaver to its tone.

Teliela shrugged. 'I don't know. But that's what she said.'

I stood staring at her, caught with resentment. Sunlight glinted off her dark hair and strong face. It was so simple for her.

'Miriam's life hasn't been an easy one, you know, and she tends to be lonely. Help her if you can. She says you're welcome to use her place at any time.'

The idea of Miriam needing help turned everything on its head. I stared down at my sandals, scuffing them on the faded wood floor. 'Thanks,' I mumbled. 'Maybe I'll do that.'

A few days later, I heard loud, boisterous laughter drifting through the window. Lying on my bed I could hear Mark, his voice raw with complaint: 'Cydney, come on, why don't you join us on our trip to Galilee next week? A bunch of us are getting together to go camping; it'll be great.'

'I gotta study during the vacation, and that's the truth. I'm falling behind in class.'

'You oughta lay off studying, Cyd. Screws your mind. Keep the channels open up there for more important matters.'

They laughed.

'Come on, Cyd, it'll be a blast,' said John.

'No, I can't.'

'Who says?' someone else asked. 'Your room-mate? She's creepier than a vine. And you know what happens when you hang around with creeps. You get creepy too.'

'Hey man, do you mind?' Cydney objected. 'She's a friend of mine.'

'She's a weirdo, a stuffy weirdo who sucks in all your oxygen so you can't breathe.'

'You oughta get off her back,' said Cydney. 'She's got enough problems.'

'You can say that again.'

More laughter. My heart went down an octave or more. A film came between me and the bright morning, and I felt hotter and crankier than I had ever been in my life.

I slammed out of the room and strode through the kibbutz to the orange groves, where large weasels lived in the bushy growth. I saw them in the distance in the road. Luckily they were far off. The day had become a scorcher, with a ticky breeze that burst out of nowhere, funnelling along the kibbutz valley, whipping me along so that I could feel the dust stinging my legs. Every gust was a blow.

I trudged along the road, angry with myself for the words I kept finding for the wind. Like 'the breath of hell'. But the only hell I had ever known was the dank environment of the convent, so what did I mean? Like 'opening an oven door'. But it was nothing like opening an oven door. This was not a wind that was going to be disciplined by words. I hated the way it hurled itself at me in raw gusts of heat. I hated the grasshoppers, humming hoarsely in the grass. Anyone with any sense was inside at this time of the day, behind closed curtains, stretched out on a bed. Except that you heard things stretched out on a bed, didn't you? Through treacherous windows. Spoken by treacherous people.

'Mad dogs and Englishmen,' I sang half-heartedly.

I was the mad fool, inching along a dusty road towards the citrus groves. Serves me right, I thought grimly. My fury mounted – fury at my own cowardice for not confronting Mark and the others for their remarks about me. Anger muttered in my stomach as I strode along, in the way water mutters as it reaches boiling point. I began walking fast, gesticulating and talking aloud, my thoughts raging to and fro in a continual din. The heat seemed to have done something to the way I was walking. My arm, swinging out in front of me as I strode along, seemed too big – or was it too small? I was aware of my knees going up and down, ludicrously like a high-stepping horse.

I checked my thoughts and came to a standstill, aware of a sound, an intense resonant hymn of insects, small movements punctuated by the quick whomp and flutter of a bird's wing rising. Awkwardly, I sat down on a pale rounded stone with my legs sticking out stiffly in front of me. The soil was loose and soft under a citrus tree that cast thin patches of shade. Many of the trees were still unharvested and bent, thick with lemons as dense as stars.

Sweat had stuck my T-shirt to my back. My toes felt slimy in my sandals. In the thick hot air, a fly hovered near my eye and I flapped at it irritably. It circled back and tried the other eye. I flapped it away again. It avoided my hand, lazy, carefree. It could do it all day, circle and land, circle and land. It could go on for ever. Like a bad memory.

Trying not to remember was harder than you would think. It took up a great deal of energy, and even then, memories sliced through the not-remembering, as sharp as ever. I felt I was spinning and wanted some great hand to emerge from the sky and lift me up and send me further and further to some anonymous place where memories could be erased. There were times when I could still smell their mustiness; in the shower I heard their murmurings, in my food I tasted the mould. This heat, too: *It was the reason why the nuns had taken us to the beach that day. They always let up on bashings and floggings during the summer break. They didn't want us exposing our welts and bruises to the outside world when we changed into our swimming costumes.*

Guilt about Frances roved sharply inside me. I must, I thought, somehow switch off the black-and-white film in my head that tried to re-enact certain scenes. I rubbed my face with the back of my shaky perspiring hand.

121

'This is ridiculous,' I said aloud, and shouted at the citrus grove: 'Ridiculous! Ridiculous! *Ridiculous!*' I hung on now, pressing my hand lightly against the bleached stone, where even in the shade, the heat beat down. I waited for the familiar arrow of fear. Only there was none. Instead a wave of calm flooded over me, sliding back, slowly. It was a first. I could feel emotion and everything was still in place, as it was before. Obscured at once by my awareness of it, the moment blurred. I could not reach beyond it. I mentally waved to my own childhood – a yearning child kneeling in church, peering into the future in which I now sat, yet unable to see me.

If we met now, would I like what I saw of myself? Was this the person I'd guessed I would become all those years ago? I was trying not to live out that child's prophecy as best as I knew how.

The silence of the citrus grove was suddenly soothing. It was as if I was the only living creature in the world. Alone had always seemed like freedom. But I didn't want it to become a life sentence. A life sentence of self-reproach.

Before class that afternoon, a familiar voice called out, 'Hey Jude!' Cydney cornered me at the door.

'What happened?' she said, biting the corner of her thumbnail. 'I thought we were going to lunch together. You disappeared.'

I nodded curtly.

'Why?'

The classroom was teeming with people. Mild hubbub. Two minutes to go before class.

I didn't look at her. 'I decided to skip lunch. Too hot.' It was true that I hadn't eaten: I couldn't face the idea of kibbutz institutional food: chicken, boiled in its skin, sitting upon waves of mashed potatoes and surrounded by shores of rice and gravy.

A streak of anger still flew through my mind at those tactless remarks I had overheard. My old restless moodiness had surfaced, as it had done on my first evening here. All morning the stream of gloominess within me had turned in on itself in dark streams and whirlpools, wearying me.

Cydney leant against the wall and lit a cigarette, squinting at me through her gold-rimmed spectacles. 'Well, thanks for telling me. I hung around waiting for you. What's your problem?'

I bristled. 'What do you mean?'

'I don't know.' She shrugged her shoulders, looking worried. She was the sincere type. She became quiet, lost in her own thoughts and I gnawed the pad of my thumb, lost too.

'What's on your mind?' Cydney said after a while, breaking the silence.

'Nothing's new, nothing's on my mind. Everything's fine,' I said. 'Don't worry about me.'

She shook her head. 'That's crap. Gimme a break. You're so out of focus. What's happening with you? You're acting – I don't know – sorta weird.'

It tripped the lever on the thing I meant not to say. 'Cydney, take my advice. You hang around with creeps, you get creepy too.'

She slapped her thigh in irritation. 'Goddam, I knew that was it. Well, why are you pissed off with *me*?'

'I'm not pissed off with you. I just feel hurt by the remarks I overheard.'

'Like hell you're not pissed off with me.' She tried to grin. 'Look, I'm sorry. Those guys are full of shit. Relax. It's no big deal. Not everyone thinks like them. I talked to Rick and he said . . .'

'I don't care!' I snapped. My nerves were raw and throbbing. My eyes felt as if they had sunk back into my head, pulling the flesh down. 'Drop it . . . leave me alone!'

The wellspring of anger erupted, engulfing us both. I tried desperately to keep my face impassive, my emotions under control.

'Aw, fuck you!' snarled Cydney fixing me with a look of utter fury. 'You can be such a goddam pain in the ass.'

And then she was gone, her feet pounding over the wooden veranda into the classroom. I imagined taking off my sandal and throwing it in her direction. Yet all I felt was a hollow feeling in the pit of my stomach, as if I had been punched: the blows of misery, remorse and rage. I had no weapons with which to fight them off. No comforting catchphrases. All my fault. I had behaved like a petulant child. I now saw what I ought to have said to Cydney, what tone I should have adopted. I had pushed her away and everyone else who tried to help. All my attempts to befriend people resulted in failure, loss. I was the outcast, the one who stood outside the circle of safety.

As I entered the classroom, all faces turned towards me. I scowled back at them. I knew that as soon as my back was turned they'd be making rueful frog-faces at each other, faces that said: *What is it with her?* I was a ninny, a laughing stock – that's how the nuns had always described me.

As I sat at my desk the person sitting behind me leant over and whispered, 'Take no notice, those guys can be complete assholes sometimes.'

I knew who he was – I'd seen him around. His eyes locked on mine. I turned away from him. I willed my face to stay calm, but the colour was rising and there wasn't anything I could do to stop it. Then slowly I let myself turn and look at him. It was a test of some kind, and I would make my face stay calm no matter what.

'They're all right,' I said aloud, because I wanted them all to hear, 'It's me who's at fault.'

He laughed and his whole face changed with that laugh. The curled corners of his mouth were amazingly expressive. His clear skin smoothly taut over the bones of his face, his cheeks faintly flushed, his eyes the colour of honey. Just looking at him made me feel better somehow. A face that definitely needed to be avoided.

Our Hebrew teacher Teliela came into the room. '*Boker tov*,' she said. Several Americans replied, 'Hi there, Teliela.' She sighed and said in Hebrew for the umpteenth time, 'No English in class, please.'

I could feel Rick watching me. After a moment I looked at him quickly. Some significant unsmiling message passed between us. Rick continued to stare. I was aware of his face. At last he said in a whisper, 'I'm Rick, by the way.'

I became tense and still, realising that in a moment he might touch me. He placed his hand between us, very polite and direct. I put my hand in his and he shook it with a firm hold.

'Hello Rick,' I said.

I tried to take my hand away, but Rick held on, as if he was waiting for more. Cold raced up my arm and into my stomach, and met between my shoulder blades. I sat there frozen, revealed to myself. Is this what I'd been angling for, with my notions of rescue? I laughed a quiet laugh and told him my name, and then he let go.

'Great to meet you again too, Judith,' he said.

There were too many people to avoid, and no place to avoid them. Remembering Miriam's offer, I began skulking over to her house like a criminal to play her records when I knew she wasn't at home. It was my only escape. It made the weight of my problems bearable.

I leaned back in one of her chairs listening to Mozart, discovering a new world: *Così Fan Tutte*, *The Marriage of Figaro*: comedies in which cries are torn from the heart. I sometimes thought that my own sense of fun was rooted in an earlier age: 1771 rather than 1971. Flipping through the dusty album covers gave me a strange feeling of time past, like an old calendar.

I wondered what it would look like inside my brain. All green and mouldy from neglect, I bet. I took down one of the books from Miriam's shelf and read blindly until the words began grouping together, forming small patterns of reason and sense. I skimmed through other books on her shelves – biographies, fiction, poetry, non-fiction – many of them by writers I'd heard about but never read.

Perhaps if I devoted myself to them now, I could stave off my sense of despair, find some answers to my problems. Deep down I had no real hope that all that reading could bear fruit for me – but I was determined to persist in my efforts. Persist, though with the same sense I'd had all my life, that anyone coming from my childhood circumstances stood no chance. Inside, I was still the skinny, helpless little girl hiding red welts on her body. It was the great wall-like fact against which, nonetheless, I persevered.

Light shimmered through the vine leaves overhanging the porch. I lingered there, contemplating the hypnotic stillness, absorbing its colours, shapes and fragrances. I felt the balm of the place close round me. It was quiet and cool, with the smell of baking bread in the air. The feeling that joy could exist came over me – I could feel it: a tentative, tangible force just out of my reach. Perhaps it was possible for me to be happy. Never mind all the people who pigeonholed misfits like me with their wisecracks, their amused, superior smiles.

I heard a confused music within myself – of memories and names of which I was almost conscious, but did not want to capture even for an instant; then the music seemed to recede, and from each receding trail of hazy melody there emerged one long drawn-out note. The record had got stuck in the groove. Two notes went on insisting, reminding me over and over: weirdo, weirdo, weirdo. I sat helplessly under the noise, pinned to the spot, accused. Weirdo, weirdo. Suddenly it stopped in mid-note. The silence that followed seemed to pulsate: big, solid, an object in its own right.

A familiar voice said, 'That record always gets stuck.'

I started, whirling around. Miriam was back earlier than I had expected. She stood behind me, wearing a large straw hat shielding crow's-feet etched hard around her eyes from years of squinting in the Israeli sunlight. She smelt of vanilla and jasmine.

'How are you?' Her smile was open and friendly. It invited me to relax.

I took a deep breath. 'OK. Fine.' It was not a lie really, just the safest thing to say for the time being.

I had dreaded meeting Miriam again, even while I felt drawn to her house. Somewhere in the back of my mind I knew that I would eventually end up talking about my childhood memories, knowing that I no longer had control over them. Press a button and one day out it will all come.

I cleared my throat, my gaze fixed on the table in front of me. I was on the point of making some stumbling gesture of apology, when the coward in me leapt up and closed my mouth. Be careful, it cautioned me. You are a loner; you must not tie yourself. Even as I surrendered to that prompting, I regretted the surrender. I knew that for a few minutes I had been happy here listening to Miriam's records.

'Would you turn that lamp on beside you?' she asked. 'Make this room a bit more cheerful.

When I switched on the lamp I turned and saw Miriam watching me. Joy and pain were both moods able to pass lightly across her face without disturbing the permanent thoughtfulness of her eyes, which seemed to regard life with a gaze devoid of emotion.

'I'm pleased you're here,' she said, 'we'll have tea, although I never quite understand why English people like tea. I'm glad to have someone to talk to – even you.'

I stared at her in amazement. Her remark came to me with the force of a wise suggestion. I decided I should make a little effort, for her sake.

'There's something I've been wanting to say to you,' I said. 'I owe you an apology for my behaviour when I first visited you. I'm sorry.'

'It doesn't matter about that.' She was obviously hesitant to say more.

I came to the point. 'I'm afraid I ran away.' I smiled. 'It didn't do me any good.'

She glanced at me while she removed her hat. 'I wasn't surprised. All those questions. Let's make that tea.'

She led the way into the cluttered kitchen and began to take out plates, cups, a loaf of bread and some butter, a kettle that she filled and put upon the stove. With proud and careful fingers she drew a caddy from the cupboard, handling it as reverently as a gold casket. I watched her as she made the tea, all wrong of course: the water not on the boil, the teapot unheated, too many leaves. A plain white tablecloth was laid on the table, and the door stood open as we sat down and looked across the Carmel Hills. I drank my tea quickly like a medicine and watched her sip at hers cautiously. For a long time we remained silent in the hushed sunlight. A pleasant drowsiness crept over me.

'Well, this is certainly more relaxed than the last time we were together,' I said. She gave a deliberate cheery laugh like releasing a little bird.

In the distance the noise of a tractor revving up, the splutter of the engine. I brooded over the thick china cup. 'Teliela said that . . . um, that you think we have a lot in common.'

She smiled, a loose strand of her reddish hair winding about her face. 'Oh, I suspect we do. I see you walking about, hiding behind your jokes, your shoulders up like this –' she demonstrated. I grinned sheepishly through a pang of painful recognition.

'You're acting just as I did when I first came to this kibbutz as a refugee from Germany thirty years ago.' She refilled my cup with tea. 'When you first arrived in this room, it was like meeting a ghost of myself.' She sighed, a sound that ached with regret.

'What do you mean?' I said.

'I had lost both my parents in the Holocaust. Years later I also lost both my husband and son within a short time of each other. My son died young from a heart attack. I learnt to hide behind a smiling mask when all I felt inside was resentment, guilt and rage.'

She did know. She really did. When I looked at her it was as if

128

my own unhappiness recognised a friend and signalled. I cleared my throat. 'That's terrible. I don't know how you managed to live through it all.'

Her blue eyes shone gently as she shrugged. 'Did I have a choice? You live through what life gives you, that's all.'

I didn't trust myself to speak more, but there were still things I needed to say. I took a deep breath, the first since I had arrived here. In a careful monotone I said, 'I know what you mean, but . . . Sometimes I feel like my insides are bundled up in a parcel tied up with a piece of string. A tightly packed parcel filled with grainy photographs. It's as if no one can get in there with me and I'm waiting for someone to unfasten the string that binds it, take a picture out and ask for an explanation.'

She nodded slowly. 'Who's in the photographs?'

I started to say 'lost children', but stopped myself. She searched my face, trying to understand. I looked away. An overpowering sense of disorder weighed on me, my mind adrift in terrible disorganisation. The drone of the distant tractor went from high to low, as if it was running out of steam, and then cut out completely.

'You know,' I said suddenly, 'for so long I've wanted someone to talk to, and now I've come this far and find it difficult to say more at present.' I glanced at the red lampshade with its burnt spot. 'Maybe I've come only to . . . to learn that I can't do it alone. Maybe that's why I came to Israel.'

Her eyes were very bright, very blue. 'To find someone to untie the knots?'

'Yes.' I traced a design on her tablecloth with my finger. 'But sometimes I can loosen up, like today.'

'Why? Did something happen?'

'It's not really important.' I didn't want to discuss the argument with Cydney. Or the way Rick held my hand. Small things, after all. To discuss them would be to make too much of them.

She got up and moved to the sink, filling the kettle again. 'I'm not a mind-reader,' she called out over the sound of the tap, 'but I'm getting a feeling from you of heavy anger or guilt about something. Am I right?'

'Yes, I . . . I suppose so.' I let out a shaky breath, and looked away as she returned. Resting my gaze on the opposite wall, I glared at the books, daring them to move from the shelves, daring the windows to shatter. 'Miriam, I – I need you to be my friend.'

She looked at me with sombre amusement. 'Am I not treating you like a friend?'

'I can't tell. I don't think I've had one for years.'

The mere thought of people probing me, investigating my background and hatching theories about it normally made me shudder with disgust. The risks were always too terrible.

Here I suddenly checked my thoughts. Well, why not? I had a sudden wish to be myself with Miriam and tell her everything, from what I was avoiding to why, but caution and a growing feeling of peace restrained me for the moment. I wanted to forget myself and cling only to this growing closeness between us in these untroubled surroundings and watch the lamplight gleam downwards into the dark amber of the tea.

'It's strange', I said, 'how often I've longed for a tea like this. Tea seems to me a symbol of what home life should be like.'

'Just a loaf of bread,' she said, 'no jam, no cakes.'

I felt then a curious anguish caused by this glimpse of the happiness I would have felt if only things had been different – could be different – but somehow sadly were not.

'The thing is, I think I can be myself with you, which I can't seem to be with anyone else.'

'Well, I'd also like to think of you as a friend of mine.'

'You don't have to say that.'

'That's right, I don't. So I won't.'

We looked at each other, and, abruptly, I relaxed, grinning.

'You appreciate there aren't many people in the queue.'

'What a relief,' Miriam said. 'I wouldn't want any rivals.'

Chapter 10

12 February
Maureen's got lice in her hair. Yvonne was looking through
it. I saw a big ant with wings running in it.

15 February
Frances made me some chewing-gum from yellow crayons.
It tasted all right. The elastic in Janet's knickers broke and
they fell down.

A bucket in one hand and a mop in the other, I pushed open the
kitchen door. I had just finished washing the floor of the
passageway next to the kitchen. Although it was getting darker
outside, I didn't switch on the lights. I didn't like the shadows
they made. Even in the daytime the convent seemed dark, and at
night when the lights were on, the darkness pervaded everything,
like a fog.

I looked into the kitchen and saw Ruth lying on the red tiled
floor, scratching it with a needle.

'All right with you if I come in and wash the floor?' I asked.
My words echoed around the kitchen.

'All right with me if you drown yourself in the bucket,' Ruth
said. 'All right with me if you drop down dead. I don't care.'

'Thanks,' I said, and dragged the bucket and mop into the
kitchen.

'Thenks!' She mimicked me, her voice mincing in a stuck-up tone.

I let it pass and worked in silence for a few minutes, twisting the mop through the wooden wringer as dirty brown suds dripped back into the bucket. Ruth whistled tunelessly through her teeth while scraping the floor.

'What are you doing?' I asked.

'What does it look like? Picking crumbs out of the cracks. I'm starving.'

'You *must* be starving to be doing that,' I said, pushing the bucket further down to the centre of the kitchen.

'Clear off!' She shoved the bucket away with her foot. 'Don't mop this area until I've done with it. If Old Double Dutch Legs could see me now, sparks would fly.'

'Who's Double Dutch Legs?'

'Sister Columba.'

'Why do you call her that?'

Ruth's brown eyes gleamed conspiratorially, a hint of warmth seeping through her icy veneer. 'Because on my first day here, she was teaching some of the kids a Dutch clog dance. She barked at them like a dog. Whenever they made a mistake, she whacked them on their bare legs with her cane. Whack, whack, clickedy-clack!'

The story didn't surprise me. Nothing the nuns did could surprise me any more. They were experts at whacking us and calling us horrible names. I shoved the mop across the floor. 'How long ago was that?'

'That was more than six years ago, after both my adopted parents died,' she said in a tone as tired as though she were speaking of six centuries. 'It was my godmother's idea to place me in the convent. Worse luck! She meant well, because how was she to know that I would spend my life like this?' Her hand in its vague gesture included the stark kitchen, the cold night, fear and her faded tunic that smelt of onions.

'All I can say is I hate the nuns' charity, but nobody else

wants me.' She scowled, flicking crumbs in the air and trying to catch them in her mouth. 'I hate needing them. I hate it. I can't wait to do another bunk from this dump. I can't wait to grow up.'

It scared me, not knowing what I'd turn into when I got older. What if I became something I really hated? How could I stop that happening?

I put the mop back into the bucket and ran it through the wringer again, hands on the top end of the handle, eyes on Ruth. This was great. The two of us alone. I had learnt not to watch her too closely, and above all to leave off from being soft in her company. So I swished the mop vigorously across the floor, letting my heart simply brim over with pure awe at having her to myself. Ruth's antics were legendary within the convent. She believed that if St Lawrence could talk back to the Romans, she could talk back to the nuns. Sister Cuthbert said he was the martyr who the Romans tied to an iron gate, and grilled over a fire saying, 'Now do you renounce Jesus?' He said: 'I'm done on this side, now do you want to turn me over?' Sister Cuthbert said he was the patron saint of cooks.

Now, without moving her head, Ruth surreptitiously moved her eyes and looked at me. She had stopped scratching the floor and was lying with her head on one side, picking at her nose. Her eyes seemed forbidding and suspicious. I wondered if I dared ask her about the day she ran away. The excitement of being with her now made my stomach smaller; it hurt. I didn't want to spoil this moment. Was it worth risking?

I said, 'Ruth, when you ran away that day, where did you go?'

'To the beach.'

'What for?'

'It was like this, see. One day I'd had enough. Strolled out of this dump to get some fresh air. D'you know what I mean? Saw the crowds in town. The lights. The noise. Look, if I tell you more, can I have a promise you'll not say a word?'

133

'I suppose so,' I said.

She jumped up from the floor and glared at me with her fists half cocked. I picked up my mop defensively and laughed. Although Ruth was the girl everyone pointed at and stayed away from, and although even in a good mood she spoke like she was only half a step away from picking a fight, I knew she never really set out to hurt. She hid the ugliness of convent life behind a shield of hard-line lingo and jokes, but Ruth, more than any one of us, was always in need of someone's smile.

'All right, all right, keep your hair on!' I said. 'I'll keep quiet.'

'OK, I'll tell you,' she said, taking one of the nuns' sauce-stained plates from the draining board, pressing her thumb on the crumbs and licking them off. 'It was like this. I got in with this bloke who had an ice-cream van on the seafront. He shovelled scoopfuls of free ice cream on to cornets for me with great swirly squirts of raspberry syrup. "Yum-yum, it'll make you nice and sweet," he kept saying and making kissing noises.'

She cleared her throat, but it was only to spit an immense dollop of phlegm on to the nuns' plates in the sink.

'Anyway, when he shut up shop, he invited me inside his van. I knew I shouldn't have because I sort of had an idea about him. I've got a nose for people, d'you know what I mean? He started mauling me straight away. His red eyes were like a wild animal's. Not an animal in a zoo, but a hunting animal. He bent down and tried to lick my mouth, like I was an ice cream. I said, "OK, drop your trousers and show us your willy." '

'What? Why?' I almost yelled.

'Well, that way I could run off and he could hardly chase me with his pants down, could he? I got away from that lickety old letch as quickly as I could. Fact is, I ran off to the nearest police station. The nuns said they couldn't come and collect me. So a copper drove me back here. The nuns went mental. Took it in turns to . . . Oh, I don't want to talk about it! Hear me? I don't want to talk about it!'

I had stopped mopping to listen. Now I resumed mopping and negotiated a tricky corner with a twist of the handle. Nobody knew what form of punishment the nuns had employed to keep Ruth under control at that time, but Frances had figured that she was kept tied to a bed in the isolation ward for a week.

'Aren't you interested in what I've just told you, or has the cat got your tongue?' Ruth said, heaving herself up to sit on the kitchen table. She brushed back her helmet of hair to get a better look at me.

'You said you don't want to talk about it.'

'Don't be so polite! Can you just stop mopping a minute? It's driving me mad. Ask me something.'

There was a slight pause as Ruth picked her teeth with her needle while I blotted out her footprints with my mop. I was dying to keep talking, to make it last longer. Say something, anything, so long as it wasn't stupid. 'Do you ever read books?' I felt like a clot as soon as I'd said it. I knew that she couldn't read properly because she'd been made to work in the kitchen and laundry for so long instead of attending class.

'Thanks a bleeding bundle.' There was another pause. She dislodged a crumb from her teeth on to the point of her needle and gazed at it intently. 'The covers of books are too far apart for me,' she said, staring at the end of her needle. 'I'm not totally illiterate. I did try to read a book once, but it was like wading through treacle. Little black dots stuck to the pages that meant nothing.'

'One day, when you're free of this place, you'll learn to read properly.'

'Yeah, freedom!' she said. 'When I first walked into this dump, I was a child. Now I'm not sure who I am. The years here have changed me for sure.'

I gave the floor a few more strokes with the mop and wondered if I had changed. I had not been physically ruined like Janet, nor beaten as much as Frances. And I wasn't the lit fuse Ruth had become. My anger was burning on a slower fuse.

It was more controlled, mixed as it was with deep fear. In my time in the convent, I never could summon the sort of courage that Ruth found to keep the nuns at bay. I saw that there would never be an end to my imperfections in their eyes, or to my doing things the wrong way; even when I grew up, no matter how hard I scrubbed, whatever I did, I knew there would always be somebody looking daggers at me.

I sighed and stood back to survey the kitchen floor with my head on one side. In its silence, the kitchen appeared serene and glistening. I looked out the window into the playground. The sun had almost gone, but the sky still retained a murky orange glow, gleaming with a few feathers of pale cloud, against which the line of poplar trees appeared black and delicately clear. I stood there realising that this was the first moment of peace in my day.

Ruth sniffed as she continued to pick crumbs off the kitchen table with her needle while swinging her skinny legs with their red knees and heavy black shoes like two pendulums. She hummed cheerfully between sniffs. I thought about her bad lungs. What exactly was TB? I tried to picture her lungs hidden beneath the billow of her tunic, like two pale spongy things in the thick darkness inside her body. They would be covered with dark bruises. It hurt when I thought about it, but TB was fascinating, like a horrible treasure.

'Me belly's fair sagging,' Ruth said rooting again with her needle at her teeth, 'I licked half of my Gibbs' toothpaste before Mass this morning. If I could have one wish at this moment, it would be for a plate of cornflakes.'

'Or just a broth of spuds and bacon rind. Anything other than those onions boiled in their overcoats we had last night.'

'Yeah, but them nuns got fried liver with theirs. I ate their leftover gristly bits that I was supposed to feed to Sister Ann's pet pusscat. What's in that blue enamel saucepan on the hob?'

I went to the ancient stove and peered at the bleachy water in the saucepan.

'Knickers, I think,' I said.

'Crikey, is there nothing for us to eat? I could do with some baked beans. Trouble is, they give me gas. Talking of gas, have you heard the joke about the drunk who sat down in the confession box and said nothing?' She laughed, the rumble of a cough starting in her chest. 'Father Holland kept knocking on the wall to get the bloke's attention. The drunk said, "It's no use knocking, mate, there's no paper in this one either."'

I laughed. 'You'll have to go to confession and tell Father Holland you said that.'

'Bollocks! Don't be soft,' she said, sucking at the crevice in her teeth. 'He'll probably give me a thousand Hail Marys. It would take me all day and night to finish them. Who is God, anyway?'

'He's a magician and he's in Heaven, isn't he?'

'And where the hell is Heaven?'

'But you believe, don't you?' I implored her. 'You think it's true.'

'Of course it's true. What else could there be?' she went on scornfully. 'Because it's the only thing that fits. Of course there's hell, flames and damnation.'

'And Heaven too,' I said with anxiety.

Ruth grinned, yawned and nodded all in one. 'Ooooh, maybe, maybe. But if Heaven is going to be filled with the likes of the nuns, well, God can have them to himself.'

Sated by her yawn, she said with tear-washed eyes, 'I wonder how much God weighs? If God is everywhere, then he's in food. I don't believe in Heaven, I believe in food.'

I looked forward to Sunday, when we had cast-off cakes and doughnuts that the local bakery donated to the convent all mixed together and baked into a big pudding. I loved it. It made a change from the daily rice pudding mixed with tea leaves plonked on the same plate as our first course.

Ruth concentrated on picking at the table and I went back to mopping the floor, moving the wet strands from side to side so that no dry patches remained.

'Was your father . . . ?' Ruth interrupted herself for an instant, and then said, 'I don't want to poke my nose into your business, but was your father rich? I mean, before he died?'

'I don't think so,' I said.

'What was he?' she asked after a pause.

'My mum told me that he was . . .' Throwing my fist in the air and extending one finger after another, I counted, 'A journalist, an aircraft fitter, a pub-owner, a gambler, a Catholic, a drinker, a story-teller, something in a factory, a football pools agent . . .'

'And now a corpse!' A coughball of laughter rattled in Ruth's throat. 'The aircraft fitter sounds good.'

Speaking of Dad made my thoughts skitter back to Mum. I had still received no word from her. Maybe she hadn't written after all; maybe Frances had just imagined seeing three letters from her in Sister Mary's cell. Or maybe she had just said it to make me feel better.

I had been here for over a year. My head throbbed, thinking about it.

As if reading my thoughts, Ruth suddenly asked with a chirpy wag of her head, 'Do you think your mum's abandoned you?'

I hated it when someone cut in on your thoughts, like they'd been peeking about in your mind.

I shook my head. 'No, I've never worried about her really wanting to leave me. Maybe that's just me being big-headed but . . . she wouldn't. At first when I didn't hear from her, I felt angry. Then I felt sad because I thought something might have happened to her, then I realised . . . well, loads of things.'

'Like what?' Ruth asked.

I gulped. I didn't want to talk about it because it always led to trouble when I did, or I'd start to cry. Crying just made things worse. It would be letting Ruth down if I were to crumple.

Ruth was the strong one.

Besides, I had stiffened myself so much on the outside, my

insides were blocked up: it was too draining even to cry, to wash things away that way.

'Well,' I began, trying to speak past the thing that had risen in my throat, 'I haven't received one letter from her since I've been here, even though Frances said she saw three letters for me in Sister Mary's cell.'

'And you still haven't been given them?'

'No . . . well, that's if she wrote at all . . . and if she did, I daren't ask for them, not after that whipping Sister Mary gave me . . .' I stopped. Everything seemed to collapse slowly inwards, my eyes drooped and my shoulders slumped. Ruth hopped down from the table and squeezed my arm roughly. I felt like a kid with an old lady's head and shuffly feet.

And then it came back, clear and sharp, the memory of a snapshot of Mum, Dad and me on the beach in Margate. I was so small then that Dad looked like a giant; I had a good view of his knobbly knees with his trousers rolled up above them. He was holding out his hand with a tiny crab on it that skittered from one side to the other in a crazy sideways dance. And Mum stood ahead of us in a white sundress dotted with small flowers, the camera up to her smiling face.

And I recalled I was happy a long time ago, when Mum, Dad and I were always together, and remembering that was so painful that I felt sick and dizzy for a moment, trying to push it away, as always. But I breathed through it. I didn't want Ruth to see me cry. I hadn't cried in front of her since the early days, when she called me grizzle-guts for being such a baby.

'C'mon, put a sock in it,' said Ruth. 'You should be like me. You'd have something to cry over then. Nothing ever happens without reason. And if your mum hasn't written to you, she must have had a good one.'

'Like what?' I sniffed and like Ruth I rubbed my nose on my sleeve.

'I don't know. Stopping you from being unhappy.'

'But I *am* unhappy.'

She looked at me long and hard. 'You poor kid. God, I hate them nuns.' I held my breath. 'They're all batty bloody cyclepaths at heart,' she hissed.

Though I could never pass Ruth's swear words over my own lips, it was good to hear them spoken.

'I think so too,' I said.

She raised two fingers and rolled her eyes heavenwards and chanted: 'They believe in the rod, the scourger almighty, creator of hell upon earth. Glory beat the Father, ran to the Son and the Holy Ghostly men. Hah! Listen, I know a good joke. How do you make holy water? Boil the hell out of it!'

I smiled even though I'd heard it before, because there was a wave of corny jokes about religion sweeping the convent. Religious jokes and food jokes. *Why did the tomato blush? Because it saw the salad dressing.*

'I'd best finish this boring old job,' I said, sloshing the mop across the floor again.

Ruth doodled on the table with her needle. 'What's the difference between roast beef and pea soup?'

I tried to think what the answer could be and then said, 'I give up.'

'Anyone can roast beef.'

'Ha, ha,' I said. Part of this ritual was mild derision of other people's jokes.

'You're doing a good job there, Judith,' she said. 'You've taken to the mop really well.'

We fell silent as we heard the pattering of feet on the heavily polished floor on the other side of the kitchen door. The swish of robes, the slight jangle of a rosary that always warned of the arrival of a nun, and then an entering form darkened the doorway.

'Norton! You lazy good-for-nothing, haven't you finished the washing-up yet?'

The light was switched on. There was a miserable glow, more like fog than like light. Sister Columba was revealed crossing the floor with a great deal of noise. Ruth leapt down from the table.

'N-no, Sister, I was giving my hands a rest because my chilblains have split.'

Sister Columba ranged about the kitchen, touching things here and there. She scrutinised the mopped floor for grime. It was spotless, and for a second I thought she was going to admit it. But no, praise might make me vain. A bubble floated from the bucket and burst wetly on her toecap. She pointed to the draining board piled high with unwashed crockery.

'The washing-up should have been finished hours ago, Norton, you idle girl!' Sister Columba squinted her eyes and screwed up her mouth, like she'd smelt an old kipper. The surface of her skin was closer to smooth, slightly dusty cardboard than skin. In the midst of this desert her two eyes gleamed alarmingly, like weedy pools. I thought almost with horror that if those eyes were ever capable of spilling a tear it would surely cut a strange furrow in the dry powdery surface, revealing goodness knew what beneath. She gave off a sweet musty smell, like old linen that had been preserved in a drawer for years.

When the nun's back was turned, Ruth made her hand snap open and shut like a beak, while she silently mouthed, 'Nag, nag, nag.'

'But I've been mopping the floor for hours. Haven't I?' she said, rounding fiercely on my shrinking form. 'I have, haven't I?' she added, thrusting her face belligerently to mine.

'Yes,' I said faintly, handing her the mop.

'If I've told you once I've told you a thousand times, don't exaggerate,' said Sister Columba. 'You tell enough white lies to ice a cake. Now, on – and – finish – the – washing-up!' The nun gritted her teeth and ground out the last words slowly, as if she were spelling.

Ruth ambled over to the sink.

'Get a move on!' said Sister Columba. 'Do you realise what time it is?'

'Yeah, I do, ta very much.'

'I've met some hard-boiled girls in my time,' barked Sister Columba, 'but you – you're twenty minutes. You're rude, retarded, incapable of learning and incapable of work.'

'But I've been sweating cobs all afternoon.'

'It's about time you accepted your condition without rebellion and without abusing those of us placed in authority over you.'

Ruth waved her hand. 'Oh, go boil your head!'

I gasped. What on earth had got into her? I recoiled against the wall, body stiff, shoulders hunched, watching as all the portals of hell blasted open. Taking a wet floorcloth covered in grease and smuts, the nun sloshed it at Ruth's head. Swish. Ruth backed away and put the table between them; another swipe and another, with no effect. Again. Swish, swish. 'That does it! I shall speak to the Mother Superior about you after tea.'

'Oh yes, must have your tea and rock cakes first,' cried Ruth, beginning to laugh and cough.

'Come here! I'll beat the stuffing out of you once I catch you,' said Sister Columba, leaning across the table in an effort to grab Ruth, who dodged out of the way. The pantomime continued at a fantastic rate; they looked like a speeded-up film with Sister Columba charging and swinging her soggy weapon and Ruth nimbly side-stepping the clumsy swings.

The filthy mulch flew in all directions, speckling the nun's white wimple. The ceiling. A large blotch landed on Sister Columba's upper lip, just beneath her nose, giving her a Hitler moustache. When I saw it, I became paralysed with horror, but a foolish giggling fit had got hold of me. I pressed my lips together so as not to laugh out loud. Tears of suppressed half-hysterical laughter began to course from my eyes.

The floorcloth couldn't withstand such violence and was soon reduced to a ragged, soggy mess. Exhausted in wind and words, Sister Columba paused, chest heaving. She threw the cloth in Ruth's face.

Ruth shuddered. With her teeth clenched, she very slowly

wiped her face. She stood there poised, frozen in a half-turn towards the draining board, with one hand outstretched balletically, and, slowly allowing a look of imbecilic delight to transfigure her features, she took one swipe at the crockery and smashed it all to the ground. The nun lurched backwards. To keep her balance she twisted about on her heel and found herself face to face with Ruth, whose teeth were chattering with anger. Picking up the soggy cloth, she threw it into Sister Columba's face. 'Heil Hitler, yah, yah, yah!'

There was one of those you-could-hear-a-pin-drop-silences. The nun glared at Ruth in the feeble light of the feeble bare bulb. Ruth smiled and stared back at her – rawly, savagely – with dark eyes a thousand years old in their wicked wisdom. Then she let out a shocking laugh as she ran past me out of the kitchen.

'Come back here, scumbag!' Sister Columba screamed. She whirled on me. 'Don't just stand there looking like a frozen custard!' She was panting, as if she had been running. 'Go and bring her back!'

I slowly put my mop away. 'Shouldn't I sweep up the broken plates first, Sister?'

'Later! Go and get Norton!'

I stood staring at the nun's sweaty speckled face. Does she, I wondered, know how much I hate her? How willingly I would allow my stare to kill her if only I had the power? Perhaps she did, because she lifted her arm and, taking a full swing, hit me with the flat of her hand with such violence that I staggered back against the wall and almost fell to the floor.

'Go now, before I have your teeth across the floor.'

The right side of my face was burning, the taste of blood was in my mouth. I ran outside into the dark, shadowy playground. It was a clear, wintry evening, with the sky freckled with stars. I suddenly remembered that once they would have seemed beautiful to me. A full moon smiled stupidly, showing no understanding of the lunacy in the convent.

I could see just Ruth ahead of me. I bounded after her. 'Ruth! Sister Columba sent me to fetch you back.'

She turned aside and spat on the ground.

'*Phth!* to her, right in her eye.'

'You must come back,' I gasped. With the tip of my tongue, I could taste the blood inside my cheek from Sister Columba's blow. I spat it out.

'You know what will happen to us if you don't –'

Ruth halted beside the nuns' graveyard, breathing hard and swallowing her breath. Her eyes were wild. She folded her arms across her chest, rocking herself. 'Well, you're wrongedy-wrong-wrong. I'll wait until she's calmed down a bit. Where shall I hide?'

I sagged like a pricked balloon. The chaos Ruth had created would inevitably affect the other girls if she didn't return to Sister Columba immediately. Yet in a way she was right – best to wait until the nun was less crazed with anger. Beatings were always more vicious when anger was at its height.

But where was she to hide? We looked despairingly about us. Shouts drifted out from the convent. We knew Sister Columba would be rallying her posse of nuns like rooks hovering in a black cloud. There was agitation and trouble everywhere, with the noise of many feet approaching from the direction of the convent.

'Think, think, think! Don't panic!' said Ruth. Behind us were the formidable figures of the nuns, ahead of us the pitch darkness of the nuns' graveyard. The nuns were more of a menace.

'I'll hide in here,' said Ruth, pointing to the graveyard. Tall cypress trees encircled it, whispering in the night.

I shivered for her. 'But it's out of bounds.'

'The nuns won't go in there. They never do unless there's a burial.'

She was right: the nuns were superstitious about it. She'd never be found in there. But even in the strongest there is anguish in the dead of night.

'Pray for me!' Ruth said, and quick as a squirrel, she climbed over the railings and hid herself in the mist and darkness among the graves.

I could hear the nuns searching the playground: the rattle of the rosary beads, the swish of the skirts, the clip-clopping of boots like hooves on the tarmac. I could see their black shapeless habits swaying as they moved and the sharp outline of the blue shadows that the moon cast behind them.

Suddenly Sister Columba called to me. 'Well, Kelly, where is she?'

'I don't know, Sister,' I lied.

Her tight face became tighter. 'Well, don't just stand there gawping, you dope. Go and join the other juniors in the boot-room.'

As I ran back towards the convent windows, which seemed washed with warmth and brightness, I heard Sister Columba thrashing her cane on the side of the railings. 'She is here somewhere!' she screamed. It was a wonder her cane didn't break.

Ten questioning faces greeted me in the boot-room. So the news had spread. We huddled together. *What's happening? Has Ruth run away? Have you heard anything? Seen anything? Where's she hiding?* I told them that Ruth had thrown a real wobbly.

'I haven't seen her so mad for a long time,' I whispered.

'Sister Columba will give us a hell of a time if she doesn't return soon,' said Frances.

'I know,' I said. 'I did try to reason with her, but it was hopeless. She was so mad.'

Of course, when I reached the point in my story where Ruth threw the floorcloth back at Sister Columba, it excited them so much that it almost belittled the main concern – Ruth in hiding.

'So where is she?'

'In the nuns' graveyard.' They all gasped in horror.

'Shh! What's that?' I whispered, 'Did you hear something?'

'When?'

'Just now.'

'Yes, listen.'

We listened in silence until our ears ached. Finally we could just hear the faint pitter-patter of boots on the stone stairs. We all quickly knelt and began polishing shoes with vehemence.

The door all but burst its hinges as Sister Columba slammed into the boot-room. We stood to attention, eyes straight ahead. She was using her usual trick of holding her rosary crushed in her hand. So that it wouldn't chink. Taking her bamboo cane from the folds of her habit, she pointed at each of us in turn.

'Ruth Norton struck me. The nuns will not tolerate such behaviour. We make the rules within this convent. And they're not to be lightly cast aside at the whim of a single troublemaker. The devil soon finds work for empty hands. There will be no food for any of you tonight. Now, Kelly, where is Norton hiding?'

I replied that I didn't know, my voice cracking from fear and nerves. I tried to avoid the nun's gaze, concentrating my eyes on her mulch-spotted wimple, still smelling strongly of Jeyes' Fluid. Everyone looked at me. I felt weak enough to faint.

Sister Columba could glean nothing from my face; it might as well have been stone. She stared furiously at me. Perfect stillness followed – not a rustle, not a breath. My heart was tearing out of my chest, its beats booming in my ears.

Very, very slowly, Sister Columba brought out her little black book bound by a leather thong. She slapped the pages backwards and forwards, giving all of us a black mark.

'Very well!' she thundered. 'If Norton does not appear within the hour,' she said, wetting the end of her pencil with the tip of her tongue and scratching in her book, 'she can sleep in the open and every one of you will receive the flogging of your life. Think about it, Kelly,' she said, strapping up her black book and stowing it away.

She left, slamming the door. Uneasiness took possession

of every face. 'What are we going to do?' we said in one voice.

Frances stood pressed against the wall beside the tiny window, looking out at the graveyard. 'It could be any of us, out there,' she said. After a deep lull, she opened her mouth and began to sing, lifting her voice to carry out to Ruth where she hid.

The notes rebounded in the small room, high and piercing. The Magnificat. We all joined in the background chorus in a deep monotone, and in an instant I found myself transported away from the present with its insane dangers, and looking at a world all young, fresh and beautiful. The gloomy boot-room vanished. For the moment, I had no fear of the nuns. The girls' kindness towards Ruth had brought me into fairyland.

The last note trembled and faded. We fell into a deep silence. Outside in the playground we could hear the constant clip-clopping of the nuns' boots on the tarmac.

One by one, we began singing again. Slowly, very slowly, the tone of our song changed. The glow passed from blue to purple, and then to angry red. Bit by bit the notes spun together till they made a fierce, restless harmony. And I knew where it was taking us. We all felt the same about the nuns. The room rang with a tremendous shout of 'Ruth!' and another, and another. All terror had gone, and fury was beating the air. Encouraged by each other, we threw back our heads to let free fly our shouts, which increased to a roar. Flushed, panting, sweating. I shouted too, until I was hoarse, releasing all my frustration and resentment towards the nuns for keeping me away from Mum. So what if they heard us? So what?

Frances, who was normally so brave, began to cry. I took her hand and squeezed it. I looked at the faces clustered around me, and realised that these girls were all that I had left in the world.

Suddenly the spell was broken. The fairytale room changed into a prison cell with its suffocating smell of boots and polish. Exhausted, breathless, our rage died down.

Quietly, Janet said, 'I wish I hadn't shouted so much. I've piddled in my pants.'

'Oh, Janet!' someone protested. 'And you've made a puddle.'

Janet reddened and then grew pale as outside the door we could hear Ruth keening, as she was pushed down the stairs and flogged. Mingled with Sister Columba's booming voice it made a sinister jarring effect inside the boot-room. Every blow seemed to cut into us.

Finally there was silence. A gust of cool wind swirled through the room as the door was flung open. Ruth came in, walking carefully, as if balancing or lame. She stood uncertainly, squinting a little, head poking forward and swinging slowly from side to side like a bewildered elephant. She sat down on the floor and leant against the wall.

'I gave myself up,' she croaked, 'I knew they'd punish all of you on my account if I didn't.' She rubbed the sleeve of her now filthy blouse across her face and sniffled. 'Besides, I'd had enough of your bloody awful caterwauling.'

Mum's letters gnawed at me. Thinking of them, I lay awake at night, sucking the tops of my arms. Had she written, or not? Sister Mary had no right to keep her letters from me, none. She had no right to flog me for writing what I liked to Mum. I lay in bed glaring at the wall that separated our dormitory from Sister Mary's cell. My letters, if they were there, were only a few feet away.

They might as well have been on the moon.

I decided not to pray to God any more. When it was time in the evening for the only prayer that was not in Latin, the Lord's Prayer, I knelt in silence, moving my lips only.

Forgive us our trespasses, as we forgive those who trespass against us.

What was the good of those words? Saying them would have no effect on the way the nuns actually behaved towards us and if they meant I would have to forgive the nuns or else go to hell when I died, I was ready to go. Jesus was a hard taskmaster. He understood our weaknesses and how difficult it was to forgive, which was why he put that in. He was always putting in things that were impossible to do really.

'It's rotten,' said Frances in the corridor after Benediction, 'for both of us to have been flogged because Sister Mary won't give you your mum's letters.'

I felt my heart filled by Frances's words and did not answer.

'We shouldn't stand for it,' she said. 'We should go and report Sister Mary and Sister Columba to the Mother Superior after collation.'

'Yes, yes, please do,' said Janet eagerly. On her cheek, dull and bloodless, was a blotch of ink.

'Yes, please, please. Tell her,' other girls said.

And there were some girls from the senior class listening and one said, 'You could do it, Judith. You've got a mother. Do it for all of us. The nuns pick on us. I looked up "sadist" in the dictionary. It said it's gaining pleasure or sexual gratification from inflicting pain and mental suffering on another person. That's them all right.'

I nodded in agreement. It sounded right. For some reason I almost wanted to giggle.

But it *was* wrong; it *was* unfair; and later, amid the clatter of plates and knives during collation, I miserably relived the flogging that Sister Mary had given me. And trembling now, I remembered another scene: the moment when I had seen Sister Mary's faint cruel creases at the corners of her smiling lips as the strokes of Sister Columba's cane beat Janet and Frances.

I hardly heard a word that was being said during collation because my stomach was churning so much. I could not eat the cockles we had collected from the beach that day due to the ordeal that awaited me. I was thinking I must do it for the sake of the other girls. I must go up and tell the Mother Superior that we had been wrongly punished because Sister Mary was holding on to our letters.

It was easy: all I had to do when collation was over and I came out of the refectory was say a short prayer for guidance, make my way to the stairs that led to the Mother Superior's rooms, swerve sharp right and then I'd be almost there. I had nothing to do but that. And every girl had said it was unfair, even the girl from the senior class, but they would not go and complain themselves. When I had decided this, I felt a little relief.

The senior girls at the top table stood up. We all stood up and grace was said. I passed out among them in the file. I must do it. I must. I was coming near the refectory door. If I turned left with the other girls, towards the boot-room, I could never go up to the Mother Superior because I would never get up enough courage again. I had reached the door and, turning quickly up to the right, passed the cloakroom where our overcoats hung like headless criminals; I glanced back and saw the girls watching me as they filed quickly out of the refectory.

By now I was in no hurry. I walked slowly down the corridor, planting my feet with care along the polished parquet floor. When I came to the narrow stairs that led to the Mother Superior's quarters, my remembering feet glided up them. I could hear no sound until I found myself on a broad creaky landing, with a carved wood balustrade behind me and several doors in front of me. They must have been the old people's rooms. The woodwork was as shiny as an apple. An oppressive silence surged through the passage like a cloud. I looked about me through the gloom and saw the saints looking down on me silently as I passed: St Jude of Thaddeus the patron Saint of Lost Causes pointing to his chest. I reached up and brushed my hand over the rough surface of the portrait for good luck.

As I approached the Mother Superior's rooms, the chill in the air was reinforced by a damp smell of mildew. My pace slowed until I stood outside her door. I was breathing hard. I placed my hands on my hot cheeks to feel. Closed my eyes. 'Calm down. Calm down,' I repeated to myself. I expelled a long breath. It was impossible: I couldn't. What would happen? I imagined the

Mother Superior's eyes looking at me behind her thick spectacles. I paced up and down, waiting to summon up the courage to enter the room, but after some minutes, I could wait no longer. Hurriedly combing my hair with my fingers and straightening my tunic, I gingerly knocked on her door. My legs were shaking and the scalp of my head trembled as though ghostly fingers had touched it. There was no answer. I knocked again, more loudly. The sound echoed strangely. Then a muffled voice said: 'Come in.' I seized the handle firmly and stepped into the room. It was long and narrow with large windows opening on to the front gardens.

The Mother Superior was nowhere to be seen. It was Sister Cuthbert who sat writing at a desk. She looked up, blinking her eyes in surprise. Letters and papers filled the entire surface of the desk. It was still and bright in the room, the sun through the window making great squares on the floor. A tinny clock ticked loudly on the mantelpiece. In the centre of the room hung a heavy gilt frame showing a picture of Christ with yellow beams of light streaming from his head. His ribcage was neatly split and with a pale pointed finger he indicated his exposed and perfectly heart-shaped heart. There was a mysterious smell of congealed gravy in the air.

Sister Cuthbert stared at me, unsmiling, her lips parted, and I stared back, blushing hotly and feeling that my eyes were as round as saucers.

'Well, child, what is it?' she said, leaning back in her chair, making it groan.

I stood still for a moment in utter incomprehension. I swallowed hard and said: 'I wanted to speak to – Will Mother Superior be back soon?'

'No, she will not be in the school until tomorrow. Is there anything I can do for you?'

I wasn't thinking clearly. All courage had left me. I swallowed again and tried to keep my legs and voice from shaking.

'No, it's all right, thank you, Sister,' I muttered; I could feel the blood rising again in my face. I turned to dash from the room when she suddenly called me back. She searched through the papers on the desk and then held up a letter with Mum's handwriting on the envelope. Of course, I still recognized her writing.

'This letter is for you. The Mother Superior must have meant to give it to Sister Mary. Just a moment while I open it for you,' she said. I went hot and cold and turned deaf and dumb for a split second, my lips parted while she unfolded the letter and scanned it.

'Well now, your mother says she's coming to pay you a visit next month. That's nice, isn't it?' She handed the letter to me. I took it slowly, like a sacred relic and put it in my tunic pocket. Mum had written. She was coming to see me! I decided that Sister Cuthbert was after all a nice nun with a really sweet face. Her coif suited her large head. I felt tears wetting my eyes and murmured, 'Oh thank you, Sister.'

I walked quietly out of the room, closing the door carefully and slowly. But when I reached the narrow dark corridor I began to walk faster and faster, saying a quick thank-you to St Jude's portrait. I did not look at the letter at once. Its presence there in my pocket was an absolute comfort. I wanted it to remain, for the moment, a lucky charm, a magic stone, a holy relic, something entirely protective. Faster and faster with my fingertips upon Mum's letter in my pocket, I hurried through the gloom. I could hear the distant choir of voices in the boot-room. I broke into a run and, running quicker and quicker with pounding steps, I leapt down the stairs until I reached the boot-room.

The girls had heard me running. Clapping and cheers greeted my entrance. They closed round me in a ring, pushing one against the other.

'Tell us! Did you see her? Tell us!'
'What did she say?'
'Did you go in?'

'What did she say?'

'C'mon on! Tell us!'

I told them what had happened and with trembling fingers showed them Mum's letter. All the girls jumped up and down and clapped their hands in wild frenzy and yelled in a chorus of cheers: 'Hurray! Hurray! Hoo-blummin'-ray! Good old Judith!' I raised my arms above my head, basking in the applause.

Some girls formed a cradle of their locked hands and swung me up and down, while the others chanted their support. And when I struggled free of them, their cheers turned to murmurs of admiration that died away in the watery green light. I looked at the envelope and felt free as I realised that it was almost over. I could leave now. All I had to do was tell Mum what was happening, and that was it, I'd be gone.

It was too earth-shaking. The world swayed as I tried to take it in.

Frances entered the boot-room. I watched her as she approached me with her upbeat, bouncy walk, and for a moment it was as though I had already left her behind. Poor Frances: she had no one to visit her. She was stuck for ever in this hellhole, while I now had the opportunity to escape. Comparing our lives made me feel so lucky it ached.

'I went to fetch these for you,' she said. 'I thought I'd give them to you for being so brave.'

She produced a brown paper bag of toffees with the smile of an amateur conjuror producing a rabbit. 'I've eaten most of them, but there are a few left.'

'Where did you get those from?'

'Sister Mary gave them to me,' she stammered.

'The greaser,' I said. 'I bet she smarmed round you after all?'

Frances eyed me guiltily and said in a shaky voice, 'I can't tell you, she would kill me. You don't know the half of it.'

'Half of what?'

'Well, any news?' she asked, changing the subject.

'Yes, the Mother Superior's not around today – and Sister Cuthbert gave me this,' I said breathlessly.

'Gosh.' Tears of joy shone in her delighted eyes. She put her hand on my shoulder and looked at my fist, clenched around the envelope, as if it might blow away. 'A letter from your Mum . . . you must be over the moon!'

'Yes. And Frances, she's coming to see me.'

We looked at each other. We knew what it meant.

My insides would have done somersaults, if they hadn't been weighed down by the prospect of what I had to tell Mum once I saw her. Half of me was excited at the idea of leaving the convent, the other half wanted to cling to Frances and tell her I couldn't leave her and the other girls. All the times we had helped each other flashed in front of my eyes.

But now my life was about to change utterly. I felt sadness, dread, and a more awful hope. Frances looked at me in a different way for the rest of the morning. She smiled anxiously, as if she was already expecting me to evaporate in a puff of smoke. Once I told Ruth the news, I could almost see green exit signs glowing in her eyes.

I held my face still to hide the guilty anticipation that swirled through me. It was like looking at someone else's life – hand-me-down clothes, all sepia and faded; snatches of Latin prayers I'd never known the meaning of; someone gently rocking my bed. My fingers touched the precious letter in my tunic pocket. The tight feeling of excitement that made my throat ache brought me back to the present and the kneeling girls around me in the boot-room.

Frances concentrated on the boot she was polishing as she said, 'We'll never hear from you again if you leave the convent.'

'I'll write to you,' I said.

She snorted, not looking up. 'It'll be impossible. You know the nuns won't give me your letters, and they won't send mine to you.'

I stopped mid-swish of my shoe brush. I hadn't thought of

that. Little shivers ran across my skin as I remembered some-thing else: I wouldn't be allowed to live with Mum in her bedsit. She'd have to place me in another boarding school, and who could say what *that* would be like? I suddenly had visions of children with greasy matted hair, grimy faces and blackened teeth who might spit and claw at me. Teachers who killed children in their care. I told Frances my fears.

'Or maybe they'll be posh with snooty smiles and speak like they've got plums in their mouths,' she said with a muffled giggle.

'And long glossy hair like American film stars,' I added in a horrified whisper. 'They'll jeer at me when they discover I've been to an orphanage.'

'You wouldn't have to tell them.'

'They'd guess it somehow. And then no one would be my friend.'

'And what if your mum can't find a boarding school right away? You might have to come back here meanwhile. Sister Mary would blow her lid once she heard that you had told your mum about what she did to you,' she warned. 'Remember what happened to Betty O'Dowd?'

'Oh, cripes, yes!' I said feeling as though my stomach was doing somersaults.

Betty's story was pathetic, and perhaps not uncommon within the convent, but I was still unscathed enough to be shocked by it. Betty never said much and when she did, she stammered. She had a round face on which she wore a timid shy expression, always a little questioning, even bewildered. Her dark hair had once been thick, but eventually fell out in clumps because more than once Sister Columba grabbed her by the hair and flung her to the other side of the room. Her bald patches were so noticeable that her Mum complained to Father Holland. Sister Columba had then beaten Betty for telling tales.

In an attempt to make her hair grow again, the nuns had smeared her head with Vaseline and wrapped newspaper around it. But it didn't work. She suffered a rapid decline in health, culminating in the occasional hysterical outburst of crying. She had great difficulty in eating, hid her food and got thinner. She began to talk of strange visions, that God wanted her to die, to go to Him, that it was His will that she should be freed from this life. After that she began to mope, talking to no one and wandering around on her own. One night she disappeared and the nuns couldn't find her anywhere. They looked high and low for her. Father Holland found her naked in the confession box. She was whisked away to a sister house of the convent in Hampshire and we never saw her again.

Frances and I looked at each other in the dim light of the boot-room, the same memory in both of our eyes. 'It was her own stupid fault,' she said, 'she shouldn't have told her mum. Just be careful, Judith.'

My misery gradually returned like an old friend. The storm within me buffeted against my ribs all the rest of that day. As night crept over the convent, I hugged the covers around myself and thought of Mum. The future wavered between being brilliantly bright to dreadfully dark. Yet a secret sun shone under my skin at the prospect of seeing her.

From then on, each day I tore a page off a small calendar I made, screwing it into a tiny ball so that the days were truly destroyed until I saw her again. Time dragged by as the distant idea of her visit grew from a stationary speck to a looming reality. At last, from counting the weeks and then the days and then the day after tomorrow, I could say tomorrow. And then a feeling of calm, almost of hope, washed over me.

I imagined myself running down the corridor to the visitors' parlour to see Mum. She'd be lounging there like a film star in her white jacket, with her Katharine Hepburn look-alike face. Was she still in love with Gregory Peck? Would she speak to me in an American accent like they did in the cinema? When I saw her, I would tremble, I would cry. She would sweep me up into her arms and take me away from the carbolic smell of the corridors, the daily pins and needles in my housemaid's knees and the skittering of terrified girls.

On the morning of her visit, I awoke early and watched the black iron bedsteads grow clearer as daylight seeped into the vast dormitory. Sister Mary's cell was attached to the dormitory, and every morning she slammed shut her cell door to awaken us. It made a booming, hollow noise that all of us hated – but today I loved this explosive sound.

I almost skipped past the sleepy girls trudging to the wash-room. There was the sound of water being splashed into the washbasins, there was the sound of rising and dressing in the dormitory, and the sound of clapping hands as Sister Mary went up and down telling the girls to be quick. A pale light showed the seniors' cubicle curtains turned back, the tossed beds. Never again would I have to rise in fear at five and scrub the kitchen and polish the refectory floors. As I looked around the dormitory at the tired faces, again there was some stop in the flow to my happiness. I didn't want to think about it. I heard the junior girls whisper among themselves about me as they dressed for Mass. She's leaving today, they were saying. Ruth gave me a sidelong glance as she cat-licked her hands and face, and then grabbed a gap-toothed comb to whisk through her thick hair.

Sidling up to me she said, 'You're dead lucky, you are. You never really knew what it was like to be dumped here like the rest of us. To be buried a-bloody-live.'

'I know I've not suffered like you, Ruth,' I tried soothing, 'but I do have some idea.'

Ruth stood stiffly holding her comb and scowling at me with fierce dark eyes as if some terrible pressure was being put upon her. She held her comb as if it were a gun; she looked strangely like some tough delinquent, brimming over with anger.

'You don't know anything,' she hissed. 'I've been stuck in this shithouse for six years. Can you imagine what that's like? No, you can't, and you don't even try to. All you care about is getting back to the bloody outside world.'

I shook my head. 'I'm really sorry, Ruth, but I do have some idea what it must be like for you.' Life, the convent, the whole damned circus was so unfair. 'I know, Ruth, I know.'

'No!' she virtually spat in my face. 'You bleeding well don't. You've no fucking idea at all really!'

Mum arrived early, just as we were waiting to leave the refectory after breakfast to begin our daily chores. I stopped in my tracks when I saw her. It was really her.

Smiling, she hurried over and we hugged. I clung to her.

'What on earth is this you're wearing?' she laughingly asked, tugging at my work-stained, faded, navy-blue tunic.

'My work tunic,' I muttered shyly, afraid that someone might hear her.

'You mean it's what you wear for schoolwork? It's very scruffy,' she said in the same loud ringing voice.

I felt myself turning red. All the girls who were lined up waiting to leave the refectory were staring. I knew from the nuns' teachings that vanity was the most shameful of all sins. I nodded and avoided Mum's eyes as they shone down on me like distant stars.

I wanted to tell her so many things, but suddenly, unexpectedly, I felt ashamed. I didn't want her to know what was being done to me. I didn't want *anybody* to know, I didn't want it to be true – I just wanted to be her little girl again. And at the same time, I knew I had to tell her.

'Would you like to spend the weekend with me?' she said, 'My landlady says it would be all right for you to stay a couple of days.'

I nodded vigorously, lost for words at the pleasure and relief I felt. I wouldn't have to decide about telling her for the time being.

Sister Mary came bustling up the corridor smiling at Mum

stiffly; she couldn't use those muscles with any naturalness. 'Mrs Kelly, please would you wait in the visitors' parlour while Judith changes her clothes?'

The nun then hauled me into the washroom, where she handed me a clean, newer tunic. She closed the door and twisted the taps until the water filled an enamelled basin fitted into the sink. The noise almost drowned out the sound of her words. Her gaze never left my face.

'Now I want you to tell your mother that the nuns are doing their utmost to raise you and the other children as good Catholics.'

It took a few seconds for her words to sink in. She grabbed a flannel and inflicted a merciless but brief scrub of my face, hands and neck and rooted into the folds of my ears. Handing me a coarse towel, she said, 'Dry yourself and hurry up. Now I'm warning you – no lies or tall stories, not if you know what's good for you and your friends. All right?'

That's what she said. Those were her exact words. I wrote them down afterwards so I wouldn't get them mixed up.

Her cheek twitched as she looked down at me. Our eyes met, I nodded, silently, my head boiling.

She watched me for a moment, and then nodded. 'Off you go then.'

She unlocked the door and I could feel the heavy sensation of the palm of her hand upon my shoulder.

As I made my way to the parlour with Sister Mary's words still sounding in my ears, I passed the refectory where my classmates were polishing the floor by shuffling along with dusters under their feet. Frances rushed out when she saw me and threw her arms around my neck. 'Good luck, Judith. Come and say goodbye when you leave. I've written a poem for you and put it under your mattress with your diary.' Then kissing the tips of her fingers in farewell, she gave me a little shove in the direction of the front parlour and, before I could say anything, turned her back and bolted away down the corridor.

As I entered the visitors' parlour I caught sight of Mum sitting in the window seat at the far end, looking out at the sweeping gardens that we weren't allowed to play in. I could smell her face powder as I stood silently for a moment, watching her. I found it very difficult to believe that it was more than a year since I had seen her. I felt so immensely older, so much unpicked and resewn and made over to a different rougher pattern, that I wondered if Mum would find I had changed.

Mum's bedsit appeared to have shrunk. The wallpaper looked like it had come to the end of its life and the brown lino was sole-weary. There were a single bed and a washstand. A yellow-checked cloth covered a small table with a jug of roses on it.

A small window overlooked the street. I peered out. You could see the tops of people's heads hurrying past. I sat on her bed and bounced up and down, but stopped when I thought my dark tunic would leave an imprint on her pale counterpane. In Mum's long mirror in the corner of her room, I stared fascinated at my head looming above the thin stalk of my neck and my twig-like legs protruding beneath my tunic. It was the first time I'd seen my reflection in a long while. My throat suddenly was no longer tight. I stopped clenching my teeth and biting my nails. I also didn't have to lower my voice. I said things for no reason, just to hear my voice booming out.

On the first morning, Mum noticed the dark rings under my eyes. 'Your eyes look like two burnt holes in a blanket. Are you sure you're getting enough sleep?'

'Yes,' I said untruthfully.

She tucked a strand of hair behind my ear. 'And you've lost some weight. What's the food like at school?'

'It's all right.' I lowered my eyes, rubbing my nose with my hand.

'You must stop doing that to your nose. You do it so often, you'll make it grow crooked.' I searched her face, scrutinising it for signs of what was running through her mind. Would she guess? I didn't know if I wanted her to or not. For a long time now, I had felt squiffy and sour inside whenever I harboured fantasies of this moment.

She was still looking at my nose, frowning. 'Did you hurt your nose? It *does* look a bit crooked.'

My hand flew to my face. 'I – I fell down the stairs,' I muttered. I flushed as I felt the hot, suffocating shame of St Joseph's cupboard again.

Her face beetled in concern. 'Oh dear, poor you. Was a doctor called?'

I nodded.

She rose and puffed up my pillows. 'You seem a bit under the weather. Perhaps you're getting a cold and should have break-fast in bed in this morning. Would you like that? If you feel like it later, we can go to Church Street market.'

She wasn't going to ask. Frustrated, I took a deep breath and pushed it out of my mind.

That morning I sat in bed playing with Mum's box of buttons and beads, listening voluptuously to the sound of her move-ments: the rattle of the frying-pan on the gas ring, the crack of the eggshell, the hiss of the frying oil. She placed a tray in front of me laden with more food than I'd seen in a month. Fried eggs and bacon! I lowered my head and ate hungrily, cramming my mouth with food and scraping my plate like I'd find the answer to my troubles painted on the bottom.

Afterwards, I lay in bed gazing out the window. The sheets were cool and soft as flowers. It seemed like I had been running for years, and had reached a place where I could rest for a while. Tired, so tired. All the weariness of months of rising at five for Mass, the drudge of scrubbing and polishing floors, living in perpetual fear of the long yellow canes hidden in the folds of the nuns' habits . . .

Now I could drink sleep. I could eat it. I could roll around in my dreams like a pig in mud. I felt my breath coming with deep slow movements, and closed my eyes, savouring them. And still I floated on waves of uncertainty. Should I tell Mum tomorrow about how the nuns treated me and the other children? I remembered Sister Mary's words: 'I'm warning you . . . If you know what's good for you . . .'

My resolve weakened and strengthened, ebbed and flowed. The thing that worried me went on as steadily as my pulse. The nuns' faces grew dim. I felt like an escaped criminal. For now at least, I had tricked and outwitted them, and they couldn't touch me.

If my mind now and again picked some faces out of the greyness, they were Frances's and Ruth's. Theirs were the only ones I allowed to disturb my thoughts.

Mum stood beside the bed, smiling down at me. She still looked like a film star to me, with her olive-golden complexion that was like a permanent suntan, and her curly hair, dark rich ochre brown.

'How are you? Would you like me to read to you for a bit?'

I nodded. She sat down on the bed and began reading aloud to me from *Reader's Digest*, while I hovered around the edges of sleep. The rhythm of her voice sounded like a prayer – a nice prayer, not the sort that we had drummed into us at the convent. A prayer that put me into a relaxed trance, and brought dreams of Frances, Ruth and myself in a nice school full of toys, with polished desks and inkwells and rooms that smelt of plasticine and new books, and loads of mashed potato for Ruth.

You needed a hammer and nails to pin such fuzzy pictures down. When I tried to re-run them on waking, they slipped away like quicksilver.

Later, propped up on pillows, I listened to the far-away sounds of Mum murmuring in a low purr to her neighbour, and to music from the wireless. Summer sunlight slanted through the window. I stared out at the sky, my mind empty, as if rocked on long waves inside a peaceful reef, beyond which crashed the roaring sea.

The distant wireless crackled a warning: 'Attention all shipping. Here is a gale warning.' I thought then about the sailors in their tossing ships on the dark enormous sea who were listening to these warnings, lifeboat men sitting in kitchens awaiting their emergency calls in the stormy coastal towns.

'Fastnet, Hebrides, Fair Isle, Faroes, south east gale force nine, increasing force ten. Imminent, imminent.'

The news that followed meant it was midday. Time was ticking by. In the pause between programmes, the space of heartbeats, the future was taking shape.

I pressed my hands to my ears. I didn't want any part of it.

That afternoon, Mum and I walked to Church Street open market, where 'Buy-buy-buy!' was the staccato advice of the stallholders. Their lingo held a great fascination for Mum, but I couldn't understand it. I caught the odd words, like 'tuppence-a-pahnd-Coxes', yet most of it was meaningless to me. My eyes passed over the glazed apples on the stall: shiny peels; the stallholder must have polished them with a rag or handkerchief.

'What do you think happens to the apples if none get sold?' I asked Mum as we passed a stall covered with fruit. 'Do the stallholders just eat them all themselves?'

Mum burst out laughing, which made me feel light-headed. My mouth was open, gasping at all the things to see. The noisy bustle and thrill of the place soon had me laughing as well. We passed stalls and second-hand shops that ran the length of the street, swarming with summery-looking people.

A sweet stall had jars of brightly coloured sugary cubes and circles. One stallholder, who wore a striped suit, a bowler hat and had two gold teeth showing in the front, like a well-off rabbit, was shouting in a high-faluting voice: 'Everything a lady needs for sewing, I have.'

An old lady sat on a chair holding several shiny black shopping bags. She sold one while we watched, taking the coins and stowing them carefully away in her old purse. In the distance, coming in veiled harmonies through the hot air were the strains of a band of buskers. The raucous music mingled with the smell of flowers, fruit and vegetables from the market stalls.

Amid the stall gazers and the press of mothers and prams, I saw a small child fall over, only to be gathered up and dusted, soothed, comforted. I stared. I'd forgotten children could be treated like this.

Mum stopped at a stall that was like a sea chest of treasure, with a dusty heap of brooches, bracelets and rings. There were also brass ashtrays, embroidered match-cases, books too shabby for the bookshop, postcard albums, an electro-plated egg-boiler, a long pink cigarette-holder, a signed postcard of Mrs Winston Churchill, and a plateful of mixed copper coins. A tiny woman sat on a high stool behind the stall. When she opened her mouth, she only had three teeth. She looked like a puckered old apple.

'Come on, love, have a look,' she said to Mum. 'I don't hold no imitations here. You won't find better.'

'That looks interesting,' said Mum, pointing to a brooch made of plaited silks.

'That's a Victorian mourning locket. They liked to be re-minded of the dead in those days. Nowadays, it's out of sight, out of mind.' She sighed, shaking her head. Her stockings were sagged at the ankles over thick black-laced shoes.

'They cut off the dead person's hair and weaved the strands into a brooch or ring. Look at the workmanship in that waving hair. What they could accomplish in them days.'

'Ooh, morbid!' Mum screwed up her face. She chose a pile of beads from a green glass bowl. The woman was selling them at tuppence each.

'Personal worry beads for my collection,' Mum said to me. She tucked them away in her handbag. 'I do worry sometimes.'

I said nothing and gave her a forced smile.

As we walked on, I noticed it was the stallholders' raw patter that held the audience. Arms akimbo, they stood on the pavement bawling with surprising speed, loud cries from gritty throats, craftily conning people into buying things they did not want.

''Ere, come 'ere! Nah then, give us another line, Jean.'

The stallholder's wife, who had a nervous facial tic, held up some chintzy plates.

'That's it, them plates.' Taking hold of several, he shuffled them like cards.

''Ere, don't muck about, give us them dozen cups and saucers as well. How about that then? These bone china plates and cups and saucers to match, worth a few quid of anyone's money. But I'll not charge you twenty quid. Nor ten quid, nor even a fiver.'

A slight pause, followed by, 'Tell you what, I'm daft! Who'll give me a couple of quid for the lot? No? Sod me, I'm giving them away. The kids'll starve this week. 'Ere Jean, gimme them dozen side plates as well. C'mon woman, stop gawping at me, we've got a living to make.'

He made as if to throw the pile of china at her. She stood frozen, trying to smile. Through the laughter and rustle of the crowd I recognised the expression in her eyes, and my hand tightened in Mum's as my stomach flinched in sympathy for the woman. But Mum was laughing too. She didn't see it any more than the other laughing punters did.

We sat inside a café while Mum drank a cup of tea and I sucked cold lemonade through a straw. It was the most delicious drink I'd tasted in a long time. Mum got out her make-up compact from her handbag and began to powder her nose in the mirror. She kept humming in a preoccupied way, giving close attention to her lips and eyelashes. Finally she smiled at her reflection and snapped the compact shut. Dropping it back into her handbag, she smiled again, as if at a private joke. Crossing her legs, she sat back in her chair and lit a cigarette, puffing a line of smoke into the air.

'Mum,' I said, blowing bubbles into my lemonade bottle.
'Yes?'
'Am I still your little girl?'
There was a long pause. 'Yes, of course you are,' she said

finally and she took hold of my hand and squeezed it very tight. 'Why shouldn't you be?'

'No reason,' I said, and went on blowing bubbles. I loved her so much, but I couldn't bear to look at her. I was afraid she would see right through me, see past the fear and shame, right through me to the truth. And part of me was angry that she couldn't see.

The bubbles made me burp. 'Oops, pardon Mrs Arden, I've got the 'iccups,' I said, trying to sound happy.

A frown touched her face. 'Your accent and the jargon you use have changed,' she said disapprovingly. 'You mustn't drop your aitches. It sounds common.'

I found it exciting to use Ruth's slang and catchphrases when she wasn't around.

'Everyone speaks like that in the convent.'

'As long as you don't use it when you're with me.' Her look scanned over me, taking in my posture. 'And your table manners have altered, as well.'

'I have to do as the others do.'

'No, you don't. You're not the same as them, you know.' She stubbed out her cigarette into a saucer, and smiled at me. 'You've taken to boarding school like a duck to water, haven't you? It shows you've got character. I knew you'd get used to it.'

As she sipped her tea, I didn't know whether to laugh or cry. I looked at her and tucked my hair behind my ears, clearing my throat. Up until then, she hadn't mentioned the convent much and I'd told her very little. She had asked me about my school-work and I had given her clipped answers, minimising every-thing, making it sound normal. 'What books are you reading?' 'All sorts of books.' 'Have you reached *The Ten O'clock Stories* yet? 'I've got past them.' Mum scarcely listened to my answers. I felt all mixed up. Should I tell her the truth now? Would she believe me? What would the nuns do to me if they found out?

'I've made my First Communion,' I said, trying to test her reaction.

Mum shook a fresh cigarette out of the pack and told me that Jesus had not been the Son of God. 'Did the idea ever occur to you that Jesus was not what he pretended to be? Did you know that there were many who claimed to be the Messiah in those days? Do you realise that Jesus was just one of a dozen men who made such a declaration?'

I did not know. I did not realise.

In the background, weary music droned from a wireless in the café, broadcast by a cinema organist. I opened my mouth to say something, and closed it again.

'I love this song,' Mum said, her eyes growing soft and wet.

The music was 'Secret Love'. It trembled across the crumby stained tablecloths, the salt cellars and sauce bottles. Yet music was just a sound. I knew the truth: all of this was just pretend, too good to be true, and she didn't really want me, she probably never did, not like I wanted her to, anyway.

I looked around me. At another table sat a family. The mother and father were talking animatedly together and their son and daughter were vigorously teasing one another. I listened to their conversation with covetous envy.

'Oh, I didn't say that, you liar!'

'Oh, you did!'

'Oh, but I didn't!'

'I heard you.'

'Oh, there's a . . . whopping great big lie!'

The mother glanced over her shoulder and smiled at me. I was surprised and suddenly felt weighed down by a feeling of loneliness, an awful lack of understanding. A sense of immeasurable sadness, of injustice, overwhelmed me. I wanted to confide, to lay down burdens. I stared into my lemonade. It was no use. Telling Mum about the nuns would have to wait until the next time I saw her. Maybe she'd want me by then. I bit my lips together to stop the tears.

I didn't speak much as the afternoon wore on. I felt too drained for words – it was the smiling that tired me out the most.

It made my face ache. That and pretending to Mum that everything was all right. Lying about everything, trying to remember where I was in the lie so I wouldn't get caught. It tired me. I needed silence and peace if I was to carry on any life at all. I dreaded my return to the convent.

When I arrived back at the convent the next day, the children were at Benediction. I sat on my bed in the dimness of the dormitory. Reaching under my mattress, I pulled out my diary. I'd stuck a picture of the Holy Family on the front to make it look like a prayer book. Inside was a black-and-white photograph of Mum with me sitting on her lap. It had been taken when we went to the circus with Nana. Mum was smiling at the camera, and I had no front teeth. Already that child seemed much younger, farther away, a shrunken, ignorant version of myself. I had other pictures of Mum, but this was my favourite, the one that could still make me cry.

'Be a good girl, Judith,' she had said as she hugged me goodbye. 'I'll see you again when I can. Keep writing to me; I love hearing from you.'

When she had stooped to give me a lipstick kiss, I felt it linger, like a gooey pearl on my cheek. Sister Mary had smiled at her, patting me on the shoulder. 'We'll see that she writes, Mrs Kelly, don't worry.' She gave Mum a vigorous shake of the hand, which obviously caused her some pain. Mum gave me a sideways glance and I smiled back at her. Then I hugged her tightly again before she went out into the sunshine and I heard the sad sound of the front door being closed and locked behind her. The sour smell of the convent surrounded me again, stifling me. The weekend away might never have happened.

Now, as I waited for the girls to come back from church, I wondered what Mum was doing. Perhaps she was thinking of me, just as I was thinking of her. But I didn't really believe it. I stared at the photograph. My hand tightened around it, ready to tear it into pieces.

I couldn't do it. Instead came the tears I had been fighting against all day. I curled up on my bed, shedding them in wretched, heaving silence. Tears only mattered to myself, and there was no one here.

So much had happened since Dad died, one storm after another, and now it was almost like a dream that he had been alive at all. Still, I felt him in my heart; I ached for him, and how could I stop that? No Dad, no Nana and Pop – and no Mum, now, either; not really.

I sobbed until I was empty of tears. Finally I wiped my streaming face with my pillowcase and returned the photograph to its place beneath my mattress. It was then that I saw it. Frances's poem for me. Lying back on my bed, I began to read it as I waited for the girls to return. I now realised that we found in each other the solace and security we could not find anywhere else. And as ardently as I desired to leave the convent before something worse could happen to me, I knew I could not. It was my duty to stay, to become part of the awful machinery. The girls trusted one another and we knew there would never be an act of betrayal among us. We had nothing else – no money, no toys, no holidays. Nothing, except each other. And maybe that was all that mattered.

Chapter 11

Miriam and I sat on her back steps, drinking coffee. The Carmel Hills were faint purple mounds in the distance, hazy in the sunset. The drone of bees stirred the air in her garden.

'I envy you living here.' I looked about me. 'It seems so peaceful.'

Her face creased as she smiled at me. 'It is now, but life in Israel is far from enviable. Remember, it hasn't always been peaceful and probably won't be again in the future. Israel knows more about war than it knows about peace.'

'Why do you think that?'

She shrugged her small shoulders. 'There is something in Jews that arouses an insanity in other people.' Her expression turned quizzical, her brow lined as if she were trying to solve a puzzle in her head. 'The German cruelty towards the Jews was a singular kind of madness – all we wanted was to live a normal life without fear and persecution. Build a better future for ourselves.'

I nodded, and we sat in silence for some time. I thought about persecution, and the orphanage, and sipped at my coffee. I wanted to tell Miriam everything. I remained silent, staring at the changing light on the hills.

My kibbutz mother and I had traded the outlines of our lives by now, but I had only given the convent the scantest of mentions – an explanation to fill in the years eight through twelve. I couldn't do more, not yet. It would break me down, and

I wasn't ready to deal with it. For the time being, the rising pressure within me seemed eased by talking of safer things: stories about the boarding school I had been sent to after the convent, stories of Nana and Pop, of my dad.

As the twilight deepened, the moon threw light on the clusters of houses scattered throughout the kibbutz.

'Houses without people,' said Miriam.

'Where are the people?'

'You're the people, the new ones coming here. But the trouble is, most of you don't want to stay on the kibbutz. You want your frivolities, your buses and your department stores and your pavement cafés. Not you, I mean. I'm talking about the others, the *sabonim*.'

I took a slow sip of coffee. '*Sabonim?*'

'The word means soap.' She traced a circle on the table with her finger, as if rummaging through some special jar full of memories.

'That's what the kibbutzniks always call the new arrivals. Like the soap the Germans made out of the ones they gassed. What can you do but make a joke? Listen, I was in Auschwitz, I know it was no joke. But we didn't all die under torture. And if we went on to live, they thought we were soap anyway.'

I held my coffee cup in both hands, looking at her.

She smiled sadly at me. 'Not much of a joke, I'm afraid. The important thing about the Jewish people is that we are here, alive, vital, together, expressing ourselves on the ruins of our near-destruction, and that is everything.'

'You're in a good mood today,' observed Cydney. 'I'd say you look like an English sunbeam. I mean it as a compliment.'

Cydney's capacity to forget petty arguments and live in the moment made her generous. She was all-forgiving and did not sulk, and in the instant that she crossed the dining hall to sit next to me for breakfast, it was as if there had never been any trouble between us.

I grinned at her. 'It's my birthday.'

'Wow! Happy birthday.' She shoved her spectacles back up her nose and smiled. 'You must like getting older, do you?'

I laughed as I picked up my fork. All around us was clatter and conversation as the kibbutz ate. 'I suppose so.'

'Tell me something,' she said. 'You spend a lot of time with your kibbutz mother. What do you guys talk about?'

I looked up, a piece of melon speared on my fork. 'Anything. I don't know. Why?'

She buttered some toast. 'Just curious. Everyone always talks about her, you know. She's like a legend here. What kinda things?'

'Whatever we feel like. She's an easy person to talk to. Once in a while she gives me a little lecture –' I leant back in my chair, and made a poor attempt to imitate Miriam's German accent. We both, laughed at my failure.

'She sounds terrific,' Cydney said. 'Hey, I'd like to join you on your next visit, maybe. What do you think?'

I shrugged. 'Sure. Of course you can.'

But I did not really intend to invite her. I had tried not to mention my visits to Miriam to anyone. I was possessive of her and didn't want to waste a moment of my time with her. After all, she was opening doors for me. Doors of perception that I would have hammered at for years before they moved an inch.

Helping Miriam sort books in the library one afternoon, she said, 'So tell me, what brought you to Israel? I don't think you've ever told me.'

The gramophone was playing Mozart, but so softly that the quiet parts were inaudible and the loud parts were a crackling buzz.

'No big mystery. I spent a good part of my childhood in that crummy orphanage. I used to dream of the world outside full of people and adventure, and I swore to see it all some day.'

'Oh? Well, you'd best get out there and see a bit of Israel, then. Your time here is over soon, isn't it?'

The thought sent a pang of apprehension through me. 'I've been asked by my room-mate to join her and two boys on a trip to Jerusalem, but I'd rather stay here.' Especially since one of the boys was Rick, who had been blatantly flirting with me for weeks now. Much too dangerous to go away anywhere with him.

Miriam looked amazed. 'But why? Take my advice: don't let your life go by without you. None of us gets any other life than this one, and it's a shame if you don't make it happen the way you want it to.'

'Yes.' I turned a book over in my hands. *Pride and Prejudice.* 'But life's not always that easy, is it?'

She shook her head with a quick grimace. 'It's not supposed to be easy. It's life.'

'No, what I mean is that sometimes there's not much we can do to stop things from getting away from us.' I groped for the words to explain myself. 'It's like an avalanche. Once events start rolling, once you make your first mistake or even just your first real decision, there's not much that you can do after that. Everything is out of your control.'

I was gripping the book too tightly. I turned away, shoving it in the shelf.

Miriam smiled softly, touched my arm. 'Judith, listen to me. I understand you. I understand what your life has been about. I know how it feels to grow up alone, without love and hope and all the things that give life meaning. I know how much that can damage you. I know how it can turn the whole concept of trust into the most terrifying thing in the world.'

My throat tightened as I looked at her. Her blue eyes were soft and kind. 'Maybe it's time we opened that parcel, Judith, what do you think? We can look at those pictures together. What we talk about is entirely up to you. I might ask you to explain something that I'm not clear about, but that's all. Basically, you decide. Is that all right?'

I nodded my head.

'It's entirely up to you.'

The weight of the past rose up to stifle me, and my first instinct was to run away again. But we had come too far for that, Miriam and I. For a moment I saw all of my roads converging inevitably to this one, leaving me no choice. I needed to do this. I needed to open up.

I took a deep breath and began to talk.

It occurred to me as I spoke how long I had carried the unshared weight of my feelings about the past: for years my waking and many of my sleeping hours had been filled with that sullen, secret ache. I had already told Miriam the bare facts of Mum leaving me at the convent; now the shadow of the emotions I had experienced passed gravely over my consciousness. The anguish, the sense of desertion, the fierce camaraderie among the girls. The terror that came with the nuns' footsteps.

'There were – well, we were afraid of almost all of the nuns, but two of them in particular – Sister Mary and Sister Columba –'

As I started to find the words for my feelings about the two monumental nuns, with their white-wimpled black uniforms, I felt nearly overwhelmed. My lungs dilated and sank as if I was inhaling a warm moist thin air, and I smelt again the warm moist thin air that hung in the bath at the convent above the sluggish pea-soup-coloured water. I saw myself rising in the cold morning and filing down with the others to early Mass and trying vainly to mouth my prayers against the fainting sickness of my sto-mach.

I spoke impatiently, gesturing with my hands as if I was catching the dark details that flocked about me. I could feel a flush rising in my neck, creeping over my jaw as I struggled to tell Miriam how Sister Mary had broken my nose, how we had all been viciously beaten at one time or another for the flimsiest of reasons. In the most intense moments of the story I still watched her eyes to see if she was listening, and I saw that her head did not move, that her eyes did not leave me, and I felt the warmth of her interest.

Finally I came to the scene I revisited in my dreams and stopped. The slippery, treacherous rocks. The raging sea. The line of children.

'The thing is –' I could not go on.

'What is it?' asked Miriam, watching my face.

I had never put into words, aloud, just exactly what the thing was. I was dizzy with the fear of it, the palms of my hands suddenly sweaty. I steadied myself with a hand against the table, feeling the wood silky under my palm.

'I had a friend.' The words seemed large and foreign in my mouth.

Miriam nodded.

'And the thing is, she . . .'

I had always tried to push away the memory of how Frances died. That way I could pretend to believe it had nothing to do with me.

'She died and it was my fault.' I took a big quavery breath. A wad of woolliness filled my throat, stopping any more words getting out.

'Yes?' Miriam did not seem disgusted or accusing. She did not even seem especially surprised. 'It's all right. Go on,' she said, as if it were normal, a child being responsible for another child's death. The expression on her face was not terribly sorry or offering her deepest sympathy, it was just a matter of geometry: an equal and opposite force.

It was what a person needed when they could not balance themselves any more. But I could not go there. I swallowed, and shook my head. Miriam looked at me for a long moment, and then squeezed my hand.

I was shocked when she said, 'I can't believe it.'

'What do you mean?'

She caught herself and patted my hand. 'Oh, I believe your

story – but what I can scarcely believe are the similarities in both our stories.'

It turned out we had a similar experience of growing up – no affection, constant fear, physical abuse – a fundamental slavery. We went back and forth, telling stories. It became easier the more I talked, until finally I realised that I did not mind the force of her enquiries.

She sat in one of her overstuffed library chairs, the late afternoon sun slicing across her freckled face. 'The nuns' habit puts me in mind of a uniform, you know. A uniform often suggests community, order, identity, with the right to have total power over others, to treat people as absolutely inferior and to assert the righteousness of violence.'

The convent had indeed similarities to a concentration camp. You could not show your suffering for fear that worse could happen. A horror that had to be endured, there being no alternative.

Miriam and I talked and talked, and at last my tears came. They fell easily, no longer hindered by shame. Miriam put a hand on my shoulder A simple gesture of affection and support. We remained like that for some minutes. Someone then banged at her door, demanding to be admitted. I wiped my eyes and left her to her visitor.

I sat awake on the compound veranda for a long time that night, smoking a cigarette, a habit I had picked up from Cydney, and staring up into the endless Israeli night. The stars blazed overhead in an icy spill as the warm wind teased my hair. Keeping my mind carefully blank, I allowed memories of Nazareth House to unroll inside my eyelids like a film.

I remembered one night when the girls were talking together in small groups in the boot-room about two nuns. Let's call them Sister Thomas and Sister Lucy.

One girl with little red rabbit eyes said: 'They were caught last night.'

'Who was caught?'

'Sister Thomas and Sister Lucy.'

'Who caught them?'

'The Mother Superior. A senior girl told me.'

'But why have they both been sent away?' I asked. 'C'mon, tell us.'

'I think I know why,' Janet said. 'I bet it's because they nicked the money from the missions box.'

'Who nicked it?'

'I dunno. Maybe all the nuns went shares in it.'

'But that was stealing. How could they have done that?'

'A fat lot you know about it,' Ruth said. 'I bet I really know why Sister Thomas and Sister Lucy have scarpered.'

'Oh, go on, Ruth,' everyone said. 'Go on, tell us. We won't split on you to the seniors.'

A ring of girls craned their necks forward to hear. A small girl with olive skin and limp dark hair thrust her face into the circle of girls, breathlessly glancing around at them as if trying to catch each flying phrase in her open mouth. Ruth raised her head to listen for an approaching nun. Then, smiling uneasily, she said, 'You know the communion wine they keep in the sacristy?'

'Yes,' replied a hushed chorus of voices in unison.

'Well, I bet Sister Thomas and Sister Lucy were caught swigging it together. And that's why they've scarpered.'

Everyone groaned in disbelief, but the girl with the red rabbit eyes who had spoken first said: 'Yes, that's what I heard too from a senior girl. Those nuns stole wine from the sacristy.'

The girls became quiet. I thought of the silent sacristy where I had stood on the day of my First Communion and even though it had been summer, a draught in the room dabbed at my ankles and climbed up my legs, as cats do with people who are afraid of them. Although it wasn't the church, you still weren't allowed to speak in the sacristy. That's where the communion wine was kept, together with the priest's vestments hung neatly on a hanger. I had waited in there, dressed in my communion veil and dress, before our procession to the altar. The white-smocked altar boy looking like the Beano's Lord Snooty with his pale doll's face and sleek combed hair, had swung the censer by the chain to keep the coals alight. He swung it gently to and fro against Ruth's bottom, but stopped when she threatened to punch him. At the altar I had raised my eyes heavenwards, opened my mouth and put out my tongue a little, and Father Holland had bent down to give me the holy communion; I smelt a slight sour stink on his breath and it had made me feel a bit sick.

The girls continued talking, huddled in little groups here and there in the boot-room.

Frances, who had been silent, said quietly, 'You are all wrong.'

We all turned towards her eagerly.

'Why?'

'Do you know?'

'Who told you?'

'Tell us, Frances.'

Frances pointed out the window across the playground where Sister Mary was pacing to and fro by herself, her rosary beads swinging.

'She knows,' she said.

The girls looked out at her and one said, 'Why, has she told you?'

'Well, of course, she's told her,' said Ruth. 'She's her pet girl.'

Scowling at Ruth and lowering her voice, Frances said, 'I'll tell you why Thomas and Lucy have gone, but you mustn't let on to any of the seniors.'

'Tell us, Frances. Go on.'

She paused for a moment and, looking nervously out the window, she said mysteriously, 'They were caught in Thomas's cell together last night.'

The girls looked at her. 'Caught? What doing?'

'Snogging.'

All the girls were silent.

Frances said, 'And that's why.'

'Vile!' said Ruth. 'Even Mary Magdalene wouldn't have got away with that.'

The film reel snagged, ran out and the memory stopped. But what more was there? We never did find out why those two nuns were sent away.

'Jude?' Cydney's soft voice.

My cigarette had gone out. I flicked it over the veranda railing and drew a hand across my eyes. 'Hi, Cydney.'

She sat down beside me. 'What's wrong?'

I shrugged. On the night air, the faint scent of citrus washed over us from the groves. We sat in silence for a moment.

After a pause, I said, 'Did I ever tell you I spent part of my childhood in an orphanage?'

I visited Miriam every day. And slowly, I found that on waking each morning there was no longer a terrible urgency to escape my thoughts. They were mostly harmless. They centred around learning my part in a play we were to perform in Hebrew to the other members of the kibbutz, a couple of letters I had to write and planning my imminent trip to Jerusalem with Cydney, Rick and Mark, small goals to purify my days. My plans became clear in my head, neat and tidy, like boxes all lined up in a row.

We stood on the side of the road and stretched out our thumbs; hoping, praying. Most of the traffic that passed was lorries with full loads of watermelons, oranges and chickens. Then miraculously, a battered red lorry with a layer of red dust obscuring the hood and the headlights, pulled over on to the hard shoulder of the road and rolled to a stop. It just stood there with its signal lights blinking. The four of us gaped back with uncertain hope, until Cydney's face contorted in that funny awestruck look she got sometimes.

'Holy shit! A ride! That didn't take long. Let's go!' And we were pounding the road.

When we reached the cabin, Cydney and I grabbed the door handle and tugged ourselves up and took our seats of honour beside the driver. Rick and Mark climbed into the open back and settled themselves on the straw amongst crates, boxes and a bunch of hippies, grime-faced and crazy. Some of them were holding on to the bars on the sides and blabbing non-stop.

'Jerusalem?' Cydney asked the wiry, grizzled driver as we climbed in.

'Jerusalem?' she asked again more anxiously as we began to pick up speed, bumping and rattling through the dust. Bent over the wheel, the driver merely raised one eyebrow and thumped his foot hard on the accelerator. We sped off down the road like riding a killer whale, weaving and surging and churning, tail-slapping whole schools of smaller cars.

The driver kept shifting his myopic eyes from the road to the instrument panel, watching the speedometer, which jerked suspiciously as we overtook everything at high speed on nail-bitingly narrow bends. Even a single donkey warranted an ear-piercing blast of the horn to signal our approach. I kept my eyes glued to the road, listening to the rattling of the old jalopy with all my senses on alert for a change of tone, a variation in rattles. It felt good to be alive and I wanted to be sure that it wouldn't all end in a splintering crash of metal at the hands of this suicidal driver.

'I'm scared shitless,' hissed Cydney in my ear. 'Is he taking us to Jerusalem, or kidnapping us?' We giggled as the sun rose slowly in the sky, heating the lorry into a burning grid. I peered through the rear window to look at Rick and Mark. They lay on their backs on a pile of straw. They saw me looking and Mark gave me an ambiguous wave, either of greeting or derision.

Despite the heat, I shivered when we passed two women

dressed from head to foot in black flowing robes, leading their flock of black goats across the scorched fields. As we reached the pine country of Jerusalem's surrounding hills, we passed an encampment of black tents with a camel or two lazing next to them. It seemed that somewhere along the way we had crossed over some great but unspoken divide.

Cydney loved it. 'Far out. Out of this world. Totally cosmic,' she kept repeating, bouncing on the seat and craning her neck to see everything at once.

Jerusalem was an emotion more than a city with its citadels, arches, domes, and minarets. It seemed to hover between earth and heaven. The fragility of the brilliant air and massive white clouds hanging over the Holy City made Cydney's commonplace 'out of this world' true enough to give my soul a start.

We were unceremoniously dumped in the Old City near the Damascus Gate and went ambling down the arched alleyways. The sun swept through the endless lanes, an obstacle course of stalls and stands bearing helter-skelter displays of peanuts, dried salted chick-peas, lupin seeds, gaudy pastries, fritters dripping with oil and honey. A swarm of flies and children, both attracted by the same wares, buzzed and shouted as they chased each other around the stalls, The stallholders, who feared for the stability of their wares, brushed both flies and children away with a single cursing gesture. Donkeys backed out of bedroom-workshop-kitchens, or bakeries, or basket weavers'. In the alleys, tailors worked away on the foot-pedals of old Singer sewing machines. Ancient beaded necklaces dangled on strings in the doorways of shops. Souvenir shops displayed clay lamps, belts, fleece-lined slippers, antique brassware, carved cherry-wood pipes, rotten teeth, coins and battered pieces of everything, including crowns of thorns and genuine slivers of the cross, laid out on the ground – a scavenger's heaven. Groups of jaded tourists piled out of their air-conditioned coaches 'doing Jerusalem' via their four- or five-star hotels, searching through the lenses of their automatic cameras for some reminder of the sensation they once had as children when they first gazed on the world. And Arabs sat in corners sipping coffee and sucking at their bubbling hookahs filled with apricot tobacco. Their hollow, saucer eyes, drooping brown, glanced briefly at us as wisps of olive-grey smoke escaped into golden shafts of sunlight. A traditional Jewish woman in a wig and babushka shuffled up the street, displaced in time, like something that had stepped from a sepia-toned turn-of-the-century photograph.

A gang of impish boys shouted frantic advice at a driver backing his tipper-lorry into a narrow lane. Hawkers offered mint tea on little brass trays, freshly baked bagels topped with sesame seeds, boxes of Turkish delight, highly perfumed and coloured mauve.

We had paused at one of the stores to look at a set of carved camels, when a young Palestinian boy, no more than fourteen, grabbed Mark's sleeve and shouted demands for shekels.

Mark shook him off. 'No.'

The boy narrowed his eyes, looking at Mark speculatively. 'Please, you give me money to buy food for my family?' he offered hopefully.

The skin around his brown eyes was red and puffy. There was blood on his forehead – not much, but a cut. Clouds of tennis-shoed tourists walked around the boy, their eyes appraising him, hardening and turning away. Some raised their cameras to buildings, focusing shutters, firing away, as the boy tried to get their attention, his arms outflung. He turned suddenly to me, his eyes wide, his underlip pouting and, spreading out his hands in a gesture of entreaty, he said, 'Lady, please help.' His voice was pure need, pure despair.

I tried to smile at him, but I could only think: How did I ever learn to smile such a cheap smile? I stood stupefied, uncertain what to do. I looked over my shoulder to see if the others were watching.

'Come on, Jude,' yelled Rick. 'Don't let him rip you off. He's only begging.'

What did he mean *only?* Wasn't that bad enough? The boy's young brown eyes and his outstretched arms seemed to me at that moment an image of guilelessness, and I halted until the image had vanished and I saw only his ragged clothes and damp coarse hair and large almond-shaped eyes pleading with me.

'Here,' I said. I fumbled in my duffle bag, found some paper money, crumpled it into his hand. I turned and walked away from him, feeling guilty but forgiving myself: nobody else had bothered with him. They got me every time; they could spot me coming, pick me out of the crowd no matter how hard I frowned. Buskers, vagrants, tramps, winos, the homeless. In the grip of the needy I was needy.

I found Rick, Mark and Cydney in a store examining some jewellery. I let myself be talked into buying some rather garish Eilat-stone necklace, which I thought Miriam might like, and, for myself, a silver filigree hand on a thin chain that the store-keeper assured me would keep away the Evil Eye. It seemed a good idea, and I laughed and slipped it on.

We continued our meandering, taking in the sights and smells that assailed us. Up until now, Rick and I had been flirting a little, making each other laugh about silly things. It was nice, it was easy, but what if I started to like him and then, boom, he disappeared?

Cydney winked at me, smiling as if she knew what was going on. I licked my lips, felling more nervous than I could remember.

'Here, Jude, I'll carry that.' Rick lifted my duffle bag off my shoulders, slinging it over one of his own. I smiled uncertainly at him. When we got close, he smelled nice. A spicy, woody fragrance. As we climbed up some steps to the Jaffa Gate, I caught his eye again. He smiled, his blond stubble sparkling in the sunshine, and I wondered if he knew what I had just been thinking, wondered what he was thinking.

The four of us decided to splurge, and booked ourselves into the King David Hotel, the most expensive and certainly the most elegant hotel in Jerusalem. The contrast with the spartan accommodation on the kibbutz was breathtaking. I turned around in the lobby, feeling like a child eating ice cream for the first time.

The lobby was decorated in the intense colours of the Middle East – azure and brick red – as well as the creamy beige of Jerusalem, illuminated by a soft yellow glow from the Art Deco lamps. Marble floors and tapestries on the walls all combined harmoniously into the perfect backdrop for intrigue, the tough political negotiations and lively parties that were part of the King David Hotel's mystique.

I luxuriated in a hot bath, my first in six months, and used all the toiletries the hotel had provided. Cydney and I were sharing a room and I tried to get some rest while she roamed around the hotel. A knock on the door awoke me. Rick. He was wearing a fresh new shirt with the collar turned up. We grinned stupidly at one another for a long minute. I wanted to stroke my fingers through his tousled blond hair. Bad, scary thought. I put my hands behind my back.

'Want to take a walk around the hotel grounds with me?'

'Um, OK . . . a walk, yes,' I said.

I was nervous. The words came out of my mouth all mixed up. He'd think I was hopelessly stupid now. A flush crept up my cheeks as I locked the door behind me. But before I had time to worry properly about how inane I had sounded, he snaked his arm around my shoulders – no one had ever done that. There was something so familiar about it as he steered me down the corridor. I tried to walk naturally, relaxed. Yes, this happens to me all the time.

Why he was interested in me was a mystery. Of course, he didn't know anything about me. I hadn't told him my background. Too serious. Too sad. Too weird. Besides, where would I begin to tell a story like mine? I swallowed hard, and walked like it was totally normal to have this man's hand flat on my back. I felt, as if I were a different person completely.

Cydney was passing through the lobby. 'Hey, you two,' she said in her singsong voice. I scrunched my whole face at her.

'Hey,' Rick called.

She gave me a little wave of her hand, her eyes all round and exaggerated behind her glasses, as if she couldn't wait to hear all the gory details.

'Let's sit in the sunshine,' said Rick as we wandered outside into the hotel garden. It was beautiful there in the gardens – the tall fir trees, the blue swimming pool with sunlight shimmering on its surface. Rick sat with his knees wide, face without any kind of expression. I pushed my hair off my face and sat on the ground, my back against a tree trunk, Rick's knee next to me.

We became silent for a moment, a strange, distant silence. Rick turned to me, his shadow blocking out the sun.

'So,' he said, 'Cydney tells me you were brought up in an orphanage.'

He said it so suddenly, I felt I had been stung. Perhaps it was the quiet of his voice, or the simplicity of statement. I put a hand up to my mouth. My lips were pressed together. To my horror, my eyes filled, as if indeed I had been stung. I couldn't speak for a moment. I was afraid to blink, afraid to move. He reached up and took my hand away from my mouth and held it.

The water in the pool lapped, slow and lazy. A chlorine dream. I took a deep breath, ready to fall into the abyss . . . but instead I found that the thought of telling him didn't panic me now.

'I wasn't an orphan,' I said to the water. I let out a long breath after I had said it. I could feel his questions in the silence. He pushed his hand through his blond hair. He was going to ask me, 'Why were you there, then?'

He asked the questions, and I answered them. As I spoke, terrible sadness, dread, an agonising desire for happiness swelled in my heart. I watched his face and felt anxious. Would he still look at me the way he did? Would he think I was different, damaged? I searched his hazel eyes for some sign that he was being put off by my story, but he just nodded and listened, watching me closely, as if he could see something with every gesture and inflection. His hand hadn't moved; it was firm on mine.

Finally I finished. He looked into my eyes, smiling. 'So what do you think?'

It made me laugh. 'Isn't that enough?'

He laughed too and in his eyes was a look something like admiration.

'Wow,' he whispered.

'It was a lot worse than I could ever describe,' I said, flicking nothing off my knee. 'But it was a long time ago. Maybe I shouldn't be telling you all this.'

'Why not?'

'Because of what you must think. It's strange, I still feel ashamed. Yet I don't know why.'

Rick moved over to sit closer to me, and made me look at him. I was not responsible for what happened to me in my childhood, he said. Only the person who had put me in that position was responsible. Did I understand that?

I tried to shrug my shoulders under the weight of his arm. I didn't understand. His closeness terrified me. Being friends was OK, friends I could just about handle, or at least I was learning to. But this –

'It's got to be difficult,' he murmured, 'for you to understand that it wasn't your fault and that you've nothing to be ashamed of.'

He began to stroke my arm with the tips of his fingers. I might have pulled it away, but I couldn't move. It was the first time someone had touched me this gently, this kindly, and I was nearly paralysed with gratitude. I felt his breath on my face. 'I mean, it was difficult enough for me as a kid, but maybe I'll tell you about that some other time.'

Rick seemed reticent by nature, not used to sharing thoughts and feelings. I thought that in this way we were alike. But although still guarded, I knew that if you cannot talk about the thing that is at the centre of your life – cannot let anything slip out for fear of revealing the entire story – you develop what might pass for natural reticence, a habit of listening rather than telling stories yourself.

The stroking of his fingertips was soothing and rhythmical, like a warm wave washing over me.

'I'm afraid,' I said.

'I know, but you shouldn't be.'

'I've never done anything like this before,' I said. 'Never really liked people touching me.' It was something I'd been thinking all day – yet was it now just an excuse to push him away?

He kissed me once, simple and careful, lips against my lips and then away. He looked at me, a question in his light brown eyes. I shivered, staring at him. When you've told someone all the worst things and they still want to kiss you . . . what does that mean? Does it mean that everything is wonderful, or that they have problems of their own?

Rick put his hands behind his head, not a care in the world, and then looked at me, one eye closed against the sun.

'I've wanted to do that many times,' he said.

I moved my fingers over my mouth and turned my head to look at him. I wanted to say, 'Me too,' but somehow I couldn't make the words come.

Chapter 12

17 March
Sister C. hit Janet yesterday in class because she wet herself.
She had to mop it up.

26 April
Some ladies came into the playground today. Sister M.
called me over. She said they liked my drawing on the
classroom wall. Sister M. smiled at me. I didn't say any-
thing.

10 June
Frances said I was shouting in my sleep last night: No, no,
no. She said I was sitting up and banging my fists on the
bed. I can't remember it.

Sister Mary called me to the front of the class. 'Judy Kelly, why
were you sitting instead of kneeling at Mass today?'

'Don't know, Sister.' Hearing my own robotic voice made me
want to cry; I didn't understand anyone any more, myself least of
all. The lack of thought, the lack of will, I had felt their approach
on and off during this time. Not too near, but on their way, like
the vague droning echo that comes from the lowest key on a
piano.

I was beginning to believe what the nuns kept telling us: we were nothing. Now it became a word I associated with myself.

During Mass that day I had seen tiny pinpoints of the altar candle lights dancing around, then rushing away from me. A faint waspy buzzing hummed in my ears. I knew that religion didn't agree with me. I whispered to Ruth, who was kneeling next to me, that I thought I was about to faint. Without moving the muscles of her face, she said, 'Judith! You've gone a funny colour. Sit down or you'll pass out.'

Then with my head on my knees I was looking at the backs of the other girls' shoes. I battled with every bit of energy I had not to faint. I didn't want to step out of my own body and lose control. Not here.

Now, standing before me in the classroom, Sister Mary's jaw tightened. 'Why were you sitting instead of kneeling?' The final hiss in her voice warned me of her feelings. She picked up her cane and brought it down on my arm, which shot up instinctively as the hard wood shivered through my elbow.

The sinking feeling in my stomach overcame me. Nausea soured my throat and I wanted to be sick, but an antidote of dull anger kept me going. When I tried to speak, my mouth clenched. It was as if my words had swallowed their tongues. I couldn't hear anything except a deep quivering pulse in my head taking on a fiercer rhythm. In a whirlpool of queasiness and fever, my forehead burning, I suddenly felt so weak I could hardly stand. My lips were dry and I longed for water.

'Lazy good-for-nothing child!' Sister Mary's eyebrows drew together as she scrutinised my face. I stared blearily back at her, wondering if she was going to whack me again. She babbled on, but I didn't know what she was talking about any more. I just nodded my head mechanically when I thought she was asking me a question.

'Well, answer me, do you feel poorly?'

I nodded my head again and everything spun about me. I lifted my hand to my forehead. I tried to find the words in the mist that shrouded me.

'The whites of your eyes have turned yellow,' she said. 'You'd best get yourself off to the sanatorium.'

The convent was a cradle of fly-bred infection at that time. With the oncoming of the warm weather, disease had crept into the orphanage and breathed its foul breath through the kitchens and refectory. Lack of food, rat-ridden dormitories and clogged drains had primed the children to catch infections. Before May arrived, forty-five out of sixty girls lay ill and classrooms stood almost empty.

It had all begun one morning a week or two before, after we had finished washing down the walls of the corridors and classrooms. I noticed with a start that Frances's face had turned yellow – copper yellow – even the whites of her eyes.

'Frances!' I grabbed her fearfully, shaking her slightly. 'You're all *yellow*!'

She shook her head. 'It could be just the dirt from the walls.' She leant back against the wall. 'But I don't feel very well.'

This was the start of what the nuns termed the yellow fever epidemic. With so many children ill, and the sanatorium filled to capacity, the girls were put in their usual beds in the dormitory when they became infected.

Sister Cuthbert encouraged those of us left in the classroom to send letters to our friends, to tell them we were saying daily prayers for them and fifteen decades of the rosary.

At last I joined Frances and some others from my class in the dormitory, as yellow and dizzy as they were. I sat on the side of my bed. I felt weak.

Ruth, standing by the door with a broom in her hand, called out, 'Welcome to the vomitorium!'

That was to make me laugh. But even her yokes were turning bad and I could not laugh because my cheeks and lips were shivery; Ruth had to laugh by herself. She was still gobsmacked by my stupidity in returning to the convent after spending that weekend away with Mum: welcoming, as she saw it, the mad bugger nuns with open arms!

'Sheer suicide,' she'd said, shaking her head.

I curled up between the sheets, glad of their coolness. My face and body felt very hot. It was as if a clock was ticking inside my head, which was held on by a piece of elastic. I was stretched to the point of exhaustion as I made the long tiring shuffle to the toilet, where the dizzy red floor tiles wavered under my eyes like chicken wire. Every time I lay down I wondered if I would have the strength to get up again.

'Will the doctor come soon?' I asked Frances. Her yellow pallor was beginning to wear off.

'No, Sister Cuthbert says we don't need one,' she said weakly. 'Don't worry, you'll only take about two weeks to get over the collywobbles and then you'll turn pink again.'

She tried rocking my bed, but the usually comforting motion just made my stomach feel dull and heavy, as if it were full of earth, and I had to ask her to stop. It was strange that the nuns had not given any of us any medicine. They usually gave you foul-smelling stuff when you were in the sanatorium. I wanted glasses of orange juice and ginger ale, the sound of a distant wireless. But these things seemed gone for ever. I was so thirsty that when Frances brought me water from the washroom it tasted like it had flowed through summer: all mown hay and lemonade. I filled myself to bursting so I wouldn't be thirsty any more and she wouldn't have to get out of her bed again.

I had been in Nazareth House for almost two years. In that time, the nuns had beaten my body and had weakened my mind. All that was left was the strength of my spirit and I knew it wouldn't take much more for that last part to go.

I had begun to think I might never make it out of Nazareth House, that my life would end within its walls. Even when I was well, I had lost interest in the life around me and went through the routine of the days with shuttered eyes, closed to as much as possible. I saw it in Frances too. The yellow fever had made her face tired and worn, her movements slow and tentative. Frances, who had been my constant companion and support in the early days, had lately seemed to be slipping away from me. Her eyes would hollow out, so that I felt lonely even when she was sitting on my bed beside me. I hadn't been able to talk to her about my uneasiness; sometimes she had seemed like a stranger.

Ruth popped in three or four times a day to sweep the floor or bring us our meals. Janet's bed was next to mine; her usually sallow complexion looked almost green now. Yet I wished I were Janet sometimes. I wished I had an interest like her frog, which she kept in a box and took care of, finding it food to eat. She said that when she was younger she broke a thermometer and ate some of the mercury in it to make herself sick so she could keep out of the way of the nuns. Or she'd stick her fingers down her throat and throw up, or she'd run and run around the play-ground to make herself hot in order to have a temperature. Sister Cuthbert twigged what she was doing and after that her ploys were harder to pull off.

'How old were you then?' I asked.

'Oh, I don't know. About six or seven,' she told me. 'When I was about four years old, I used to sit on a chair facing the wall of the playroom. I used to think that if I kept very still and out of the way and didn't say anything, I would be safe.'

'Safe from the nuns?' I said.

'Just safe and sound,' she said. 'I used to get into trouble a lot with the nuns for wetting my knickers every day. They'd lose their tempers with me and make me stand with my wet knickers over my head in the dormitory. Sister Cuthbert would be all right, but you never knew when one of the others would blow their top about it.'

Janet's face dissolved, re-formed, and something in the sudden change in her expression made me feel sorry for her. She'd been here since she was two years old – throughout all that time when I'd known happiness with Mum and Dad and Nana and Pop.

Suddenly it was unbearable to listen to Janet any more. It

made me feel even more nauseous. I felt it everywhere around me, in the walls, in the very air I breathed. I closed my eyes. In my head there was a square of flickering darkness, in the centre of which was a bunch of broken purple flowers.

Cold sunlight filtered through the dormitory. There would be cloudy grey light over the silent playground. I wondered if I could die just the same on a sunny day.

Lying there, I remembered the story of the last agony that had been given to the First Communicants. At that time, in the peace of Father Holland's sunlit room, with leaves blowing across the windows and the birds singing outside, it had seemed too remote to be very terrible. But now, sick and aching, I felt the words crowd back into my head. I would die someday. Perhaps very soon. It was as if Father Holland's words were playing on a gramophone record in my head. It was odd, because I had only half listened; I had been watching Frances sketch the outline of the priest's profile with her finger on the flyleaf of her prayer book: white bushy eyebrows, the gold-rimmed spectacles.

Father Holland had asked us to imagine what it would be like to convey ourselves to the bedside of a dying person or to the side of a grave ready to receive a coffin. To ask Our Lord for a fear of death and the grace to be prepared for it every day.

What was it to die? Was it to melt in the sun or be blown away by the wind? Would it be like walking into a dark cellar at night? I huddled in my sweat-damp blankets, fever pounding at my skull. Father Holland had said a good Catholic should always be ready and willing to die. He said that dying was to say goodbye to everything in this world . . . to riches, happiness, relatives . . . a sad, final goodbye. He told us to imagine our own funerals. To picture everyone dressed in black, all with sad faces. We would be thrown into a small hole in the ground with no clothes but a sheet and no company but worms. Father Holland said that we had been dying ever since the day of our birth and every hour of play or schoolwork brought us a little nearer the end of our lives.

My boiling brain now seethed with his words. Were they true? When I had proudly told Mum that I could now recite the catechism by heart, she had replied that she didn't believe in brainwashing children. She said that when I was grown up I would be able to make up my own mind about religion, which was responsible for a lot of wars and unhappiness in her opinion, as well as unfairness and narrow-mindedness.

That night Frances stayed by my bed watching over me. I wanted to jump out of bed and kneel on the cold floor and pray, but was too weak to move. I kept pushing the blankets away from my legs. They felt as scratchy as dry turf. The sweat trickled down me in never-ending streams. There was nothing Frances could do, except stay with me and try to make me drink more water. I grew increasingly hot and then I shivered as if I had cold slimy water next to my skin. At one point, Frances was tempted to ask Sister Mary to fetch a doctor. I quickly dismissed the idea. I didn't want to cause any trouble.

When food arrived, it consisted of large fibrous potatoes. One had the mark of a spade in it, which when cut oozed yellow juice from its sticky core. I was sure I would never eat another potato again.

One morning, several days later, I awoke feeling well enough to enjoy life in the dormitory. A wonderful happiness spread through me like magic. I was alive. It would be nice getting better slowly. You could get a magazine to read then. The icing on the cake was that, for a short while at least, I would not have to carry out my daily chores and get whacked.

Perhaps for others in the outside world, life was like this all the time – natural. We were allowed to play with some old jigsaw puzzles. They were very puzzling indeed, since about a third of the pieces was missing. We had also been given some tattered magazines to read, and the competition for these was very keen. Some of the pictures had been cut out, and at the top of each one was written in a nun's handwriting: 'Certain photographs of this magazine have been censored, as the matter they contain is unsuitable for the minds of children.'

But what the nuns hadn't cut out was a picture showing a small boy dressed in a short coat and a cap, staring blankly at the camera, his arms raised in surrender as a soldier trained his machine gun on him. Beside him was a woman who may have been his mother; her arms were also raised as she looked anxiously over her shoulder at the boy.

In another photo a pale, thin man clad in striped pyjamas stood vacantly looking at a pile of dead bodies.

I stared at the grainy black-and-white pictures. I was living in a world of lies – lies that grown-ups pretended to believe in. I hated them for it. The horrible things that they did to each other were endless. I lived in a world where it was all right to kill people for no reason, but to climb through a nun's cell window to read your own letters was a punishable offence. A world where landlords and landladies did not allow children to live with their mothers.

The thing that was bothering Frances had her in its grasp again. After we had all recovered from the yellow fever and returned to our daily routine, Frances was still complaining of bad headaches. She looked changed, confused, like a small bird with big eyes and a sharp beak. Sometimes she stood rocking herself rhythmically from the tips of her toes to her heels and back again, her hands thrust deep in her tunic pockets. As I watched her swaying form, I tried to say kind things to her, but it was as if she no longer knew the language of kindness. Everything I said irritated her into spiteful replies. After a while I simply stopped trying to speak to her. There was a nightmarish barrier between us through which neither of us could pass. The bounce in her walk had disappeared. I longed for her to be the old Frances, to look up at me and smile or say something nice.

In the refectory one evening, Frances leaned her elbows on the table and closed her eyes. When she re-opened them they seemed muddied with something more than misery. Ruth and I looked at each other and then looked away. We had never spoken about what was happening to Frances, but now I knew that we both had the same thoughts raging through our brains. Something or someone had pierced the protective shield Frances had developed against life in the convent, and we had a good idea what it was. We often heard shuffles and whispers in the dormitory at night. Sometimes we heard Frances softly murmuring the Hail Mary over and over. In the morning, her tumbled bed showed how sleepless she had been. During the day, we could see the attachment Sister Mary had for Frances growing steadily. But recently, things had changed and we'd often see Sister Mary having a go at Frances, poking her finger against her chest and ranting, telling her to snap out of her strop.

'Frances, I need to talk to you,' Ruth said. 'What is that creep doing to you?'

Frances took a deep breath and stared at Ruth, her jaw set, her hands flat on the surface of the table, her eyes confused and darkened.

'I don't understand what she's doing to me,' she said. 'I just feel bad because I know it's not right somehow. She always wants to kiss and cuddle me after a beating. She sits me on her knee and tells me the secrets of the convent. She says she loves me like a daughter and sometimes at night we lie on her bed together. At first I didn't see any harm in it, but lately she wants me to kiss her back and things.'

'And things?' said Ruth. 'Don't you see? The dirty devil's trying to teach you the blummin' goose-step.' She placed two fingers under her nose and raised her arm in mock salute. 'Heil Mary, full of grease!'

'Stop it, Ruth, it's not a joke,' I said.

Frances was shaking, her eyes goggling, her jaw trembling. I felt nervous for her, of her. I was afraid she might break down in some alarming way. My voice was deliberately calm.

'You must put a stop to it, Frances.'

'I can't. I don't know how to. What can I say to her? Please don't tell anyone,' said Frances. 'She mustn't find out that I've told you. I feel so mixed up.'

'But why,' Ruth asked, 'did you ever get caught up with her in this way?'

Frances bent her head and muttered very low. 'I've thought about this a lot. I honestly believe she was just trying to be kind and I used to think I liked it, especially when she'd give me sweets and things. Now she frightens me and I don't know how to stop it.'

Ruth's face creased itself into a sneer and she sniggered out loud. Her laughter seemed to confuse Frances, who hesitated as if trying to shake off the weariness that clung round her brain and clogged her thoughts.

'OK, go on,' said Ruth.

'Well, I don't want to make excuses, but I thought if I carried on with her, it would make life easier for everyone else. I was just a child when it first started,' she added, as though she was an old woman chatting about a far-distant past. 'She was a sort of mother to me. And, you know . . . I thought she felt sorry for me . . .' She stopped and shook her head.

Ruth screwed up her mouth as though at a sour taste. 'God, you poor sod.' Her voice oozed contempt for Sister Mary.

Frances drew herself up, moving away from us. 'I don't expect anyone to understand, because even I feel muddled up,' she said. She had been speaking with a soft whine of misery quite unlike her usual voice. Now she lost control of herself and hissed, 'You have no idea how much I hate the way she touches me! I really don't want to feel her hands on me ever again. I want to be left alone and not worry whether she's coming to get me. I *hate* it. I feel so dirty. But it's probably all my fault, I know that.' With a deep sigh she rose from the table and walked out the refectory, the knife with which she had been eating still in her hand. We all watched her in astonishment. She'd forgotten to wait until grace had been said.

'That gives me an idea,' said Ruth. 'I think I know how to put a stop to all this.'

'Whatever you think of, it won't work unless we're all in it together,' I said. 'The only one who can make it happen is you, Ruth.'

Ruth said nothing for a long time. Then her lips curled up in what I could only assume was a smile.

'Leave it to me,' she said.

Ruth was in the centre of the huddle in the boot-room, staring at the faces around her.

'It'll be dead easy,' she said. 'Don't worry. I'm just going to put the frighteners on her a bit. It's the only way.' She became very still, her mouth in a hard, thin line.

The door of the boot-room opened violently as Sister Mary, cane in hand, thrust herself in. The bold metallic eyes stared about and the harsh voice said, 'Up to the dormitory, all of you.'

I tried to imagine what demons in her own life had driven her to the point that the only pleasure she sought was beating us children. Between she and Sister Columba there was a spirit of rivalry about it. Malice marked their facial expressions, and a kind of greed from the satisfaction they derived from humiliating us. There seemed to be no limit to their cruelty. I more than hated them – I had passed that stage months ago. They disgusted me, their very presence epitomising the ugliness and horror I felt each day at Nazareth House.

'No,' Ruth said. 'We're not going to the dormitory yet.'

The nun stopped and they looked straight at each other; Ruth seemed to be gritting her teeth so tightly that her strained jaw jutted through her skin. Sister Mary slowly moved towards her. Janet quickly closed the door and held on to the doorknob.

'Don't come any nearer,' said Ruth, retreating and looking with horror in her eyes at the nun's face. 'You monster!'

The circle of girls that had formed around the boot-room looked stupefied as they waited breathlessly to see what Ruth would do next. A few carried on polishing shoes, afraid to look up. Into the goggle-eyed awful silence broke only the gasping of Ruth's breath through her open mouth as she turned her back on Sister Mary and took something from one of the pigeonholes. When she turned round again, she had a bread knife in her hand. Someone shouted, 'Look out! She's got a knife!'

The world tilted and stuttered into slow motion. I was paralysed. Sister Mary caught her breath and instinctively re-coiled against the wall, her back pressed into it in the hope that it might suck her in, away from the knife, its bright point hovering and now almost piercing the black stuff of her habit. There was an enthralled hush as the circle of girls inched in closer and the ones polishing shoes stopped, sensing that what they wanted to see was about to take place. No one breathed, our attention focused on the first rebellion within the convent.

'You little slut, Norton,' Sister Mary said, her face crimson, more with surprise than fright. She stood rigid, as if pinned to the wall. 'What on earth do you think you're doing?'

'It's time for justice,' Ruth said, her face tightening into a sneer. 'It's our turn to watch *you* squirm for a change.'

'Where did you steal that knife from? You've no business with a knife,' said Sister Mary, speaking more rapidly. 'Do you seriously think you can get away with this? I shall have you all arrested.'

'Then we've got nothing to lose,' said Ruth. 'We already live in a prison.'

Frances grabbed Sister Mary's cane and held it in both hands. Her lips were wet and trembling and tears spilled from her eyes.

I looked at Ruth and saw something in her face that had never been there before. It was swollen with hatred, twisted, dripping venom. Ruth scarcely ever altered expressions: instead she changed faces like donning a mask. And the face appeared and stayed in position without changing while she spoke. Then it would fall, detaching itself from her.

'You can't kill her, Ruth,' I said.

'Watch me,' Ruth said, looking at me without appearing to see me, as if I was a stranger who shouldn't have been in the room. 'Just watch me. Someone's got to put a stop to her.'

'Be careful, Ruth,' Frances said.

'Listen to your friend, Norton. She's talking sense,' said Sister Mary. She was almost incoherent with anger and fear. Her crimson jowls shuddered and her thin mouth twitched in nervous curls of disgust. How could Frances let that mouth kiss her?

Frances took a deep breath and shoved the point of the cane into the centre of her tormentor's stomach. We watched the nun flinch from the blow, her lungs wheezing for air.

'Shut up!' Frances said, her face emptied of its sweet-eyed appeal, a resting place for all the ordeals she had endured.

In so many ways, she was no longer the Frances I had known when I first arrived at the convent. Sister Mary had done more than bully her and beat her flesh into rags; she had taken her beyond mere humiliation. She had broken her down and pulled her apart. She had ripped into the gentlest heart I had known and plundered it of feeling.

'Stop it, Ruth,' Frances said. 'She's not worth it.'

Ruth lowered the knife.

'I'm relieved that one of you is seeing sense at last,' Sister Mary said, getting her wind back. 'I shall, of course, have to report this appalling incident to the Mother Superior and to the police.'

'You won't be tipping off any coppers,' said Ruth.

'Of course I will, you have assaulted and threatened me with a weapon. You're evil, Norton, and I'll make sure you'll suffer for this.'

'You're not only not going to report me,' said Ruth, raising the knife again, 'you're never going to touch any of us again. You're cruel, you're like Hitler and you deserve to be sliced for what you've done to us, especially Frances. If you report any of us, then we'll get you for all the low, filthy tricks you've been using on her.'

For a moment, Sister Mary searched for words to match her anger, her head thrust forward, her stammering mouth covered with spittle. 'What kind of lies have you been telling them, you little brat?' She glared at Frances. 'I'll never forgive you for this. Never, never, never.'

'Don't put the blame on Frances! This isn't just about her,' said Ruth. 'This is about all of us. We've all had enough of your cruelty. You leave us all alone, do you hear me? Or you're for the chop. I mean it, I'll kill you.'

The threat was so unexpected, so shocking, and so horribly voiced that it froze us all completely. The nun and Ruth gazed into each other's eyes.

'Oh, you devil!' said Sister Mary, in a misery of help-lessness. 'I hear you, but I'm never going to forget you did this.' Shaking a pointing finger at all of us, her face twisted with spitting fury, she added, 'Do you understand? I'm never going to forget this.'

'That goes for us too,' said Ruth. 'Here's a bargain for you.'

We all held our breath, our eyes fixed intensely upon Ruth. 'Our silence against yours. Is it a deal?'

A soft murmur of approval swept over the boot-room. Sister Mary gave Ruth a sharp sideways look and with a nod of her head, she waved her hands dismissively.

'That makes us quits then. It's the devil's deal, isn't it?' Ruth said, her voice rising. 'Go away! Clear out of here!' and she drew the knife back in her hand as if she would have thrown it at the nun.

I had a last vision of Sister Mary sidling along the wall, crab-like and cowering, her breath coming in long shrieking gasps as she got herself out the door.

'What's the devil's deal mean?' I asked Ruth, awe making me feel weak.

She enlightened me. 'First one to forget gets burnt. Good and proper.'

Chapter 13

I lay in an ambient trance on the grass outside a disco in the local village. I opened my eyes and saw through the chequer-work of leaves from overhead trees the big moon looking down on me, clear cut and intensely bright.

I had begun to wear clothes that allowed me to blend in with the kibbutzniks: shorts, T-shirts, kaftans and beads. I could relax and take pleasure in the fact that I was at last starting to shake off that awful closed-in sense of myself. I was like a teenager, falling in love with everything and everyone.

And now even the colour of the night sky knocked me sideways. Flopped out on either side of me were Rick and Mark, all of us tipsy and giggling.

'Let's light up.'

After weeks of saying no, I took the joint from Rick and propped it in my mouth.

'Watch it!' Loose tobacco threads caught fire. A flame and acrid smoke lit the air.

'Go on, inhale and hold it in,' ordered Mark. My chest caught fire as I let the smoke from the burning herb cruise through my lungs. A mellow buzzing filled my ears: Aleph, Beth, Ghimel, Yom Kippur, Hanukkah, Bar Mitzvah, Meshuuuuggah.

People massed around the entrance to the village disco, from which an amplified voice boomed, followed by heavy thrumming music that earthquaked from the speakers. Everyone hollered and whooped their approval. Within minutes, I ventured inside and stood, fascinated as dancers with bodies bumping and grinding all over the place showed off their new moves and party pieces. The music dilated and swelled like a waterspout. It filled the room with its metallic transparency, crushing time against the walls. I was carried away by the noise. Orbs of silver revolved in the mirrors flashing rainbows across the room; rings of smoke encircled them and spun around, veiling and unveiling the hard grin of the light. I drank the wine the volunteers urged on me – joy juice. It held all the answers, unlocking something inside me. It was fun to test myself against new things, I began to understand: that's what freedom is. The right to experiment, to see what fits, what doesn't. It was how one learnt who one was and who one wasn't. I danced with the others on the crowded dance floor. A party started inside my head as I slipped into an ecstasy of sweat, saliva and pelvises, slinking and shaking to head-thumping sounds. In shadowy corners, couples danced with hands slinking up and down backs, skulking around hips, vanishing inside clothes.

Amid the music and laughter, all eyes turned my way when the Rolling Stones' 'Jumping Jack Flash' was played. British music. 'Go, Jude! Let it all hang out!' yelled someone. I laughed, pulsating to the music. My eyes were out on stalks like a stoned snail. What the hell had been in that spliff I'd smoked? *It's a gas, gas, gas!* I'd never heard music played like that before; I suddenly understood the secret of its magic. The room seemed to expand and contract, like some crazy accordion, my soul steeped in cosmic schmaltz.

I could feel Rick's eyes on me all evening. I led him a merry chase. I danced too often with other fellows, elated by my new power, but he was the one who later walked me across the tinder-dry grass back to the kibbutz. It felt so natural to lean into him and have him slip his arm around my waist. With the music fading behind us, it was as if we were the last pair of souls on earth, with just the buzzing crickets for company.

This feeling became swamped under a new, exciting throb of desire. It was a struggle to walk in a straight line, dizzied not just by drink but by thumping suspense – I could feel his breath on my cheek. I was on cloud nine. But something held me back.

'What do you think?' Rick asked, laying his hand over mine as we neared the kibbutz.

'Noisy,' I said. My heart was beating so fast and it made my voice sound unsteady. I took a deep breath, not daring to look at him.

'I don't mean the disco,' he murmured. He put on a low serious voice that made me want to giggle, even as it filled me with dread. He held my gaze a little longer than I could stand. Desire suddenly drained out of me.

'I'd best be getting some shut-eye,' I told him in a whisper as we reached my room, 'Up at the crack of dawn tomorrow, you know.'

He frowned. I had been leaning against him all the way back, pressed snugly against his arm. 'Well – don't you want to sit up for a while? I don't bite, you know.'

I shook my head. 'No, seriously, Rick. I'm really tired. Look, we'll have a rave next time, OK?'

'You're strange,' he said, 'but in a nice way.' He touched my cheek lightly.

I was in the habit of making up rules and pretending they had been imposed upon me; now I convinced myself that I didn't like the idea of the night going on and on. Yet my heart still turned over in disappointment as I made my decision to continue playing the safe game, the orphan game that made me a loner.

He took my hand and gently kissed it. 'I'm always here for you,' he whispered.

As I watched him walk away it was like moving from a black and white movie into colour. It was unreal. It was just a fantasy. That was all. It will pass, I told myself, it will dissolve and go away eventually, and all you have to do in the meantime is keep a firm grip on yourself and not behave like too much of a ridiculous fool. After all, what did he see in me? It had all crept up on me and knocked me out before I was aware of what was happening. My feelings were like a force of nature that couldn't be checked, an avalanche, a mudslide, breaching my carefully built defences.

Later, I awoke, queasily despondent from a burning, sheet-grinding dream. Wild with wine, I staggered to the bathroom, Rick's face flickering inside my eyelids. I swung back into sleep and dreamed of sharks and guppies in the sea.

Summertime was the best time. Not knowing what to do with us during the long holiday, the nuns regularly took us to the beach, and let us splash and play in the waves. They sat on the beach, shapeless black-and-white forms.

The yellow cliffs had warning notices with pictures of falling rocks. I didn't care. They held an odd fascination for me, and I had wanted to explore them from the first time I saw them. When I saw my chance I slipped away from the others, not looking back at the group of children and nuns on the beach. None of them paid any attention to me. The girls were too busy splashing and having fun, and the nuns always talked among themselves, not watching us.

I looked up, squinting into the sun, which was fierce, and saw how, at the top of the cliffs, seagulls soared far above with sunlight on their wings. I started to climb, clinging to the bleached grass, stepping from ledge to ledge. A gull watched me. I flapped my hand at it, and it took off, sweeping down towards the beach.

I braced myself against the rocks and looked around. The sense of the sheer drop below suddenly pierced my body. I began to hear the distant beating of the sea. Stick-like figures of children scampered along the beach beside the dark lumps that were the nuns. The seagulls mewed and yelped. It was safe enough to stand there as long as I kept still. But I'd amazed

myself, climbing as high as this. Climbing so far seemed to open
a fresh door in my mind. I felt I was able to see past the jumble of
daily tensions and realise that, if I could do this, I could do
anything.

Cautiously I looked up at the top of the cliff, wondering if I
could climb all the way. But craning up at the blue-white sky
made me feel dizzy. I clutched the rocks on either side of me,
but they crumbled in my hands, and I wavered, more frigh-
tened than if I had not tried to hang on at all. I quickly pressed
my back against the cliff face, feeling sick and unsteady. I
closed my eyes as the wind tore at my hair.

'Hey you!'

A man was approaching. I stood still until he was near to me.
The noise of the sea was so loud that it was difficult to hear what
he was saying.

'You mustn't climb those cliffs. Can't you see the notice?'

Almost in tears now, and determined not to understand him, I
said, 'Why not?'

'You mustn't climb up there,' said the man, as if he had not
heard me. 'You'll fall.'

'I won't,' I said, but I knew I was defeated.

'Someone fell from there only last week,' said the man.

'All right,' I said shortly. I turned my shoulder to send him
away and he moved off.

Frances had wandered away from the group, and was running
towards the cliff, beckoning to me.

Relieved, I started to climb down, step by step, holding on to
clumps of grass. When I reached the beach, Frances grabbed my
arm.

'The nuns sent me to fetch you. They said it's dangerous to
talk to strange men.'

I sat on the baking front steps of the children's house waiting for
my co-worker to arrive. Today it was an Israeli girl called Avatel.
She was twenty years old and had recently completed a two-year

army stint. We were planning to take our five charges swimming in the kibbutz pool.

I breathed in the citrus-tinged air. Everything looked bright and fresh today. I liked my new job taking care of the kibbutz children. I sat enjoying the sunshine, letting happiness touch me.

Because I had realised something after my trip to Jerusalem – no, before the trip, as if I knew it all along – there are no secret passages to strength, no magic words. I was strong, I was able, because I *was*. The freak in the sideshow no longer fitted.

I smiled ruefully at myself. So, what was the catch? Some danger of which I was not yet aware? What would I have to pay for this, for thinking well of myself? Whatever the price, it was worth it. Even for ten minutes, it was worth it.

I glanced at my watch. Avatel had forgotten. I hoped for a moment that she had, then prayed that she hadn't. I would have to take the children swimming on my own. Abruptly I jumped up, walked up and down.

A thought nagged at me, threatening to surface. I shrugged it off.

When Avatel finally arrived, grinning apologies, we changed the children into their bathing costumes and set off for the pool. When we got there, Avatel's boyfriend Ben arrived, which gave me the opportunity to return to the children's house to get some soft drinks from the fridge. I was wearing shorts, and as I set off, the backs of my legs were slick with sweat.

It was a perfect day. My head sang with an intricate, melodic line – Beethoven? Mozart? I couldn't remember, but I loved those fresh unfamiliar instruments – the recorder, the harpsichord – those simple statements of truth. And tonight I would be going to the barbecue disco with Rick. Thinking about it made my skin ripple pleasantly. A feeling you get going up in a fast lift. I shouldn't plan ahead like this, I thought, I shouldn't expect good things to last long. The lift could hurtle down again and you could thump to the ground. I wandered to the house by a roundabout route, keeping to the shade of the trees. Dazed with the heat, with the sun on the blistered roofs, the paths, the burned grass, I walked slowly.

Squinting, I could just make out a corona in the whitest part of the sky. It reminded me of something, but I tried to deflect the memory. Suddenly fear surged through me. I stopped walking and stood glued to the spot. The children in the pool! Avatel and Ben weren't watching them properly; they were too wrapped up in each other! Images scintillated, shone, disappeared. I had no idea where my panicked certainty came from, but the world seemed gently to crack about me, its appearance unchanged, yet on the brink of falling to pieces. Disaster is not quickly understood. I spun around and ran to the wire-mesh fence surrounding the pool. I saw four of the children standing waist deep in the water. There was a slight lull in their chatter as they looked warily at something at the end of the pool which I could not see. I thought from the way they were huddled together and the looks on their faces that they must have been watching Avatel and her boyfriend kissing. Slight relief slumped through me – and then I realised that I couldn't see the fifth child, a girl called Danah. I gripped the wire fence.

'Avatel!' I had to call twice before she knew where my voice was coming from. 'Avatel! Where's Danah?'

She jumped up from beneath the tree where she and Ben had been sitting. She looked around the pool and then slowly spread her arms wide and shrugged her shoulders. 'Don't know!'

Her unconcerned gesture and lack of urgency were probably my invention. The crippling fear I felt when I noticed a child was missing from the group – even while I was telling myself she must be in the shallower water – must have made Avatel's movements seem unbearably slow and inappropriate to me; the tone in which she said 'don't know' was heard by me as monstrously casual.

Then she stiffened, pointing to the deep end of the pool. 'What's that?'

There, just within my view, a small pink bundle, floating and agitating below the surface of the water. Why did she *ask* what that was? Why didn't she just dive into the water and swim to it? I couldn't swim. I ran along the edge of the pool, my sandals slapping against the concrete.

Avatel's boyfriend got there ahead of me. The water surged as he jumped in and pulled Danah out. He just had to reach and grab her because she was floating somehow, with her head underwater, moving towards the edge of the pool. He hauled the dripping child from the water.

The only person aloof from the situation was Avatel, who still hadn't moved from the shallow end, where she stood transfixed, clutching a Coca-Cola. Danah had not swallowed any water. She wasn't even frightened. Her hair was plastered to her head and her eyes were wide open, golden with amazement. She rubbed the water out of her eyes and said, 'I swimmed to the deep end.'

'She could have drowned!' I clutched Ben's arm. 'Couldn't she? She could have drowned!'

Avatel walked slowly around the pool, her eyes wide and frightened. 'I don't know how it could have happened. One moment she was in the shallow end, and the next she wasn't.'

'It's OK,' I said to Avatel, who was nearly crying. 'It's OK, she's OK.' I took a deep breath. 'Well done, you swam,' I said to Danah.

'Yes,' she replied. 'I never drownded.'

The real shock didn't hit me until later that evening. Then, as I was eating dinner in the canteen, my body went numb. My head filled with strange sounds. A roaring noise. Shouts.

'Judith? What's the matter?'

Cydney was standing over me, 'Are you all right?'

'I'm all right.' I could hardly hear myself; the sounds inside my head were so loud. Someone began to talk with Cydney – broken bits of conversation that I could not follow. I made my excuses and headed for my room, holding myself stiffly upright. I saw myself putting my feet one in front of the other. My body felt nothing. Just a scare, that's all. Delayed reaction.

Fully awake, I lay on my bed with the curtains drawn, a nothingness washing over me. Whatever was happening to me was my own fault. I had done something wrong. Something so huge I couldn't even see it. I was inadequate and stupid, without worth. Through my neglect, Danah had almost drowned. I was a fool. I might as well be dead. My eyelids felt dry and scratchy as I fell asleep.

I was dreaming.

For miles and miles the sand stretched in front of me in the moonlight, a cool smooth beach. I fruitlessly tried to identify the place. It was nowhere that I'd ever been in real life, but whenever I dreamt of this beach I sensed it was familiar.

A night breeze bent the spiky beach grass flat. I felt so tired. I lay down, put my head against the sand and felt its grainy coolness under my cheek.

When I raised my head I saw Frances sitting on a rock in her red swimming-costume. She looked happy to see me. I held out my hand to her.

'You need to come with me, Frances.'

A smile broke out over her, like the sun had pierced the clouds. 'Can't Judith. Can't swim.'

Now she was in the water, her chin craning up as she struggled to keep it raised over the waves.

'It's bad out there! You have to come back!' I stood on the slippery rocks, reaching for her. Suddenly other children were behind me, pulling me in a long hand-to-hand chain. Darkness. Only darkness. The full moon failed to cast a reflection on the diesel-black water, yet somehow I could see every detail.

I could do nothing to bring her back, and watched helplessly as she struggled. Shouts, children tugging at me as I felt the sea lap against my ankles. Suddenly the tide engulfed me, sweeping me away. I convulsed with panic.

'No!' I screamed, 'I can't swim!' I tried to keep afloat. Something or someone was struggling to pull me to the surface. I couldn't breathe and twisted violently on to my back. Then water filled my eyes and my screams came back to me as echoes from the bottom of the sea.

I tried to scream and woke myself with the utterance of a tiny sound. I felt first relief, then the security of my room, then remembrance. I sat up in bed, tousled with the nightmare, hugging myself. I could hear the echoes inside my head as the smell of the sea haunted me again. I looked at Cydney's side of the room. She hadn't stirred.

The blood tingled in my veins, hot and cold. I felt as if I could shatter into a million pieces. No good to think about it. Don't think about it, don't.

It was nearly morning. It would soon be five o'clock. People on the kibbutz would be waking up. Still too early to call on Miriam, though. I scrambled out of bed, quietly tugging on my clothes. Outside I walked swiftly in the cool morning air, without direction. To calm myself. To get away from dreams, because there were worse ones and I didn't want to remember them, didn't want to think at all. There were lights on in some of the houses, but no one in sight.

I leaned against a tree, pressing my forehead against the gnarled and fissured bark. I must get less intense, but how to do it? To concentrate on it was to accomplish the opposite. A phrase attached itself to my mind: *Nuns Pray at Sea Rescue.*

A swift, sinking feeling clutched the pit of my stomach as I remembered the newspaper articles. The newspapers had pounced on the nuns' praying, pointing out that they had done nothing to help us. But none of the papers had explained why, or followed up the story.

Oh God, *why* then? What purpose had been served?

I lunged off the tree and started walking again. The sun was coming up, the air around me already hot, but I was shivering, my skin clammy. I made my way down to the citrus groves where the soil was loose and soft among the trees, the leaves glossy, the ground itself fragrant. To sprout such leaves and be hung with oranges would be a blessing. I wished a fibrous woodiness would enter my limbs: I wanted to take root and stay here for ever in this most temperate of places.

The sea was warm as a puddle that day. Frances and I shaded our eyes against the sun, ankle-deep in the water. I could hear laughter and shouts on the breeze. There was Ruth, her sleek, brown head like a seal's, far out in the water.

'She's swimming!' shouted Frances.

'No she's not, she's just floating!' I shouted back.

'Come on in, it's smooth as a moth's nose!' yelled Ruth, as if she owned the sea.

Frances laughed and waded towards her, stumbling a little on the shifting sand, her dark hair ruffled by the wind. The water was warm, soft, but as I watched, thoughts not quite grasped made my stomach tighten with unease.

'Hey Frances, wait for me.'

I squinted my eyes and scanned the beach, looking for a strange seashell, seaweed, anything I could seize to make sense of this vague shudder of anxiety.

Nothing.

Noisy seagulls dipped and flapped inland on the high wind, and an angry light was forming out at sea beyond the black rocks where Ruth was floating.

'The weather's changing,' Ruth yelled, looking up towards the veiled sun she hurled a curse at the sky. 'Damn! It's as uncertain as Janet's bladder.'

Rain clouds began to roll in the sky. Frances was dancing in the waves, leaping over them as they crashed into the beach. 'Judith! Come on!'

As I followed Frances into what now seemed an enormous sea, I hesitated a moment, my feet beginning to sink slowly in the quaking sand. Turn back. I ignored the warning in my head and pulled my feet from the suck as I walked in further. By the time I reached Frances the sea was up to my thighs. We squatted down in the water letting the waves wash back and forth over our shoulders.

'Shall I teach you both to swim?' Ruth called over.

'No thanks,' I shouted across the water.

'You're not scared, are you?'

Yes, I was afraid but did not say so; I was spellbound by the solitude between the sky and the sea, one as vast as the other. When I glanced back, the beach seemed like an invisible line, and the two nuns in charge of us were like distant dots. With the beginnings of panic, I pictured the immense dark depths below, where I could sink like a stone.

'I can do the crawl stroke, watch.' Frances splashed up and down in front of me, screwing up her eyes and kicking her legs.

'That's cheating! You've got one foot on the ground!'

'You're not supposed to have noticed that. It's easy, you try it. Just hold your breath and close your eyes. Ready, steady, go – and away!'

I closed my eyes but kept one foot firmly on the ground thrashing violently with my arms. Gasping then yelping, 'Oh, cripes, I'm almost swimming!' I opened my eyes, blinked away the spray and saw the blue-green, white-flecked crests of the advancing waves. It seemed we had moved further into the sea. The water swirled around my chest, thick and dark. You could hear the sea thumping the rocks, like a boxer's fist against a punchball in training for someone's jaw. Frances yelped with laughter. We held our arms above our heads and jumped up as each wave approached. Now the water seemed warmer than the air, yet the sea seemed to have become fiercer in the short time since Frances and I had entered it. The noise of the waves was overwhelming. The sun had clouded; the high backs of the incoming rollers were now almost black. I turned around to-wards the shore again and over the flecked jumping wave-crests

I could see a distant figure running across the sweep of sand towards us.

Finally it was seven o'clock, late enough to call on Miriam. I stood motionless on her veranda. I could hear her moving around inside. A cracking headache exploded behind my eyes. My throat ached. I pushed open her door. Miriam had her back to me, reading something. She looked over her shoulder, her face creasing in concern as she took in my expression. I stood in the doorway, silent and staring.

'What's the problem, Judith?'

Her gentle use of my name freed me, shattered me. The relief of being here, of seeing her, washed over me.

'Can I come in?' I said, my voice a whisper.

Before she could reply, I stumbled forward, slumping into a kitchen chair, and without warning began to cry. I hunched forward as sobs wrenched out of the deepest part of me. The tears were fossilised, older than time. I held my hands over my face, crying like a small child.

'Something happened yesterday –'

'All right,' Miriam said. She touched my arm. 'You can tell me.'

But voices from the past still controlled me. I shook my head fiercely, wretchedly, and covered my face.

Irresponsible, the Mother Superior had said. And inexcusable.

As Ruth, Frances and I turned and headed towards land, we heard Janet's distant voice calling to us. Then I recognised her green-spotted cozzie. For a girl with legs as thin as willow sticks she had reached us at a remarkable speed. She plunged towards us, beckoning, shouting something I couldn't hear above the roar of the sea.

'Janet, you'd best go back. It's getting too rough out here,' I yelled above the crash of the waves.

'I've been sent to call you and the others in,' she shouted, battling through the tide. 'Can I stay and play with you a bit?'

Before I could reply, the water hurtled against us, pushing us apart. A wave swept over my head. I fought my way to the surface, gasping and swallowing sea water. My hands reached out for something to clasp, but my arms felt like lead. I was choking and spluttering; absorbed in the task of taking the next breath, I began to understand the strength of the waves – their great size and how violently they broke. I tried to make my way towards the stark rocks that loomed out of the water, but the current seemed to be taking me out to sea. I tried harder, spurred now by fear.

I called 'Frances! Ruth!'

Somehow I reached the rocks, stretching out a hand to claw at them. 'Get on to the rocks!' I yelled.

Mindlessly Frances tried to obey, choking as water washed over her. I heaved myself up on to the craggy rocks, grazing my arms and legs. My only thought was one of survival. Ruth was already there with several other girls, all of them crying out to Frances. Yelling and screaming everywhere. Foam boiled around the rocks, swift and powerful.

'Judith!' Frances's eyes were wild. I knelt down, stretching out and grabbing hold of her arm, but she fell back and tugged away from me, her feet swept from under her.

By this time, Janet had reached Frances. We watched as Janet grabbed Frances's hair trying to keep her head above water. Then when a wave's crushing curling descent engulfed them, Janet's head disappeared from view.

I stretched out, groping towards Frances, the sharp rocks cutting into my knees. 'Take my hand! Take my hand!'

I felt the fierce sea clawing at me. There was no room for fear as she siezed hold of my hand. 'Don't let go!' I shouted.

The sky above us was lumpy with dark clouds. Frances stared up at me with land-longing eyes. Ruth grasped my other hand and I saw that she and the other girls were forming a human chain across the rocks.

'Pull her out!' someone cried.

'I'm trying!' I yelled, but as I tugged at Frances's hand I experienced, like an unexpected blow, a sudden exhaustion. What had happened to the strength that I had a moment ago? My body was coated with a profound, numbing weakness. 'I can't! It's impossible!'

'It's impossible!' I dropped my head on my arms. 'I just want to stop the memories coming. Frances kept a photograph of her mother under her pillow so that her image wouldn't be taken from her.'

Miriam hesitated. 'Why is that relevant?' she asked softly.

I raised my head, holding myself taut. Control. I had to keep myself in check, or all would be lost. I fought back the tears that were rising again. I swallowed hard and took several deep breaths. My body heaved, drowning, drowning. I put my head on my arms again, the comforting warmth of my own breath against my face.

'So many memories just keep returning. Night after night, I can't turn my anguish from the exact moment Frances died. I can't seem to stop it.'

'Why not?'

I lifted my streaming face. 'I don't know! I'm sorry, I must talk about this and get through it! It's like a dark cloud hanging over me!'

'Why is it hanging over you?'

'I don't know,' I shook my head, confused. 'I just need to talk – I need to be free of it all.'

'Free of what? What did you do?'

I began to cry again. 'I let Frances die!'

'How? What happened?' Miriam asked.

But it was coming from some part of me that was separate and unknown. It was useless; I could no longer fight it. I slapped my hand on the table.

'I don't know, but I did! Frances, Frances, I'm so sorry!'

Head cradled on my arms again, I rocked back and forth.

Couldn't think. As a great wave of hot, fierce rage swept through me, I didn't understand why I was so angry.

How did it happen, the moment Frances let go of my hand? Did she think it was all over? What was going through her mind? Did she think she was about to die and go to hell, as the nuns had said she would? Why did she let go? Maybe she wanted to die?

I stared at Miriam as if the answer to my question might change everything.

No! Frances's eyes had screamed to me in horror as she fell backwards into the sea. Slowly, ever so slowly – but it can't have been that slow, could it? It can't have been that slow?

'Judith,' Miriam said. 'Stop it! It's not happening now.'

I widened my eyes. I felt like I was dragging myself back from a long distance and blinked at her several times.

'I just don't know how to live with this burden. It's all so unfair.'

'That's right, it isn't fair. Your mind is boiling over with anger and remorse and black pain because Frances let go of your hand. And it hurts to be angry with her, doesn't it?' murmured Miriam. 'Everyone has grudges, everyone has anger. You tried to keep everything inside, but you can't; it always finds a way out. It's good to turn your anger outward at last. It's a powerful emotion that pushes you to discover the truth. But what is it that's really bothering you?'

I felt drained and sick. My head still pounded. 'I've never spoken to anyone about all this before. I've had nobody to tell. No one to trust.'

'Well, you have now, ' said Miriam. 'I'm your friend. You can tell me.'

'Miriam, it's not that easy.'

The early morning sun glinted on her reddish hair as she sat back in her chair.

'Let's go through it all step by step. You had hold of Frances's hand on one side and held on to the human chain on the other, so you were being pulled in both directions. Is that right?'

I nodded and sat up. The kitchen was cluttered and homely. Home. Soothing sounds – the clink of cups, the creak of a chair; comfortable smells – coffee, baking bread; the red lampshade with its scorched spot, the dusty books. I stared at Miriam through sore eyes.

'And Frances was older and bigger than you?' Miriam said.

'Older, yes, but I wouldn't describe her as sturdy,' I whispered.

Miriam smiled sadly. 'But don't you see? It wasn't your fault.'

My voice shifted, cut through thousands of pages in hundreds of books. 'But it was! It was! The nuns told me it was.'

Miriam's eyes were a sharp, stinging blue. She had the calm of someone who had spent a great deal of time pondering problems like mine. What would it be like to feel that way, how did you get there? She was quiet for a long time, but I could tell by the way she nodded to herself and held her hands together that she was thinking.

Finally she said, 'How long are you going to punish yourself for surviving?'

My throat went dry. 'What?'

'That's what you're doing, isn't it? Judith, you were only a child. The nuns were responsible for you and the other children. It was not your fault that those two girls drowned; to have put the blame on you was hypocrisy. The nuns must have been wounded and they passed their wounds to you. What do you think you could have done to help Frances any more than you did?'

'Pulled her out, or – not let go –' Tears flooded my eyes again. I wiped them quickly away with my hand. 'I don't know! Something!' It was always this way. My mind shut down. I could not get past this burden, so immense and overpowering that it was useless to look for a source.

I slumped my damp cheek on my hand, and mumbled, 'You don't understand. Her dying was all so pointless. She was a special child. It should have been me, not her. Or what was the point of it?'

'The point of it,' Miriam said, 'is that it happened. I'm sorry. I do feel sorry for your unfortunate friend, but you were the nuns' scapegoat. And you cannot spend the rest of your days as a tragic scapegoat.'

I jerked up. 'No! That's not it! I wish it were that simple. There's more,' I said, reaching across the table, as if to get her attention.

Careless, the nuns told me afterwards, but they didn't come into the water to help with the rescue. They thought praying was sufficient. When Frances let go of my hand and fell back into the water, a man jumped into the sea fully dressed to rescue her. I watched in a daze. Where had he come from?

I still held on to the human chain. They pulled me over the rocks and dragged me through the water to safety. When I reached the beach, I collapsed, lying face downwards on the sand. I coughed, wheezed and moaned quietly with relief. Some-one began pummelling me with a towel and asking me if I was all right, but I was still in another world. I listened without thinking that I might be able to answer, preoccupied with the wonder of finding myself alive. Giddiness overcame me as I sat up and I covered my eyes for a moment. As I withdrew my hand I noticed several rescuers plunging, linked together, from the shore, dragging more girls to land and while all this was happening, the two nuns knelt on the sand and prayed.

'Sweet Jesus, save them!' they shrilled.

I squinted my eyes to look for Frances. The man had managed to lift her out of the violent sea. He carried her across the rocks slung over his shoulder. Her hair dangled like dripping seaweed down his back. Water poured out of her mouth. The man handed her over to a waiting crowd on the shore. They reached out hands to her, lifting her in a gentle gesture that from a distance looked almost like love.

The scene was unreal, pictures painted on a flat screen. If you kicked it, it would tear open, showing only a black emptiness behind. The eerie pale-green light played over everything. It crept over the group of waiting children, the nuns kneeling in prayer. It crept over the man trying to tug Frances back to life as she lay on the wet sand.

Someone ran up the beach shouting, shrill, like a train whistle before departure. Janet had been spotted in the water somewhere between the rocks. Some of us ran down to the sea again, and stood in the water up to our knees, ignoring the surge and suck round our legs. 'Janet!' we screamed. 'Janet!'

We called her name till our throats were parched and our eyes wind-dried and stinging. The sea took on a green fluorescent glow beneath the dark dome of the sky as we stood straining our ears over the thump of the waves. A voice – I think it was mine – said, 'Janet's gone, she really has gone.'

We scanned the shoreline, finding the place where she was last seen. The wind whipped the black water over the area into a great explosion of spray. It was true; she had vanished. We staggered back to the beach, dazed and numb. Several of the smaller girls remained scattered along the water's edge, casting anxious glances at the praying nuns. When they began to sob, crying in a terrible, pitiful, hopeless way, some of the senior girls ran down to them and hustled them back up the beach.

The sand was now dark with spectators milling to and fro. The crowd surrounding Frances huddled together, their voices inaudible. I pushed my way through them. Was she alive? Somewhere was the memory of my dying father, and I dreaded what I might see. Someone in the group of strangers tried to grasp my arm to hold me back, but I shook them off.

I stood and watched for a slight rise and fall of Frances's chest – but there was nothing. I reached down and took her cold hand. 'Frances, Frances, it's me, Judith.' I could not tell if she was hearing me. Her face was immobile, almost purple. I squeezed her hand, willing her to breathe.

The man who had saved her drew a hand across her face. 'You have to go now,' he said to me. 'We'll take care of your friend.'

I started to leave, but Frances held on to my fingers for a heartbeat, so light and brief that it might have been a reflex. I squeezed back, careful not to hurt her.

'I'm sorry,' I said.

Tears of grief this time. I twisted my handkerchief round my fingers, my thoughts spinning around and around.

'Judith, listen to me. Life is not fair always, or sane, or good or anything. It just *is*,' said Miriam. 'I'm no analyst, but it is clear to me that Frances was a pretty, gifted child who was able to cope with the terrible circumstances of her institutional life, but you were thrown in at the deep end and found it much harder. She was your role model and during your time at the convent, it seems you tried to copy her in order to survive.

'For a time it worked. After all, you were probably a very good actress. Then along came the drowning incident, and the impossible happened. You, as the inadequate child, survived. Your friend, the one you had patterned your whole life after, wasn't so lucky. You couldn't make sense of it. In your eyes it seemed so unfair. Am I right?'

'Maybe. I don't know,' I said dismally. 'All I know is that her voice was as near to music as any voice I've ever heard.'

Miriam touched my arm. 'Listen, it makes sense that you've tried to become someone else. For everyone. For the nuns, for your mother, your friends, and, most of all, for yourself. Only, that's been a terrible burden, do you see? But how could you rid yourself of it? Well, you couldn't. That's been your dilemma: a problem without a solution. And so, because you weren't able to work out how to deal with the problem, you decided to hide from it, bury it, carry the burden alone.' Miriam leant forward. 'Does any of this make sense to you?'

'I've no idea,' I said. 'I'm sorry, Miriam, I don't understand what you're saying.'

'Judith, you were acting in self-preservation. You must understand that no one needs you to be perfect. People will like you, faults and all, if you just be yourself.'

'But I no longer know who I really am any more!' I cried.

'Yes, you do,' Miriam said. 'You do. Judith, that person is trying hard to get out, and she's never going to be the one to hurt you, believe me. Let her talk. Let her tell you what you did that was so bad. Listen, do you know what you did? You hung on to the human chain that your friends had formed on the rocks. That's it. You survived. That's your guilt. You can live with that, can't you?'

I could not answer, did not have to answer. I leant back. I felt as if I was seeing Miriam through a hazy curtain. The air shimmered between us. I was light-headed, my bones brittle, without substance, like scraps of paper.

'What's bothering you,' Miriam said, 'is plain to see. Not letting yourself connect with your own feelings. All your stiff-upper-lip way of dealing with these memories is tearing you apart, leading you off on paths that don't lead anywhere. What happened today?'

'One of the children in my charge fell into the deep end of the swimming pool yesterday afternoon,' I said. 'She was all right, but it shook me up. And then I had that dream again about Frances.'

'So you didn't get much sleep last night.'

I shook my head.

'Have you had anything to eat since yesterday?'

'No . . .' I began to say that I was not hungry, that I was too tired to eat, but Miriam was on her feet and heading for the kitchen before I could protest.

'It's good to voice your feelings. That way you'll feel easier. Grief requires time. In your case, extra time.' Miriam stopped then. 'Are you with me?' she said.

I nodded my head and sat looking at my fingernails. Ugly, ragged. I'd started biting them again recently. Narrowing my eyes, I blended everything to grey in Miriam's room – the curtains, the walls.

She placed before me orange juice, bagels, fried eggs and coffee. '*Eat*,' she urged, and I obediently took up my knife and fork. 'You'll feel better once you eat.'

But I was too restless to eat. Restless with her calm, restless with my own story laid out between us, restless with myself. I shifted in my chair, elbows on the table. I took a few tentative bites of the eggs and pushed the plate from me. Too risky. Too nauseated.

'So you don't think I'm potty?'

'No,' she said, 'of course not. Just eat.'

'I'll try.' My stomach felt in poor shape and my legs were suddenly frail and rickety. 'I don't know what I would have done if I hadn't come to see you this morning. I felt so lost.'

'And now?'

I closed my eyes. 'Like I've lost sixpence and found a shilling.'

Miriam put her hands together, resting her chin on them, scrutinising me with moist, friendly, blue eyes. She smiled, and her expression embraced me with all the motherly concern my heart at that hopeless moment longed for.

'Listen, Judith. It wasn't your fault that as a child you were small, vulnerable and needy. It wasn't your fault that your friend drowned. You've been bound to those memories by a sense of guilt. What happened this morning was that you let go of yourself and felt some pain. That's good because feeling is not selective. If you can't feel pain, you aren't going to feel anything else, either. And the world is full of pain. Also joy, anger and revenge, humour, good and evil, vanity, jealousy, humility, horror and love. The strong feelings are all around you and they aren't always pleasant. Shutting yourself off from all feeling won't make the world any safer. Some things can't be foreseen or understood or blamed on anyone – they can only be endured.'

With an effort I sucked air into my lungs, clenching my fists, breathing slowly. The wave of anger receded gradually, leaving me with a tightness, a burning sensation in my chest.

She went on, 'I found you awkward and hostile when I first met you and you made me feel awkward too. Yet I knew that once you started being open with me it would be quite easy.'

I said in the same tone, 'I know, I think I was very stupid. But I'm glad I didn't run away.'

'You almost did. I'm so glad you came to me this morning.'

'And so am I.' I felt a blissful sense of power, which was at the same time a frenzy of appreciation. Now I felt I could act humanly, think, wish, reflect, speak. I got up from my chair, moved to the window and stared over to the distant hills. Behind me, I heard Miriam pour herself a cup of coffee. I turned to watch her. Then it happened without warning. A tiny seed opened slowly inside my mind, revealing the answer in all its clarity and detail. A rush of blood went up to my head; I was suddenly alert, electric with precision, as if something dangerous had just missed hitting me.

'Oh, my God!' I said. 'I think I've just worked something out.'

'What's that?' Miriam asked.

'Who really is to blame.'

I sat beside Miriam, my back against the wall, knees up, holding a cup of coffee in my hands. 'God, I'm so tired,' I said.

'Well, that's quite a big secret you've been keeping from yourself.'

'So what do I do now?'

'Well, you've done it, haven't you? You've taken a step in the right direction. You've discovered your mother wasn't perfect, but be aware of her limitations. Yet what I still don't fully understand,' she said, 'is why you never spoke with her or anyone else about the convent afterwards.'

'Would it have made any difference if I had?' I said. 'Why should I have told the truth and then be called a liar? Why should I have to wear such a story around my neck and be such a tragic figure to the world? I was ashamed of what happened to me, I wanted to disown it. I wanted to be light, to be new, to be free of my guilt and shame. Besides, sometimes I wondered if my mother ever gave a damn. I know now why she hardly ever visited me at the convent. *I know!* She was too busy having a good time with her new-found freedom, why should she care if the nuns were beating me to a pulp? Maybe she never really loved me.'

'No, more like she loved you as much as she was able. Maybe she was afraid, maybe it was her circumstances or maybe it was hard for her to give love. You've built a cage of needs and installed her in the empty space in the middle. Don't blame her. Maybe she couldn't show you the way she felt. She must have had her reasons. Human beings are endlessly ingenious about encouraging their own misery. Even in a catastrophe, mysterious barriers can isolate them. Perhaps you should find out why she didn't get on with your grandparents. Then when you've understood her past, you'll have nothing to do except forgive her and I know that will be well within your capacity.'

'But I've always loved my mother, even what's awful.' I closed my eyes. A jungle in there, inside my head. I became silent, feeling an immense tired cloud rising out of me.

'You look exhausted. Stay here and get some sleep,' Miriam said. Her eyes were fixed on me, a tender and compelling blue.

'I can't. Teliela has warned me that if I miss class again, I'll be scheduled for work in the dining-room every morning instead of Hebrew class. I can't take more pressure.'

'I have to visit someone in Kibbutz Mishmar Hasharon today, so you can stay here if you wish. I'll have a word with Teliela.'

I sat up. 'Thank you.'

Miriam laughed. 'How are you holding up with so little sleep?'

'I'm beginning to fade,' I admitted. Tears welled up again behind my eyelids. I wiped my eyes. 'Do you mind if I lie down outside on the veranda until you get back?'

'Of course not. Stay as long as you like.'

No need for any more words. I lay down on the canvas bed in the shade. The air was warm and sweet. Up in the sky, a flock of birds heeled sideways. They went on turning and wheeling, catching and sending the light through the air. The sky with the dipping and turning birds in it seemed like a great bowl of light above the earth. In that moment I felt so safe, floating in the calmest of seas.

Chapter 14

When we returned to the convent we were herded into the senior classroom, a group of trembling, shell-shocked children. There was a shift in the room, a hush, and the Mother Superior came in, glaring at us.

Taking off her glasses and wiping them on her sleeve, she said, 'I want you to very quietly and reverently kneel down beside your desks and pray for the soul of Frances McCarthy, and that Janet Dover will be found soon.'

Everyone knelt and bowed their heads, but I sat lower in my desk and crossed my arms. I didn't want to pray. Frances was everywhere – on the surface of my skin, a whisper in my ears, even the beat inside my own heart. I didn't have one thought that wasn't about Frances. Since we had returned from the beach an hour ago, we'd been retelling the specifics of what happened, going over it again and again, but I had pulled myself away from all the talk and turned silent.

Now I closed my eyes, seeing Frances's last moments as if they were my own. A thick pain lifted up in my throat like a stone. I stayed in that moment where I held Frances's hand for the last time. What was happening to her now? Were they anointing her eyes and ears and hands with holy oil, representing the forgiveness of the sins she had committed? Wash and shampoo. Clipping her nails and hair? They'd grow all the same afterwards. I tried to picture her in the sky. Her face under its halo was not full of love, but resentment. And who could blame her?

'In the name of the Father, the Son, and the Holy Ghost. Oh, Merciful Father, in Thee we trust when dangers threaten.' The Mother Superior lifted her head, her mouth pursed. 'The nuns are most distressed, you know. There has *never* before been such a tragedy at the convent,' she said to us in a tone that was purely conversational, as if she thought the news might interest us.

Someone coughed. Someone else blew her nose. I couldn't bear to listen any more. I turned my face to the evening sun pouring in the window, burning brightly in the blue sky outside. I let it fall over my face, its warmth on my skin, and closed my eyes.

'Janet Dover hasn't been found yet. We are all praying very hard for her.' She scanned us, lips tight. 'It was their own fault, of course. Such foolishness, not paying attention to the rules, staying out in the water too long.'

I looked around at the faces in the classroom. Did they believe such lies? They couldn't, they were there too! But they didn't even blink at them.

'That's not true, Reverend Mother.' I was almost too breathless with fear and anger to speak. 'Janet was sent back into the sea to call in us other children. She said so.'

Silence. I knew it was wrong; I knew I'd get in trouble for it. But I also knew I would be angry for ever at Frances's death, at the nuns, and most of all, I would be angry with myself if I didn't speak up. A stirring rustled around me as the others looked at me, expectant. Their eyes were shouts of encouragement. I watched the Mother Superior, not breaking my gaze from hers.

She stiffened, her eyes narrowing behind her thick glasses. 'Hold your tongue! You're all worthless; you'll never amount to much. Especially *you*, Judith Kelly. Why, I'm told that you let go of McCarthy's hand, and that's the reason she drowned! But for your carelessness, she would still be alive.'

My fault. Yes, it had been my fault that Frances had died. My skin prickled with fear and my stomach knotted as I remembered that moment when I let go of her hand. I felt as if I was seeing the Mother Superior through a curtain of mist. I wrapped my arms over my stomach – such a cold feeling in me, like I was turning into a block of ice right there in front of the Mother Superior. I sat down again, defeated, covering my face with my hands.

'You must all swear to me, on holy obedience, that you will never say anything about what has happened today,' said the Mother Superior. 'We need to conduct this whole business quietly and without any fuss. There are people out there who may ask you questions. Don't you dare answer them. Do you understand? We don't want the convent's good name dragged through the gutter press. I'll tell you briefly what I think of newspapers: the hand of God reaching down into the mire could not elevate one of them from the depths of degradation – not by a million miles. The most truthful parts of any newspaper are the advertisements.'

When she left the room, everyone immediately began talking in hushed tones. Some girls fell on their knees, moaning quietly in sorrow. I couldn't get away from it, couldn't escape my guilt. It kept me in a cold shiver, so that I hugged myself wretchedly, unable to feel warm.

The girls cried and comforted each other as we waited for news of Janet. The only news we heard was that every corner and crevice among the rocks was being thoroughly searched. One of the nuns began screeching in the corridor.

'Jesus! Oh Jesus! Jesus!'

I shook the sound out of my ears by an angry toss of my head until she stopped.

I spotted Ruth watching me. I moved over to sit next to her. 'Ruth, it all seems like a bad dream.'

'It's not a dream. I wish it was. The sea wasn't safe today. That wave knocked us clean over.'

'And sort of sucked us under too,' I added.

'Listen, I've got a plan.'

'Uh-oh!' I said. 'I always worry when you say that.'

Her brown eyes narrowed as she glanced around. Then she thrust her face close to my ear and began to tell me a string of intricate plans, given over in a breathy whisper with a great many 'and-then-we'll . . .'

At last, she leaned back and looked at me doubtfully. 'Well, what do you think?'

'I'd like to, but . . .' I blurted.

'Do as you like. I'm not forcing you.'

I felt a chill crawl up my back and into my hair.

'Oh come on,' cried Ruth, 'It can't be that frightening, can it? Think of poor Janet out there all on her own. Besides, that frog needs her.'

I nodded silently.

'Let's do it,' said Ruth 'I mean, if we go together we can protect each other.'

I licked my lips. 'When . . . when were you thinking of going?'

'How about around midnight?' whispered Ruth.

'We might get into awful trouble if we're caught.'

'Might! Better say we would! But I don't give a shit.'

In the dormitory that night, what had been Frances's bed was now just a bare mattress. I couldn't look at it. I lay awake and waited in restless impatience. There had still been no news of Janet. A lot of the girls sobbed quietly, so rhythmically that I could predict each gasp. I lay there, tense, listening to each one. I didn't dare let go myself.

I fell into a chaotic dream-filled sleep, and was just about to be attacked by a horde of anxious faces when I felt myself being gently shaken. I gave a short start and opened my eyes. Ruth.

'Do you still want to go and look for Janet?'

I nodded. I was lying. I wanted only to stay where I was, but I couldn't let Ruth down. In a single minute I was dressed and creeping down the stairs with her. We tugged at the bolts of the back door, and held our breath as we drew them back; then Ruth pulled the door shut behind us and we raced out into the waiting blackness of the playground. Although it was barely midnight, there was not a light showing in the convent. Everyone was in bed and asleep. I felt resentful; I had expected a vigil for Frances, and for Janet.

A faint wind moaned through the trees. 'It might be Frances's ghost, urging us on,' whispered Ruth. She put her finger to her lips and gestured for me to follow. We crept through the forbidden gardens, running from tree to tree for cover. My heart racketed against my chest as we dashed down the driveway and out of the convent gates. Our pace gradually slowed. When we reached the road we came to a stop.

There were no lights in the road that led to the beach. We stood in silence in the light of the clouded moon, our shadows thin and dark blue as we stared uncertainly into the darkness. I told myself that I could go back if I liked, and be warm again in bed, where I had made a dummy of myself of pillows. But we'd look right fools getting caught on our way back because we'd turned chicken.

Ruth pulled my hand. 'Come on. We can't let a little dark stop us.' We ran, our feet barely skimming the ground, my heart beating loud enough to burst my ears. The road sloped gently downwards. The wild hedgerows flashed in low dark lines beside us. The trees looked huge, big gnarled branches hooking out towards us with leafy hands, like they might grab hold of us.

We didn't stop running until we reached the beach. When we eventually halted, I had a stitch in my side that stabbed me with every breath.

The dark beach spread endlessly around us, sweeping out to the moonlit sea. I felt very small. There was something so much bigger and lonelier about the beach at night. Somewhere in the Channel, a boat blew its siren and another answered, and another, like dogs waking each other at night.

Ruth seized my arm. 'Look!'

'What is it?' I gasped as we clung to each other.

'Look at the sea! Do you see them?'

'I –'

'There!'

Lights appeared in the distance, flitting back and forth. Shouts burst over the beat of the waves, sending hollow reverberations to our ears.

'There are some people getting out of a boat. Let's run!'

'Keep still! Don't you budge! They're coming right towards us.'

We stretched ourselves on the sand, not lifting our eyes, and lay waiting in a misery of fear. Torches approached out of the sea. Half a dozen of them. Every now and then one of the beams swung sideways and lit up the pebbles on the beach.

'They must be the coastguards searching for Janet,' I said. 'They're coming this way. What shall we do?'

'I dunno, Judith. Do you think they've seen us?'

'Oh, they'll see us, like cats do in the dark.'

'Don't be afraid. We'll stay here. Keep perfectly still, they won't notice us.'

'I'm trembling all over, Ruth.'

'Listen!'

We put our heads together and scarcely breathed. A muffled sound of voices floated up over the noise of the sea.

'Look, see there!' whispered Ruth.

'What is it?'

'Oh, Judith, this is awful.'

We hid our heads as some vague figures came scrambling slowly up the beach. They were breathing hard and uttering little grunts as they struggled with the awkwardness of the stretcher they were carrying. The load looked white and lumpy in the moonlight. One of the coastguards shone his torch on it, and we could just make out a red swimming cap.

We didn't need to say anything. We knew.

The noises died away until once again there was no sound left in the black, bandaged darkness but for the long drawn-out sigh of the sea.

Neither of us felt like returning to the convent. We walked for a mile along the coast towards some cliffs, and climbed up a rough pathway that had been hacked out of the grass and bracken. Once we reached the top we carried on walking until we came to a small opening in a clump of gorse. My worn shoes were hurting my blistered feet. I didn't mind. The throbbing took my mind off other things.

Finally we scrambled down another rough pathway and came to a sheltered and sandy cove. In the moonlight, we could see the cliffs curve round on either side of us, like the arms of an enormous armchair. We stumbled down to the shore, our feet sinking in the silted sand. I closed my eyes to hear my shoes squeaking pebbles and crushing shells. When I opened them again I had the strange feeling that Frances was so close that if I just half-turned my head she'd be there. See now, she was there all the time. And ever shall be, world without end.

'No, no,' I whispered, shaking my head tearfully. 'No, no. She's not here. She'll never be here.'

With an angry sob I picked up a large pebble and threw it into the water. Wildly I picked up anything I could find, hurling broken bits into the sea. I felt so racked with pain that I no longer cared about anything but the tight knot that seemed to pierce the very centre of myself. I was angry that Frances and Janet had died. Angry with Frances for going away and leaving me. I wanted to see her again so I could say sorry.

'I hate you, God! I hate you. You hear me? I hate you, I hate you.'

I stood yelling and screaming at the sky until I sank, exhausted and weeping, to the ground.

Ruth put an arm round my shoulders.

'I'm sorry, Ruth,' I said. 'Sorry.'

'Poor Janet. If she hadn't been sent back into the sea by the nuns to call us in she'd still be alive. I don't think I shall ever get over it.'

'Me too. It's just that – I could have helped Frances and didn't.' My eyes began to smart again. 'She wrote a poem for me once. Now it's all I have left of her. I hope my mum will take me away from the convent once she hears what's happened. Then maybe I'll tell her about what's been going on.'

'There's nothing to tell,' said Ruth tiredly.

I gaped at her profile in the moonlight. 'There's *lots* to tell. Maybe if people knew what goes on in the convent, they'd do something about it.'

'I don't want anybody to know, Judith.' Her eyes filled with tears. Ruth, who never cried. 'Not your mum, not my god-mother. Not anybody. What's the point?'

And all at once I knew she was right. It would be a waste of time. The nuns had been treating kids badly for years. Nothing changed, nothing ever changed. I used to think that however cruelly they treated us, they were on God's side, and we shouldn't question their behaviour towards us. As Frances used to tell me, without the nuns where would she have been?

But now she was dead. And I knew in my heart that I had always felt that the nuns were dangerous.

'I want it buried,' said Ruth 'I want it buried as deep as it can go.'

I nodded slowly. 'You're right. Because we've got to live with it, and talking makes living it harder. But my mum might ask.'

'Let her,' Ruth said, standing up, brushing the sand from her tunic. 'Let her ask, let her think. But the truth stays with us. Just be glad you'll soon be back with your mum. Forget everything else.'

'What do you want to forget most, Ruth?'

'I don't want to wake up feeling frightened ever again,' Ruth said in a voice coated with despair. 'Or scrub any more floors. And I don't want to be beaten. We put a stop to Sister Mary that time in the boot-room, but Sister Columba's got worse since then. Every day it's just worry and worry, and sweat and sweat, and wishing you were dead all the time. I want to be able to sleep, not worry about what's going to happen next. I want to wake up every day at the crack of noon. If I could get that, I'd be happy. I'd be in Heaven, or close to it.'

I hugged myself as a chill wind swept over the sea. 'I hope my mum can let me stay with her for a while. If not, I'll probably have to go to another boarding school. But nowhere could be as bad as the convent, could it?'

Ruth looked at me. 'I'll feel lonely without you. Let's make a pact to meet up one day when we're grown up. We'll have a God's own beano and then we can talk about what's happened and do something about it.'

'All right,' I said. 'We'll meet in Trafalgar Square and eat a packet of cornflakes together.' We both sighed at the thought.

The sea looked cold and black. Heavy lumps of seaweed, the occasional stick of wood, the odd broken beer bottle, rusty tin cans, a solitary old leather shoe, bits of plastic, corks and straws had washed up on the shore.

Grown-ups were so destructive. There was no kindness in them, not even towards nature.

I was too hungry to sleep. We huddled together for warmth in the shelter of a beach hut. The endless night slowly retreated. I awoke with a start, filled with dread, shivering and uncomfortable, unable to remember falling asleep. The dawn inched up, lighting the sky, streaming over the poisonous bottle-green sea, mottled with seaweed. The salt wind smarted on my lips.

Ruth was sitting up, staring out across the dark wash of water. She began to cough: a steady hack, hack, hack towards the sea. An old man went stooping down to the shore, very slowly, turning the stones, picking among the dry seaweed and shingle for whatever rubbish he could find. The gulls, which had stood like wax candles down on the scummy sand, rose winding and screaming in the sunlight. The old man picked up a boot and stowed it in his sack as the gulls swooped down on a broken crab – half vultures, half doves.

'Let's walk into town and buy some food,' Ruth said, swivelling her eyes on me and continuing to cough.

'With what?'

She jingled something in her pocket. Then with a grave gesture she extended a hand and, smiling, opened it slowly to my gaze. Two silver half-crown coins shone in her palm. 'See, I've got five shillings. I've been saving it for a rainy day, but I didn't know it was ever going to get this wet.'

Huge white clouds sagged and sailed in a blue sky. The stooped figure on the beach looked up at us as we left. We walked down flowering lanes, listening to the gab of birds. The high hedges were thick with dog roses, mostly a clear pink, sometimes white with yellow-gold centres. The roses were thickly entwined with wild honeysuckle trailing and weaving among the pink and gold. Neither of us had ever smelt or seen such wildflowers in so small a space.

'We'll have to decide later when to go back to the convent. Or if,' said Ruth.

The convent. The convent. It was like a poison jetting through the nerves. Until that moment, it had seemed to recede from my thoughts and its influence upon me had seemed to wane, but now I felt empty, as though the day itself had lost its colour.

We wandered slowly into the town, which had still not awoken. Birds jabbered everywhere – from eaves, trees, on telegraph wires, rails and fences. We walked through the dozy streets like waifs who had emerged from the sea, shrugging off seaweed and water. We walked past old bow-fronted houses, their sea-view doors sealed tight. Trim gardens squatted tidily in neat rows along hilly streets.

I imagined eyes peering at us from behind net-curtained windows. Ruth laughed. She said she could hear someone snoring in one house.

'It sounds just like a giant pig slobbering and snorting – making the windows rattle.'

I managed a smile. 'The beds shake.'

'Getting up too early in the morning is like a pig's tail. It's twirly.'

A church clock struck faintly in the distance, like a sound from another world, but I didn't count. The wind cascaded over us, sweeping time away.

The day was growing sultry, and in the windows of a shuttered baker's shop loaves and cakes lay bleaching next to the sleeping form of a large tabby cat. To our surprise the shop was open and we bought some biscuits and bread rolls which we ate hungrily as we wandered through the quiet town. We couldn't find a dairy, so we went into a newsagent's shop and bought a big bottle of lemonade. The sun went in behind some clouds and left us to our jaded thoughts and the crumbs of our feast.

Up the street, outside a dilapidated public house, we smudged the pane of the window, white noses flattened, gazing at the sunlit bar. The gilded-lettered mirror behind the bar where wine and ale glasses shimmered flashed our own images back at us: two shabby strays. Even in the street the bar sent out whiffs of beer and stale cigarette smoke. At the back of the bar, the clock said twelve o'clock. Twelve o'clock was opening time. 'I bet the hands of that clock have stayed at the same time for the last fifty years,' said Ruth. 'It's always opening time in this pub.'

'Like my Dad's used to be.'

'You're too young and too early to be going in there!' boomed a bone-rattling voice behind us. We turned, and saw a large policeman looking down at us. 'Not running away, I hope?' He smiled so widely it was a wonder his teeth didn't drop out.

'Morning, constable,' Ruth smiled, imitating his smile with lots of teeth. 'No, we haven't run away. We're visiting my aunt.'

'You'd best come along and tell that to the sergeant at the station,' he said in his buttoned, blue voice, and taking us both awkwardly by the hands he led us round the corner, up the stone stairs and into the little bare over-heated room where Justice supposedly waited.

'Handcuff House,' whispered Ruth to me mournfully.

Justice was a bald-headed sergeant trying to hide a tin of fruit drops behind a telephone. He showed his tartar-coated teeth in a fatherly smile and sent the constable to fetch two glasses of milk. Opening his desk drawer, he hastily pushed back a half-eaten sausage roll on a saucer and brought out a pad and pencil.

'Names?' he asked stabbing the paper fiercely. At Ruth's reply of 'Margaret Rutherford', he raised his head and said sombrely, 'I'm a very busy man and have no time for games.'

There were two trays on his desk marked In and Out, but the Out tray was empty and all the In tray held was a copy of a newspaper. Waving his pencil at Ruth, he said, 'Listen, I've been a policeman for thirty years. Thirty years. I'm not Sherlock Holmes and all I need from you is the answer to certain questions. Now then, I'll take a guess that you're a couple of runaways from the convent. Don't you girls know it's unsafe to be roaming the streets on your own?

'We'll ring the convent up and say you're safe. They'll fetch you very soon. The nuns have enough to worry about without having to deal with runaway kids as well.'

The constable who placed two glasses of milk before us watched us closely, noticing when Ruth winced away from questions.

'What made you run away? Playing truant, eh? Think how anxious your parents will be.'

'I don't have any,' Ruth said.

That question went home. I pictured the Mother Superior's eyes looking down on me accusingly. I began to cry.

'Now, now, now,' the sergeant said. 'No need to get hysterical. That's not going to do anybody any good now.' He obviously didn't know what to do.

'Don't you think it's funny,' the constable said, 'that there haven't been any reports of missing children from the convent?'

'They think they're tucked up in bed.'

'You're scared, aren't you?' the constable said. 'What scared you?'

'I don't know,' I said.

'Somebody scared you, didn't they?'

'I'm scared of the nuns,' I said. I felt a catch in my throat, for even to speak the word 'scared' was to feel it, and summon up the awkward questions, the nuns, St Joseph's cupboard and the shadows of the night. The responsibility for keeping it all hushed up weighed on me heavily, making me miserable with the unfairness of life. I didn't want to keep any more secrets – I was finished once and for all with grown-ups. Never, never again would I share their companionship or trust them.

Ruth was staring at me, begging, pleading. 'No, sergeant, I told you, we're visiting my aunt.' Her voice wavered out unconvincingly. 'She's ill. My friend's crying because she wants to get back to her.'

The sergeant rolled his eyes. 'I think perhaps we'd best find a police car to drive you both back to the convent.'

Ruth looked frantically around the police station. 'Wait. There she is.' She pointed to a thin woman standing outside. 'There's my aunt, she's come to look for us.' The smile returned to her face, the show of teeth. She ran outside, waving and yelling. The woman raised a small gloved fist, yawned gently, tip-tapping her open mouth and looked blankly at Ruth.

'She doesn't seem to know you, does she? I think you'd best wait here while I go and speak to her.'

'I'll talk to her,' Ruth said.

'Oh no you don't,' said the policeman, grabbing her arm. 'You both wait here.'

But we were already through the door as he approached the woman, Ruth glanced at me quickly, and we both charged across the forecourt with our heads down. A car horn blared as we ran across the main road, a car swerved to avoid us, and I glimpsed the angry man at the wheel, and the frightened face of the woman beside him.

My legs were shaking as we passed a parade of shops, and my hands felt strangely light, as though I'd lost some vital ballast. We ran past fish-and-chip shops, stationers selling newspapers, dingy hotels with open doors. Only when a woman at a bus stop carrying a parcel called out to us, did I realise that I was making a lowing sound, like a sick animal. Ruth and I didn't exchange any words; we were desperate to keep moving through the streets until we could find somewhere to hide. We caught up with a knot of children running away from something or somebody, laughing as they ran; we were whirled with them round a turning, then abandoned.

We couldn't have been more lost, but Ruth hadn't the stamina to keep on. At first I feared that someone would stop us; after an hour I hoped someone would. We couldn't find our way back to the police station or the convent, and in any case I was more afraid than ever of the nuns. I felt like a terrible coward for almost breaking my promise to Ruth and spilling the beans to that police constable at the station. We wandered aimlessly through back streets. Families were sunning themselves in doorways, the rubbish bins had been put out and bits of rotting vegetables were squashed on the pavement. Further up the street, a washing-line with two crucified shirts fluttered in the breeze. The air was full of voices, but we were cut off; these people were strangers and would always now be strangers; we were marked by the nuns' behaviour and shied away from them.

We sidled past another police constable, a young man who was chewing nervously at the chinstrap of his helmet as he directed the traffic. He started to walk towards us. We decided we didn't trust him; he wasn't a match for the nuns. Ruth grabbed my hand and yanked me down a side street.

'I don't think he's following us,' Ruth gasped.

'Look again!'

'Don't run. Just walk normal.'

'I think we should run.'

'Come on,' said Ruth. 'Just keep walking.'

We veered round a corner and came to a large cornfield. My feet were tired by pavements. We did not speak or look or stop, but plunged on through the cornstalks. Our feet made swoosh noises going through it and then another noise burst in front of us. We stopped as a long bird shot up out of the corn, almost brushing against our faces. I could feel its wings beating. We watched it fly away and, when we thought we were safe, we sat down in the quiet field and looked at each other.

'We're up the creek,' said Ruth.

I glanced over at the tall, dense rows of corn, the blue sky above. Insects crept in the dust, their backs and heads powdery with dirt.

'I think maybe we should hide again tonight.'

'Hide? Hide where?' Ruth looked around.

'Anywhere,' I said. 'We'll lie low. When it's dark enough and late enough we'll slip away.'

'No, Judith. We're bound to be caught eventually. I've decided to go to Guildford and find my godmother. I'd rather die than stay in that prison camp. In fact, I have to go before I do die.'

'Can I come with you? I'll be no trouble, I promise.'

She looked at me without smiling, but the severe mask was changed, softened into a sort of regretful relieved exhaustion. She looked suddenly very relaxed and tired, like someone who had travelled a long way.

She said, 'A person only has a chance to get clean away if they're by themselves. You'd better go back to the convent. Your mum is bound to take you away from that dump when she sees the newspapers. Remember the old Latin motto: *Illegitimus non carborundum?*'*

*Don't let the bastards get you down.

Her words touched me so poignantly that I was even more determined to cling to her.

'If you're not going back, neither am I! I'll be no good without you. What's the matter? You've got guts, haven't you?'

Abruptly, I stopped. What was I saying? This was Ruth, one of the nicest, bravest people I knew. She was just being sensible on my behalf. But something told me that sensible made no sense in this situation.

Ruth looked at me intently. I could tell she was hurt. She shook her head and then stood up. A flock of birds exploded from the field. 'Come on, I'm so hungry I could eat the dates off a calendar. See them red berries over there.'

'They look scrummy,' I said.

'Well, if you eat them you'll get guts-ache and die. They're deadly nightshade and they're poisonous. Let's find a blackberry bush, but don't eat anything till you've shown me. Look, there's a good one,' she said pointing to a hedgerow dripping with blackberries. 'You pick there, I'm off to find a patch of my own.'

An hour later, after scratching our arms and legs and staining our hands and mouths with juice, we sat down in the grass and passed the bottle of lemonade that we had bought earlier back and forth.

'Ruth,' I said softly, 'I'm sorry.'

She burped and, putting her hand up to her mouth, said mechanically, 'Manners! I blame the radishes.'

'I still think that maybe we should hide for another night,' I said.

She shook her head. 'I'm telling you, no! The police won't give up until we're caught and then there will be hell to pay.'

'There's going to be hell to pay even if we return to the convent today, I can tell you that!' I said.

'If it could only be just like this for ever and ever amen.'

We started walking. I was scared, scared for Ruth as much as for myself. Scared for the girls we'd left behind in the convent.

246

Would Sister Mary go back to her old bullying ways without Ruth there to shield them? By running away we had put the girls in peril, laying them open to retribution from the nuns who had power over them. This was a thought so agonising that I almost had to bend over with the pain. A blast of wind swept into my face and I shivered at the remorseful accusing thoughts that buzzed in my mind. What kind of reception would await me at the convent when I went back? How would the nuns treat me? What would they say to me about this piece of irresponsible lunacy? Ruth squeezed my shoulder firmly as I walked with her to the railway station, expecting a policeman to loom up with a pair of handcuffs at every step. But nothing happened. Ruth bought me a platform ticket and we sat on a bench and gazed at the empty oil-spotted tracks.

'Don't forget to write, Judith,' said Ruth huskily. She took another swig of lemonade with shaking hands.

'Yes, Ruth. I promise I'll keep in touch somehow.'

She gave me a sharp look. 'You might feel different when you get home. I suspect your mum missed you. Probably why she didn't write much.'

I nodded.

A cloud of smoke drifted upwards from a clump of trees in the distance. We watched it getting nearer and heard the sound of the approaching train grow louder. We stood up. The train rounded the corner like a clattering caterpillar.

'Now, don't let the nuns get you down before your mum comes to get you.'

I nodded, and my eyes became misty. I blinked. Tears fell down my cheeks. I gave a sniff and brushed them quickly away.

'Thanks,' I said. I swallowed the lump in my throat.

'I'll miss you,' said Ruth.

'Me too.'

The sound of the approaching train vibrated on the still air as it drew into the station. A crowd of children and parents were

247

hanging out of the window. The guards in their dark blue uniforms went to and fro, opening, closing, locking and unlocking the doors. Ruth opened the door. One of the mothers caught sight of the anxious look in Ruth's eyes and helped her on board.

'You can sit with us,' she said kindly.

Ruth thanked her and hung out of the door window. A whistle blew and the train began to move away.

'Abyssinia!' yelled Ruth and we waved to each other till the train and platform were out of each other's sight.

It was past seven o'clock in the evening when I walked into the front entrance of the convent. I was in a daze, covered with dirt, my eyes swollen. The building seemed empty. I walked about aimlessly, scarcely aware of where I was or taking in my surroundings. Only the cold inside me was a reality. It cut through me like a knife, turning my blood to ice.

I made my way to the church. A faint, familiar waft of incense drifted out of the door as it creaked open. The interior was dimly lit. I walked with echoing steps. All around me the shadows stretched into an infinity of gloom. Alone. Unconnected.

How can I bear it, I thought, how can I go on bearing it without turning mad? I saw my future life flash past. I'd always be on the move, restive, without a single connection to family or friend of any kind. A drifter. The light was fading outside the windows. The red sanctuary lamp winked and glinted from the altar. Candles burned low in the nuns' area of the church, casting shadows over the statues lining the walls. They looked like living people making beckoning gestures in the gloom. Why am I here? Where am I going? I walked heavily forward like a statue might move, half-flesh, half-stone. It seemed a gigantic effort to place one foot in front of the other, as if I were wearing iron weights under my shoes. Around me the shadows leapt and grew. I prayed for pardon for being the cause of Frances's death. I uttered the words meekly, kneeling in the darkness. I did not bother my head about God's wrath or indignation, I knew there was no such thing. All I cared about was the burden of hurt and damage and remorse I had inflicted on the other girls.

I vowed then that I would never allow anyone to get close to me again. That way I wouldn't get hurt, nor could I hurt in return. There were no tears now. No pain. Just that strange icy coldness inside me.

I leant back against the wall of the church and slid down to the floor, my face in my hands. There were no thoughts at all, just a black hole pulling me down and down. Everyone had either disappeared or died. There was no Dad, Nana and Pop, Frances or Ruth or even Mum. How could I bear it, I wondered, and how could I bear it *alone?* I was the only one left in this awful life that felt worse than hell. And no one from now on would ever know what it was really like to be me.

Sister Cuthbert found me in the church when she came to lock up. I don't remember much about it. I was holding on to one of the wooden handrails near the altar and seemed to have got stuck there. She had to force my fingers open. She asked me what I was doing, but I wouldn't answer her. I felt curiously unwilling to speak; it seemed so difficult. Or maybe it was just that I didn't see the point of talking any more. Eventually she managed to put me to bed in the isolation ward.

Father Holland came, asked me a lot of questions and called me his little roaming Catholic. I made an effort to speak, opened my mouth and began 'I'm –', and could go no further. Mostly I just nodded or shook my head. The next day the Mother Superior arrived carrying a tray. She smiled nervously, peering at me through her cracked spectacles. I watched her with un-easiness; I wasn't going to be drawn into answering any questions.

'Glory, glory,' she said sitting on the end of my bed. 'Here's our little wandering Jew. Why don't you try a bit of this nice pudding I've brought you? If you like, I'll bring you up some jam for it.'

I shook my head.

'You ought to eat something,' she said, taking hold of my hand.

It wasn't right for her to look so merry. It made her seem human in the way that I was human. I didn't want any grown-ups in my world. It was enough that they came at me in dreams: the faceless witch who stepped out of the trees, the man with a knife who chased me.

Eventually, she shook her head and hurried away with her tray. I listened to her soft, determined footfalls disappearing down the stairs.

Father Holland returned. More questions, over and over again. I lay on the bed with my back to him and said nothing. It was amazing how easy it was not to react. Easy – and somehow safer. I was afraid that if I let go I might fall completely to pieces. So I said nothing and felt nothing. Then they left, abandoning me to the two holy pictures on the walls; from one the Virgin looked at me with an expression of detached pity, in the other an angel was arrested in mid-act of announcing the good news to the maiden Mary.

I tried to keep Frances's face clear in my memory. The pure tone of her voice, soaring effortlessly above the others in the choir. If I could only die, I could be with her, I thought. I tried placing my hands around my neck and squeezing hard. Really hard. It didn't work. So I tried to end it with sleep, black deep sleep, if only for an hour, and lay shuddering by dawn's blue light until fatigue and fear, hunger and shame, wore me out and closed my eyes.

When I did fall asleep, my dreams were desperate. A black sky and galloping waves, like wild ponies tossing their tumbling manes, hurtling along the beach. I awoke trembling, damp with sweat. The salt smell of the sea haunted me. I longed to forget, but the bubbles broke to the surface and I couldn't stop them.

Frances dead. Janet dead. At least Ruth got away in time. I clung to the thought; it warmed me. But later I heard that her godmother had sent her to a different Nazareth House orphanage in the Mumbles in Wales.

It was a grey and blue day when they buried Frances and Janet, with a wind blowing and rain clouds banked on the horizon. Mourners formed a circle around the small hole in the ground. As they crammed the two small coffins into the damp earth, there was a weird sound. We girls turned sharply. The nuns stood stiffly in a row. Behind them was the figure of a woman who looked like an older Frances. She was swaying, bending forward and putting her hand to her mouth. I thought for a moment that she was overcome by tears, but then I saw that she was laughing. Monstrous giggles convulsed her from head to foot, turning, as she tried to stifle them, into wet spluttering gurgles. Tears of laughter wetted her cheeks. The graveyard echoed with it.

'Schizophrenic,' I heard one of the scandalised nuns mutter. Suddenly the woman rushed forward pushing the priest out of the way. She fell on her knees, clawing at the earth with her bare hands and tried to embrace one of the coffins, her face twisted and contorted. She let out a high-pitched, doleful wail, rising at first like a tendril of smoke into the sky, gathering momentum as it rose.

I put my hands over my ears. Sister Mary was yelling, 'Get rid of her, get rid of her!' In a hurry to bury. Frances's mother was quickly removed from the scene.

The next day Mum turned up. She stood in the visitors' parlour clutching her handbag, staring at me. 'I saw the newspapers,' she said. 'Judith, I've come to take you . . .' she hesitated at the word 'home'. She put her hand on my head and peered at me like she was trying to get me in focus. I was so cold that I couldn't stop shivering. She kept asking if I was all right. She said: 'You look so different, altered.'

I told her a few things about the nuns and she burst into tears.
'Why didn't you tell me all this before?' she asked.

251

'I didn't want to leave my friends.'

'I left you here in all good faith believing that the nuns would take care of you,' she said, wiping her eyes. She had a thousand questions to ask, she said, but they could wait.

When I said goodbye to the girls in my class, they were polishing the refectory floor with dusters under their feet. The swishing to and fro movement stopped when I appeared. The room was motionless as they numbly returned my gaze. They seemed shy of me. A shock of despair ran through me. Not mine, but theirs. They knew I was leaving for good, and I knew I'd never know friends like them again. But I had to leave them. The convent was killing me.

Later, when Mum and I walked down the path away from the convent, she clutched my hand so tightly it hurt. 'Poor little souls,' she said. 'I wish I could take them all with me.'

They still have one another, I thought. Yet I knew we would all carry something out of here that would still pulse in our brains come old age, linking us in a rare way and binding us to the same memories for ever.

Mum never asked me one more question about the convent, let alone the thousand.

Chapter 15

My months at the kibbutz were over. Part of me wanted to stay in Israel for ever. Here there was no past beyond yesterday, no future beyond today. But no, my own future awaited me back in England.

The fresh, balmy air caressed me, and the stiff grass gave off a mossy odour. There was a rich newness everywhere. Overflowing with it all, my freedom and a floating sense of high, yet with everything sharp and clear, each grass blade, the buzzing gnats, I walked happily, inhaling the sweet air. It was the first time in my entire life that I had felt that way, my nerves uncluttered. No one to save, nothing to be, no one to escape.

I had spent the morning packing, and now Rick and Cydney were waiting on Miriam's steps to say their farewells to me. They watched as I strolled towards them.

Rick pushed himself to standing. I tried to smile. I felt nervous at saying goodbye to everyone. Exposed. It was like meeting them again for the first time.

Cydney took in my outfit and grinned. 'You look more American than I do now.'

'You mean I'm just as hip and full of shit as you lot.'

It was true, I wasn't so different from them now, at least in my looks. I wore a kaftan, bell-bottoms and several layers of beads around my neck. But in my case, I still didn't give a toss about the Bomb or what happened in South-East Asia. I didn't chant mantras, or read the right books – Kerouac, R.D. Laing, Jung. I didn't sit around the volunteer camp and drink beer or chew the fat with the best of them.

In short, I was still weird. I knew I was still damaged in some places, ugly in others, but I didn't mind. I no longer felt any shame in myself, nor any sense of judgment from the world in general. I was at peace with it, and with myself.

Rick didn't say anything. He took long strides down the steps and covered the space between us, encircling me with his arms, pulling my face into his neck. He said my name, as if he were calling to me back across the years. My name, spoken in that way, made me laugh – not a real laugh more like a cough. I hid my face in the hollow of his neck, and for a moment, he rocked me slowly, gently in his arms. Gratitude came as a physical pain, and then I felt an easy tiredness that was pure joy. He sighed and looked at me with puzzlement.

'You seem happy,' he said almost accusingly.

'No, just real. I can see a bit clearer now.'

'Couldn't you see before?'

'No. When I first arrived on the kibbutz, it was like I had a black veil tied round my head. Now I'm able to see the world and love it.'

'Yeah, that's cool,' and ducking quickly away, he turned and left. I watched him go, my whole body shifted by that hug. For a minute, I couldn't speak. I felt suddenly relaxed, like someone who has travelled a long way and arrived. A feeling of intense happiness went coursing through my body in a dazzling quiet stream.

Cydney sat forward, wrist balanced on her knee and cigarette smoke curving a line up in front of her face.

'Was that odd or is it just me?' I said.

She shook her head. 'He's just freaked out.'

'Freaked out? By me?'

'He told me he was nervous about saying goodbye to you,' she said. 'The guy's crazy about you.'

'Me? Oh yes, I'm sure.'

'He is. He told me he was. He said you were the only together person on the kibbutz.'

'I can't believe he said that. Why doesn't he tell me himself?'

Cydney shrugged, and took another drag on her cigarette. The heavy smell of Miriam's flowers hung in the warm air around us. 'He's shy. He has a bit of an inferiority complex.'

'Tell him to join the club.'

'You tell him.' She grinned and waved her hand in the direction Rick had taken. 'He's too shy to tell you that he's passing through England on his way home to the States next month.'

I don't actually remember the moment I said goodbye to Miriam. Was it that morning? The afternoon before? I don't recall, and it pains me.

But I remember one day towards the end of my time there. I was helping her sort the books in the library, as we had done together so many times before. The conversation was easy, laughing. I was trying out some of my hard-won Hebrew on her, and she was tutting at my pronunciation.

Suddenly – I remember this clearly – she stopped shelving books and put a hand on my arm. 'When you go back to England, promise me something.'

'Sure,' I said, startled.

'Seek out the other girls from the orphanage. Will you do that? You need each other. And confront the nuns, if you can.'

I slowly put down the book I was holding, keeping my eyes on her lined, freckled face.

She nodded to herself. 'Go to the nuns and get some answers to your questions. And talk over your past with the other children, so that you can let it go and maybe some day understand. If you want to, write your story. It will help you. And more importantly, get to know your mother better. Find out about her past and discover the answers.'

Chapter 16

Bloomfield Terrace,
London,
SW1

The Mother Superior,
Nazareth House,
Hammersmith Road,
London,
W6

19th August 1977

Dear Reverend Mother,

I am trying to trace two friends of mine who were residents with me at the convent and should be most grateful if you could assist me. Their names are as follows:

> Betty O'Dowd
> Ruth Norton

Also any information you could provide me as to the whereabouts of Sister Cuthbert and Sister Mary would be most welcome.

Many thanks,

Judith Kelly.

A reply from the convent arrived about a fortnight later. I was curiously unsurprised by the arrival of the letter with its familiar heading 'JMC'. It was as though I had been expecting it. The previous memories had warned me: we are after you, out of the past.

Nazareth House,
Hammersmith Road,
London,
W6

Judith Kelly,
Bloomfield Terrace,
London,
SW1

2nd September 1977

Dear Judith,

Thank you so much for your letter to the Mother Superior, who passed it on to me.

You will be pleased to hear that Sister Mary is well and living here at Nazareth House in Hammersmith. If you wish to visit her, then you will be very welcome to come along at any time and I'm sure she will provide you with the contact addresses of your old friends.

God bless you.

It had taken me years to follow Miriam's advice, but at last I was here.

The receptionist was a large, chubby nun whose full-moon face looked as if it had been rubbed raw with a Brillo pad. She moved nimbly despite her bulk. The room she sat in was overlaid with crucifixes and reproduction holy pictures in dark frames. On the window sill opposite her were two black-and-white closed-circuit television monitors.

She glanced at me and then, barely stopping for breath, began a lengthy tirade in an Irish burr: 'Sure I haven't had me a moment to drink my tea – look, it's cold now and the bug in my stomach is playing up something rotten. It must have been the fish I ate last night. Sister Catherine said it was so off it might have been in the desert forty days. It seemed all right to me, but then I usually have a superb digestion. Young nuns nowadays are too pernickety.'

She took a key from her pocket and unlocked a desk drawer.

'I've a bottle of water here from the Well at Lourdes.'

She took a stoppered flask in the form of a cross from the drawer.

'I have to keep it under lock and key. I can't trust the char-woman. The water's reputed to have miraculous powers. I have a nip whenever I have an upset stomach.'

'I'm sorry?' I stood uncertainly, wondering if she had mis-taken me for someone else.

'See these two screens? I have to watch them constantly for visitors. Had them both mended recently, well, I say mended, that is, a bearded hippy in filthy jeans strutted around as if he owned the place fiddling with the aerials, but that's the *Yellow Pages* for you. There's the blessed doorbell again! Who's that? I can't make them out, the screen's all blurred. If it's not the doorbell, it's bang, bang, bang, as someone assaults the knocker.'

'I'm here to –'

'Why are you standing? Sit down, sit down! Well, I can't stop here chatting, much as I'd like to, how might I help you? Keep it brief, I've the phones to answer.'

'I have an appointment with Sister Mary.' She nodded and bleeped her on the switchboard. Time went by and no reply came. She asked a young man who came in to go and find Sister

Mary, and meanwhile continued her diatribe about her job, workmen, the stream of visitors, occasionally taking a swig from her flask. I shifted in my seat, not commenting.

Finally the phone rang; she popped a segment of orange into her mouth as she answered. 'Sister Mary's on her way to meet you,' she informed me, picking up some leaflets from her desk. 'Take these devotional reflections with you. Should you wish to contribute to our leprosy mission, you'll find a box in the hallway.'

My mouth became dry with dread. I could feel my throat tightening, and an ache along my jaw line. Stay calm. But a nauseating sensation of fear and shame came over me. It was a familiar feeling. I used to get it every time I had to face Sister Mary. I'm an adult, I thought, why am I still scared of her?

After what seemed like an age, an elderly nun with a clenched-fist face came into the room. She gave me a dubious eagle-eyed glance.

I rose. 'Sister Mary.' As she stood in front of me I felt a desperate nervous flush on my cheeks. Gone was the austere black wimple of old and in its place the milder Mother Teresa tablecloth style.

'I don't recognise you,' she said curtly.

'Of course not,' I laughed. 'I was all skin and grief when you saw me last, hardly a description that fits me now.'

I handed her a small bunch of violets I'd brought to prove that I bore no animosity about the past. I almost shrank back at her reaction. She looked astonished and inexplicably annoyed, and didn't thank me. I immediately felt diminished in her presence, as if I were a child again – the same ashamed awkwardness, the same fear, the same childish compunction to please. I tried to straighten my spine and remind myself: you are no longer small, vulnerable, a rag that can be torn apart with both hands. Yet now I was a word or two away, the oddness of the situation pressed in on me. Eleven. That's how old I was the last time I saw her. Yes, that long ago, and after all this time it might seem to her now that I was some menacing thing, a figure from an anxious dream come walking and talking across the wilderness of years to find her.

The receptionist held up a phone message. 'Sister, could I have a word?' Sister Mary turned away from me for a moment, and I was given the opportunity to study the nun who had haunted my thoughts for so many years.

So here was the unforgettable Sister Mary. The same sharp expression resided in her steely pale eyes, dimmer now in their burnt-out sockets. She was wiry and lithe, her jowls lined and paper-white. The most striking thing about her was the feeling of suppressed fire. It was very impressive in one so elderly, yet I could sense that any intimacy with her would be difficult.

Finally she led me through a corridor into an oak-panelled parlour with velvet chairs, glossy teak furniture and framed prints with their dull-gold backgrounds.

'In, in,' she said, with a fussy little gesture of her hand.

On the mantelpiece a great marble clock ticked loudly. An overwhelming smell of beeswax polish filled the air. She beckoned for me to sit next to her on a settee. She seemed uneasy, her body language suggesting a double barrier with both arms clutched tightly around her waist and her legs firmly crossed. She looked at me without seeing me, as if considering what to say.

Her first words stunned me.

'Why do you refer to me as Sister Mary, when I have always been known as Sister Magdalene Ita?' Peevishly she added, 'You must have me confused with Sister Mary of Nazareth.'

I stared at her familiar features. 'No, not at all – I recall Sister Mary of Nazareth went to South Africa as a missionary shortly after my arrival in Bexhill.' My nervous laugh felt foolish, echoing through the room. How strange that she spoke to me in just the same tone of voice, as if nothing had intervened or changed in all those years.

She drew back, her eyes glittering in surprise, and for a moment she was speechless. However, she soldiered on and said I must therefore be confusing her with a Sister Mary Therese, who had died two years previously. I couldn't recall knowing a nun of this name. Yet she was relentless in her denial that she had ever been known as Sister Mary, and her conviction that Sister Mary Therese must be the nun I had known.

We were at cross-purposes. I was here to discover the whereabouts of my old friends, and she was here to defend herself against some imagined attack. If she didn't want to see me, then why had I been invited?

As I sat facing her, trying to understand, she drew herself up on the settee, her pale eyes wide and threatening. I stiffened. I thought she was about to burst into one of the screaming rages that had terrorised that part of my childhood. At that moment a hundred memories were freeze-framed and thrust forward, blown through a narrow tunnel to the present.

Always out of control of her anger in those days, today she was very much in charge. So how was I to obtain an admission as to her true identity? All the nuns I had made contact with recently had alluded to her as Sister Mary, including the receptionist. A burdensome silence weighed awkwardly between us.

'About my old friends who I'm trying to find –' I started.

She shook her head tightly. 'I have no contact with any of the former children from the convent.'

'But I was given to understand –'

'You must have misunderstood. I have no contact with them.'

A door slammed shut within me and the key was about to turn in its lock when she asked me something that made me stop breathing for a second.

'Do you remember Frances McCarthy?' She asked the question without expression.

The light was fading, and I could not distinguish her features. From the sunset through the window, bright glints caught her hooded eyes, and the eyes looked straight at me, sharp and mocking.

'Yes, of course I do. She was my best friend.' My voice was tense.

She shifted in her seat, watching me. 'Does it bother you that I ask that question?'

'It doesn't,' I said curtly. 'I no longer feel any guilt about what happened.'

'What about Janet Dover, do you remember her?'

I forced myself to sit without trembling, to stare straight back into her eyes. 'Of course. They were both friends of mine.'

Between us at that moment their names were suddenly like a flash, like a physical manifestation. Our former selves appeared for a moment like ghosts, and Frances and Janet's ghosts were with them.

There was a moment of silence in which only the seconds could be heard as the marble clock marked them in its circular trance. The room with its yellow aftertaste of polish almost hummed with tension. Suddenly I wanted to rip apart the fabric of our shared experience.

I held my voice tightly, not letting it shake. 'Why did you and the other nuns punish us so severely?'

Her eyes burned as if the last drop of moisture had been scorched out of her body. She snorted. 'We did what was necessary. You must understand that some of those children were very rough and headstrong and would take advantage of any weakness in us. Some of the nuns, especially Sister Mary Therese, believed in the old school of thought regarding discipline. A rap over the knuckles or a box on the ear wasn't sufficient to break an obstinate child's will and remould it in God's way.'

Her mind, as if magnetised by her speech, seemed to circle slowly round and round the subject of disciplining children. As she spoke I involuntarily glanced at her face. As I did so I met the gaze of her metallic eyes and something in the tilt of her head or the angle of her profile gave me a sharp impression of the younger nun I remembered. I turned my eyes away again.

'But there are kinder ways of teaching children to behave.' I forced my voice out with immense effort, as one tries to scream in a nightmare.

The icy voice continued. 'We were only God's implements. We had to act before your whole natures became warped. A life of vows is a difficult one, particularly then, when we had no control over any of the decisions that were made. We had no choices and times were tough, yet those were the glory days for the Catholic Church. Nowadays, churches are closing. Saints are superfluous. Priests face their congregations like television presenters on a cookery programme, abandoning the Latin liturgy in favour of pop-song Masses. Humiliation and discipline are a thing of the past. I miss the old traditions. Those dear dead days beyond recall: St Christopher medallions on car dashboards. We had everything then. Now we have nothing,' she sighed.

I found myself almost sad for her, almost believing her.

'I think the nuns were very capable in taking care of the children. We acted as your nurses, your teachers, your social workers. We had to be with you constantly, we never had a moment to ourselves except during prayer time and at night. But it was the Lord's will and we did our best.'

I could find no words. When I did not reply immediately, I could see that she took my silence for acceptance. She sat pale and composed, lit with a singular, quiet exhilaration. Her words sounded rehearsed, precise. Unrepentant. She must have prepared them for my visit.

'We were devoted to the children, you know. We were just following our order's rule, which is based upon strict lines of self-denial, poverty and obedience. We tried to combine a life of work and prayer for you in imitation of the Holy Family.'

I managed to swallow. 'So you're saying you were merely obeying rules, is that it?'

She shrugged her shoulders and nodded.

I wanted to fling at her example after example of vicious cruelty, demand answers and extract penitence and contrition even if I had to shake them out of her. Yet I could hardly think, could hardly take in what she was saying.

'But that kind of obedience . . . it must have been destructive to the nuns, and – and so unjust on the children.'

So unjust. The words echoed weakly.

'Unjust, unjust? My dear, you were all charity cases. Charity is not entirely about mercy, and little to do with justice. We were carrying out that work for the sake of our own salvation. It was a way of detaching ourselves from acquisitiveness and greed.'

My voice raised. 'In other words, you were doing it for your own benefit, not ours. I accept that life must have been difficult for the nuns as well. Yet didn't you ever question whether such punishments were wrong?'

Her pale eyes snapped at me. 'We had to do what we were told. We did try to find other solutions, such as the punishments of silence, but the minute our backs were turned you'd all be playing up. As you know, many of the children were orphans and lacked parental authority. Many of them were wayward. It was up to us to teach them the rule of obedience. We *had* to use harsh tactics.'

Since I made no reply, she must have felt she was beginning to make her point, for she kept on in the same vein for a good while. She consoled herself with clichés, and more than once it was as if she totally forgot to whom she was speaking. Her small face gleamed with fierce pride as she said, 'We couldn't allow ourselves to be faint-hearted, you know.'

I could read the sharp disappointment in her face when I cut in at last. Now I knew why I was here.

'You do realise you are speaking about innocent children here? Where was the justice in those two twelve-year-old girls losing their lives?'

My words touched her face like a soiled hand, dabbing her

eyes and cheeks with smudges of anxiety. She tried to speak but couldn't.

Several seconds passed before she answered. 'Oh, I've had enough! I'm not going to sit here being quizzed about something that happened so long ago. The nuns loved the children, but you only had yourselves to blame, you wouldn't come out of the sea when you were called. Yet it's delightful to think that Frances and Janet are in heaven together.'

She let a little laugh escape between her teeth, as if a joke had been made.

I leaned forward, holding her eyes with my own as I said clearly, 'The nuns knelt in prayer and did nothing to help us while we were in difficulties and Frances and Janet were drowning.'

A wild dilating fire appeared in her eyes. She shook her head. 'The time had come for those two children. Besides, there was little those two nuns could do. Do you remember those cumbersome habits we used to wear? Can you imagine what it was like to be dressed in twenty pounds of gabardine and starch in the middle of August? Those habits made it impossible for the nuns to effect any kind of rescue. In any case, I believe one of the nuns was held back from entering the sea by several children.'

I became silent again. What was I hoping to hear? Even I didn't know. What did it matter? As she said, it was so long ago. Maybe to hear a trace of real sorrow, an explanation as to why the nuns put the entire blame for the drownings on me? And why had the two girls been buried in an unmarked grave? And why had it been hushed up that Janet, as a non-swimmer, had been sent into the sea to call in the other children? And why had there been no mention of Janet's courage when she sacrificed her life trying to rescue Frances?

The silence between us was far from empty. It was hostile. Full of unspoken words.

'What is it you want me to say?' she demanded. 'Why are you really here?'

I stared down at the parquet floor and pinched my nose between my fingers. The years slipped away as I was whisked back towards the unhappy playground.

'Look at my face,' I said, raising my head. 'Look closely. Take your time. It'll come to you.'

I let my own eyes dwell on the sagging skin of the nun's cheeks; she raised her head briefly, but then dropped it again, as if her veil had suddenly become too heavy. Go on, I silently challenged her, look at me. She then lifted her head again and stared at my face. Her face remained neutral, her eyes continuing to reflect the sunset through the window. I sensed the tension in her body, as if she felt cornered. Her staring eyes travelled across my nose. Then a violent flush spread across her face as if a warm cloth had been thrown round her head. She drew in her breath sharply.

'It's understandable why you don't want to remember me,' I said softly, 'but I can't forget you so easily, however much I'd like to.'

'It all happened so long ago.' Her words came out with a struggle, tinged with anger. 'What's the matter with you? Why do you need to dredge up the past in this way? What is it that you want after all this time? I suppose you're waiting for me to apologise?'

'What's the point of an apology?' I said, turning away from her. 'You destroyed my faith, but that really doesn't matter any more.'

'It does. And I do apologise. Now I'd like to ask you a question,' she said. She was flushed with distress and annoyance. 'Are *you* free from sin?'

'I'm as free as anyone else.'

'Well, you're in good company. I know I could get into Heaven any time I choose.'

I felt shattered, reluctant to delve deeper. Silence fell on me in droplets. Behind Sister Mary's head there was a picture of the Virgin and Child in a bevelled burnished gilt frame. The Virgin looked infinitely sad, but detached. As though she knew that all the concern she felt for the pathetic human scene taking place under her calm sad gaze could not alter human nature by one iota. Her high round brow, the tendrils of her perfectly curled golden hair, gave her an implacable beauty.

Sister Mary's brow on the other hand was not visible beneath her veil, and no strands escaped from that prison. Any hair that did show would be grey and wispy, if not white. Nuns' hair had been a fixation when I was at the convent. The thrill when Sister Cuthbert had appeared in class with a distinct curl of brown hair that had the nerve to emerge from its captivity. As nuns were not allowed to look in the mirror, she was probably unaware of her mistake. Another thrill at the idea of Sister Mary's tart scold when the rogue wisp was glimpsed. It all added up to the fact that the nuns were not bald and did not shave their heads; they simply cut their hair conveniently short.

Looking at Sister Mary now, beneath the tumble-locked Virgin, I found that I had not altogether lost my fixation with nuns' hair. Or their appearance in general.

Finally I said, 'I was given to understand that you were in touch with some of my friends from the convent. I would very much like to have their addresses or –'

I was interrupted by a knock at the door. I had for some time been conscious of a noise outside in the passageway, a low shuffling, a type of impatient snuffling.

'Yes, come in,' said Sister Mary impatiently. 'Well, Sister, what is it?'

'Oh, I'm sorry, Sister, I didn't realise you had a visitor –' A slightly breathless voice behind me. I turned round and saw a young nun with a wide ruddy face and intense eyes. She scrutinised me with unsmiling objectivity for a moment or two. I turned away and I could hear her muttering something in a low voice to Sister Mary, who gazed over my head at her visitor with barely concealed annoyance. I could feel myself becoming red with embarrassment and I twisted round, trying to see what it was that the nun was saying.

'As you can see, Sister, I'm rather busy at the moment,' said Sister Mary quickly.

The nun departed and Sister Mary frowned. I noticed that she suspended speaking until there could be no question of the recent intruder overhearing us.

Then at last she said, 'Unfortunately, I lost my address book in one of the many moves I made over the years from convent to convent.' Her voice sounded weak and slightly hoarse. 'I used to have a lot of photographs of the children as well, but they also got lost in the moves.'

Just circles and more circles. And endless unspoken questions. My head ached, and my eyes felt strained and sore. Nothing was resolved. I slipped into a morose silence. Her fire had faded, and she sat looking tired, old and vulnerable. The sight of her almost moved me to pity. But I had to be careful in my compassion, for vulnerability can be like snow on a sharp rock, and melt away at the first sign of a thaw.

My voice was low and tense as I asked her again: 'So you have never been referred to as Sister Mary?'

And she denied it a third time.

I stood up abruptly, looking at my watch. 'I'm afraid I need to go now. I'll come back if I may another day.'

She looked up in surprise, her eyes vague. 'You'll do nothing of the sort! Another day I may be underground. I'm dying with curiosity to know the real purpose of your visit today. I shan't sleep tonight unless you tell me. Sit down and relax.'

I sat down again and looked at her doubtfully.

'I'm trying to contact Ruth Norton,' I said. 'That's why I came.'

'Ruth Norton,' Sister Mary repeated with careful diction. As she spoke, she grimaced and delicately rubbed the tips of her fingers together as though she had been dabbling them in something unpleasant.

'I wondered if you might have her address. I believe she may live somewhere in Guildford.'

'Ah!' She nodded thoughtfully. 'And why, pray, would you want it?' she added, still staring at me.

I held her gaze determined not to be intimidated.

'As you know, we were friends . . .'

'And all these years later, you intend to . . . what? Drop her a line? Turn up on her doorstep? Gossip about the old days and cause trouble for me? You two were always trouble together. Ruth Norton in particular was a rebel. Has she ever contacted you?'

I couldn't take her staring eyes any longer. I looked away from her and concentrated on the view out of the window.

'Well, has she?'

'No,' I replied, but the word came out so quietly that even I couldn't really hear it.

'Let me give you a bit of advice . . .' To my surprise I discovered that she had risen from the settee and was standing beside me. I turned my head to look at her. I saw her now as an elderly woman. I wondered why I was still wary of her. She paused; she was gazing out the window and seemed unaware of my attention.

'I just want her address,' I said eventually, breaking the silence.

'Well, I'm giving you some advice instead,' she said. 'Everything that happened in the past should be laid to rest and not dragged into the daylight after all these years. If I knew Norton's address – which I don't – I wouldn't dream of giving it to you.'

I stared at her helplessly for a moment and wondered what she was afraid of, but she wouldn't meet my eyes. The smell of beeswax, the denials, the lack of success in discovering the whereabouts of Ruth – all combined to give me a feeling of nausea. It reminded me of the nausea of jaundice. I dream of it sometimes and awaken with a start, thankful to find myself with no yellow aftertaste.

'I'll go then,' I said. 'Thank you for giving me your time.'

'No, no. Let me show you the church. The Lord has been very good to me. He has allowed me to spend many years taking care of it. I cannot complain if now He feels that my work here is over.'

She took me along a plain corridor with a series of alcoves containing garish statues of assorted saints. When we reached the church she turned to me and whispered, 'Remember to cover your head.'

'I haven't got anything,' I said with annoyance.

'A hanky will do,' she said, smiling encouragement.

I fumbled in my pocket and found a small, not very clean tissue, which I laid on top of my head. Sister Mary looked at me with amiable satisfaction and opened the door to the church. Several small children who were kneeling in prayer turned to look at us. Sister Mary dipped her fingers in the holy water.

I felt overwhelmed with concern. 'Do those children board here?' I was aware of the palpable dismay in my voice.

She shook her head. 'They're day pupils.' She genuflected to the altar. When she raised her head, she added in a whisper: 'We have to use a good deal of discipline to keep order.'

On our return to the front door, the nun at the reception desk glanced up at us furtively as she took another swig from her flask. Sister Mary opened the door on to the Hammersmith Road where, for some reason, she touched me, a hand on my elbow, and the touch startled me. Her fingers were cold on my skin.

'I have to get back to the church,' she said, guiding me towards the door.

That unwelcome touch made me eager to get away, to be gone from the dark memories. She then shook my hand. Her palm felt dry and cold against mine as I held it for a moment, looking into her pale eyes. What was that strange sense of unity against the outside world that I felt with her? I was overwhelmed with a mysterious gratitude that I had survived the threat she once posed to my sanity and my life. I had been spared, and as I faced her finally, I bore no hatred, only pity.

Yet if she had been candid, we could perhaps have built a mutual empathy in order to bury the ghosts, not the truth, from the painful past. Filled with sadness, I bent down and made a pretence of kissing her cheek.

'It's all right,' I said to her. 'You can go back to your church now.'

She seized my wrist in her sinewy hand and in a lowered voice said, 'You obviously have no clear memories of those times and that's understandable, for children forget very easily, don't they?'

Emotion rose up into my mouth, pounded against my skull. Rage. I suddenly felt I was being monstrously put upon, that the whole thing was an outrageous farce, designed to humiliate me.

I looked into her eyes and, with a wicked surge of pleasure, said thickly, 'Oh no, Sister Mary. You see, I kept a diary when I was here. So I shall always remember.'

Epilogue

12 July 2001. I find their grave with the help of the cemetery officer. As I expected, there is still no gravestone to commemorate their short lives. It is simply a small mound of purple heather and weeds. Yet the memory of this place stops me still. Time shatters around me as I stand motionless amongst the graves. No one has been here before, of that I am sure. Time, like an ever-rolling concrete mixer, has left the graveyard an island entirely surrounded by DIY megastores, video factories, fast-food joints and suchlike cultural boons. It's just another high street facility. Where once it had been surrounded by green fields, it's now a place, as Ruth would say, you'd not want to be caught dead in.

I don't know what to say, or do, or think. So I stand and recite the poem that Frances wrote for me all those years ago. The words are of little comfort.

It is time for peace; time to give things a rest. Find a spot where I can shut my eyes and not have to revisit the places I've been. Maybe I could get lucky and forget I was ever there.

I reach in my bag and bring out a small white stone I brought from the Wailing Wall in Jerusalem years ago. I place it on their grave.

A Dream

When we grow up and reach the age of 20,
We'll meet again in the outside world
And take a seat on a bird with a motor
Where we'll rise and soar into space.
Then we'll fly sail and SING,
Over that lovely faraway world
We'll glide over the hot deserts of Arabia
And mysterious land of wizards
And when we free ourselves from the
boiling heat
We'll stroll over icebergs in the north
Then flying again we'll cross the island
And the jungles of Africa of kangroos
And the Holy Land of the Bible
We'll soar slowly floating and singing
and basking in the magic of this world
To Heaven we'll soar and climb
On a cloud my sister on the wind my
friend

The poem that Frances gave me. Although I cannot think how Frances would have known it, 'A Dream' turns out to be strikingly similar to a poem by Avraham Koplowicz, a Polish child who was killed in Auschwitz. The poem is now held in the archives of Yad Vashem, the Holocaust Martyrs' and Heroes' Remembrance Authority, in Jerusalem.

My **mother** remarried in 1958 and died from lung cancer in 1990.

I had no further contact with **Nana and Pop** after my mother and I left them in 1951. In the year 2000 I discovered from the Family Records Office that Nana had died from melancholia five years later. Pop remarried and died in Brighton in 1971. In 2002 I found evidence that my mother had been born illegitimately in St Pancras Workhouse. Her real mother had been a Roman Catholic. Nana and Pop were her adoptive parents.

After managing to escape from Nazareth House at the age of nineteen, **Ruth Norton** taught herself to read and write and bluffed her way into the publishing industry. She has one son and lost her husband five years ago. In 2001, we kept our pact and eventually met up again in Trafalgar Square where her first words to me were: 'I'm still trying to get over my childhood, and now I'm ready to go into an old people's home.'

Sister Mary died in the 1990s. **Sister Cuthbert** and **Sister Columba** died a few years before her.

Cydney is now an attorney in San Francisco. She is married and has a son.

In August 2000 Sister Alphonso of the Sisters of Nazareth was found guilty of maltreatment of children within **Nazareth House** homes, Scotland.

In January 2004 former children from **Nazareth House** homes in Australia and New Zealand received an apology and compensation for the abuse they suffered whilst in the care of the Sisters of Nazareth.

A Note on the Author

Judith Kelly was born in Southampton. After leaving
the Catholic orphanage where the events of *Rock Me
Gently* took place in the mid-1950s, she moved to a
new school where she was encouraged by her English
teacher to read widely and develop her writing. Some
years after she left school, Judith spent time on a kibbutz
in Israel. When she returned to England, she was
accepted into Chelsea College of Art and thereafter
worked for the Keeper of the British Collection at the
Tate Gallery, London, until she began her career
in television production at TV-am, Reuters and BSkyB.
Now retired, Judith Kelly runs a support group for
those who were abused by priests and nuns within
the Catholic Church.

A Note on the Type

The text of this book is set in Linotype Sabon, named after the type founder Jacques Sabon. It was designed by Jan Tschichold and jointly developed by Linotype, Monotype and Stempel, in response to a need for a typeface to be available in identical form for mechanical hot metal composition and hand composition using foundry type.

Tschichold based his design for Sabon roman on a font engraved by Garamond, and Sabon italic on a font by Granjon. It was first used in 1966 and has proved an enduring modern classic.